THE SON OF GROUCHO, Arthur Marx is the author of a number of successful biographies including the long out of print *Groucho* (1954), material from which is incorporated in this volume and *The Nine Lives of Mickey Rooney* (Robson Books, 1987). He has also written works of fiction and several hit Broadway plays, including *The Impossible Years* and *Groucho: A Life in Revue*, which played in London at the Comedy Theatre in 1987, where it was nominated for the Laurence Olivier Award for Best Comedy Production. In his youth, Mr Marx was also a ranking tennis player in the US. He is happily married to Lois, and makes his home in Los Angeles, California, where the two of them share a hilltop house with two poodles and five canaries.

Arthur Marx

MY LIFE WITH GROUCHO

A Son's Eye View

PAN BOOKS
London, Sydney and Auckland

First published in Great Britain 1988
by Robson Books Ltd
This edition published 1991 by Pan Books Ltd,
Cavaye Place, London SW10 9PG
9 8 7 6 5 4 3 2 1
© Arthur Marx 1988
ISBN 0 330 31132 8

Photoset by Parker Typesetting Service, Leicester
Printed and bound in Great Britain by
Clays Ltd, St Ives plc

TO LOIS

MY BEST FRIEND

Preface

My Life With Groucho had its genesis in a magazine article I wrote for *Collier's* in 1951.

At the time, my father's television show, *You Bet Your Life*, had just become one of the most popular radio and TV programmes in the United States of America, and he, in the vernacular of the trade, was suddenly a 'very hot property'.

I, on the other hand, was not very hot at all. In fact, you might say I was lukewarm. I was thirty years old, married to Irene Kahn, the daughter of Gus Kahn, the popular song lyricist, had two kids, a bungalow in the Pacific Palisades, and a writing career that didn't seem to be going anywhere very fast.

I'd sold a few magazine articles to national publications; I'd written a novel called *The Ordeal of Willie Brown*, about an amateur tennis player, which had had very disappointing sales. So disappointing, in fact, that in order to make a living I was working at MGM studios in the shorts department, writing Pete Smith Specialities.

Pete Smith liked my work, but it was a dead end job.

Then, one afternoon when I was in my office on the lot, I received a phone call from Ted Strauss, who was the West Coast editor of *Collier's* magazine. He was wondering if I'd be interested in writing a profile of my father. They'd pay me $750. It was twice the amount I'd ever received for a single magazine piece before, almost as much as I'd made from the publication of *Willie Brown*, and the equivalent of three weeks' salary writing Pete Smith Specialities.

Nevertheless, my immediate reaction was to say 'No'. I thanked Strauss, but said I'd spent most of my life trying to avoid being known as the son of Groucho so people wouldn't accuse me of trading on my father's name, and I didn't think I should change that policy now.

But Strauss begged me to reconsider. He said that Groucho was very hot copy as a result of the enormous success of *You Bet Your Life*, and he felt that a piece written from his son's angle would have a wide audience appeal. 'Look at it this way,' he continued, 'who else but you could write this particular piece? You're not only his son, but a professional writer. You've already had a novel published.'

I told him that flattery would get him nowhere, but on second thought I would write the article for him.

I had an ulterior motive. I figured that if *Collier's* liked the job I did on Groucho, they might put other assignments my way. And even if nothing else came of it, I'd at least have picked up 750 bucks for a few nights' work.

Besides, I was sure I could write a better, more revealing article about Groucho than anyone else, for the obvious reason that no other writer knew, or was likely to find out, the things I already knew about him without an interview.

When being interviewed by the average newspaperman or magazine writer, Groucho could be terribly witty and incisive in his observations on the world scene. If his Boswell also happened to be a girl with big breasts and nice legs, he'd be exceptionally charming, and she could be certain he'd make some clever remarks about sex, and a number of quotable wisecracks on the hopelessness of any two people living happily together as man and wife. ('Marriage is the chief cause of divorce.' 'The trouble with marriage is you have to marry a woman – the last person in the world you could possibly have anything in common with.') Chances are, he'd even try to date her.

But it would take a Bob Woodward to worm anything out of

him but the most superficial information about his personal life. In his autobiography, *Groucho and Me*, he divulged less about himself than you could learn by looking him up in *The World Almanac* or *Who's Who*. In fact, in Chapter 22 he admits receiving the following note from his publisher: 'Up until now you've written 80,000 words and your readers still don't know a damn thing about you.'

At his publisher's insistence, he then confessed to being the father of three children. He also admitted he had a wife. But except for a few lines about my tennis career, and a plethora of anecdotes illustrating my half-sister Melinda's precocity, you wouldn't know he had a family, a home life or any normal human feelings.

That's the kind of fellow Groucho was. He'd rather have a smart wisecrack attributed to him than a kind word or deed. The real Groucho persisted in hiding behind a smoke-screen of jokes.

I'm not knocking him for that. Most actors live in a world of illusion. Few will own up to their correct ages (even to themselves), or reveal anything about their lives that might detract from their superstar image, even though it might be of interest to readers or theatrical historians. I'm just pointing out that very little of what you read about a celebrity bears any resemblance to the truth.

Bernard Shaw once said, 'No man is bad enough or good enough to tell the truth about himself during his lifetime.' That certainly applied to Groucho. And it may even apply to me, though I'm at least not denying I had a father named Groucho.

At any rate, I didn't set out to do a hatchet job on my father for *Collier's*. I wanted to show him as he actually was — amusing, eccentric, lovable, difficult, impossible and completely unpredictable. At the same time I wanted to be informative. Plenty of things had happened in Groucho's life since he'd last been the subject of an important magazine article.

When I had finished writing, I debated whether I should show the article to him before publication. Not that I expected him to object to any of the material — I felt I had done a very benevolent piece, showing him as an eccentric but lovable and sometimes misunderstood martinet around the house, a doting parent, and a good provider. And in appraising his talents I'd been as laudatory as I could without seeming unduly biased.

My hesitancy stemmed from the fact that in the past, whenever I'd showed him unpublished work, he found much to criticize. He had hated my first book, for example, and predicted that no publisher would accept it. As my father, and being a writer himself, he expected me to write everything his way.

However, since it was a profile of him that was to be published in a national weekly, I felt I had an obligation to show it to him. Which I did reluctantly, and he took me completely by surprise.

'It's quite good,' he admitted, handing the manuscript back to me with just a few minor corrections pencilled in the margin. 'It's not full of the cliché'd, formula Groucho-banter everyone thinks of me. I don't come off as a caricature.'

So the piece went in just about as I had written it, and the editors were so pleased they gave me $1500 instead of the $750 they had originally offered.

I also started writing regularly for *Collier's*. As a result, I quit MGM to do magazine work full time.

I'd been a magazine writer for about a year when Jack Goodman, the editor in chief of Simon & Schuster, asked me to write a full-length biography of Groucho.

On first impulse, I turned him down, for the same reason I had initially shunned Ted Strauss's offer to profile Groucho for *Collier's* – I didn't want people to think I could only write about my father.

'Once I might have agreed with you,' argued Goodman, 'but now, between *Willie* and your *Collier's* articles, you've proved you can write about other things, so how can it hurt you? And you might make some good money.'

Between his persuasiveness and the fact that a novel I'd been fooling around with in my spare time wasn't really panning out, I finally consented to write the book. At least it was a definite commitment, with a contract and a $2,000 advance.

That evening I phoned Groucho and told him I had contracted to write a book about him.

'You probably won't make any money on it,' he said. 'Why waste your time – just to have your name on another book?'

Despite his lack of enthusiasm, Father was extremely co-operative with me during the many months it took to commit his life to paper. He didn't have anything to do with the actual writing – even the footnotes that appeared in the original edition, signed 'Groucho' and apparently his humorous comments on the text, were entirely my own work – and he never saw a single word until I'd finished the whole thing.

I'd go to him, however, if I were in need of a bright quote, or perhaps a piece of factual material about his or his brothers' early lives with which I wasn't totally familiar.

During *Life With Groucho*'s gestation period Irene and I would usually dine with Groucho a couple of times a week at his house. At these get-togethers he'd often relate a funny anecdote I'd never heard before, or drop a piece of character-revealing information that would be good for the book. Sometimes his candour would surprise even me.

One evening, when my wife and I were having dinner with him and one of his numerous lady friends, I happened to mention that I'd written a passage about his first marriage in my book that afternoon.

'What'd you write about me?' Groucho asked suspiciously.

'I said you were a very good father, and a faithful husband,' I replied.

'That's not true,' he corrected me swiftly, almost proudly. 'I was a good husband, but never a faithful one. I cheated on your mother all the time.'

When I expressed surprise that he had been unfaithful to her even in the early days of their marriage, he got up from the table and took us into the playroom where there hung a large, framed photograph of the cast of *Cocoanuts* taken in Denver, when the show had played there in 1927.

'See that little cutie,' he said pointing the tip of his cigar at a pulchritudinous blonde flapper, standing in the back row with some other ladies of the chorus. 'She was my girl.'

I'd never accuse Groucho of being strait-laced. But it was puzzling to me how he could equate being a 'good husband' with one who cheated on his wife from the beginning of his marriage.

It was just as well that he was single with that attitude, for he certainly wasn't capable of maintaining a relationship with any member of the opposite sex – in marriage, anyway. He was a man's man, preferring the company of Norman Krasna, Arthur Sheekman, George S. Kaufman, Nunnally Johnson and Harry Ruby, all of whom were successful playwrights and/or screen-writers.

'What can a man possibly have in common with a girl once you're not in the hay?' he would often exclaim. 'And you don't have to get married for that!'

'Anyone who gets married a second time doesn't deserve to have lost his first wife,' was one of his favourite quotes from a long-forgotten vaudeville monologist.

Paraphrasing it to fit his own circumstances, he used to say, 'And anyone who marries a third time doesn't deserve anything at all, which is exactly what he'll wind up with.' He sounded sincere, anyway.

Since there was an abundance of material on this one subject alone, I devoted an entire chapter of the book to Groucho's bachelorhood, his experiences as a Don Juan, and his pro-nouncements that he was content to live out his life as a single man. (He had divorced Kay, his second wife, and mother of Melinda, in 1950.)

One of my favourite stories concerned Groucho, the six-year-old Melinda, and a couple of bit-part actresses who doubled as hookers on weekends.

Because she loved horse-back riding, Groucho often took Melinda to the Alisol Dude Ranch in Santa Barbara when it was his turn to have her for the weekend. One Saturday, according to a prearranged plan, film producer Irwin Allen, a close friend of Groucho, brought the two actresses up to the ranch for him and Father to amuse themselves with while Melinda was out riding. Allen arrived at the ranch a few hours after Melinda and Father had checked in, and knocked on their bungalow door. At the sound of the knock, Melinda raced for the door and opened it.

Seeing Allen with the two brassy blondes, Melinda quickly turned to Groucho and asked, knowingly, 'Which one is yours, Daddy?'

So how else could a six year old find out about sex in those unenlightened days before the Sexual Revolution.

Between his second and third marriages Groucho was a good bet for hostesses with single women on their hands. Often this resulted in some unlikely pairings.

The hostess of a party once prevailed upon him to squire Clare Booth Luce, then Ambassador to Italy, to her home in Bel Air.

Groucho always had a difficult time finding his way around Bel Air, even under ideal weather conditions. It was extremely foggy the night he was chauffeuring Mrs Booth Luce to the festivities, and soon after he drove through the main gate of Bel Air, he and the Ambassador were lost.

They finally had to get out of the car and fight their way through some dense shrubbery in order to find a street sign. As the pair emerged from a thicket of oleanders at the corner of Stone Canyon and Capricio Drive, they found themselves face to face with the writer Charlie Brackett, who was taking his nightly constitutional.

'Well,' quipped Brackett, eyeing them speculatively, 'I never thought the day would come when I'd catch Groucho Marx in the bushes with the Ambassador to Italy.'

'Why not?' retorted Groucho. 'Isn't Chico an Italian?'

To write approximately 100,000 words about a man I admired and loved as dearly as Father, and still remain objective, wasn't the easiest assignment in the world. But when I finished the book nine months later, I believed I had achieved a good balance of warmth and truthful reporting.

When I gave the completed manuscript of *Life With Groucho* to my wife to read, her only criticism was, 'It's very good, dear. I just hope it's not too full of hero worship.'

If that was her only comment, I was sure that Groucho would have no complaints. So I packed up the manuscript and mailed it off to Naomi Burton, my literary agent, in New York City, without first obtaining my father's approval. Not that I

13

was worried about what his reaction would be. The book was written in the same style and tone as the *Collier's* piece, which he had liked very much. I just figured, knowing his predilection for rewrites, plus his low opinion of most of my writing, that it would be safer to show him the book after I'd had a professional assessment — either from my agent or my publisher. Once he knew that someone he respected had given it the stamp of approval, he'd like it too.

One further note: my father was still alive when I wrote *Life With Groucho*, hence the style and tense in which the book (which forms Part One of this edition) is written. Although I wrote it over thirty years ago, and from the point of view of the young man I then was, the book remains true to its subject. Though our relationship was often marred in later, darker years, I have seen no reason to make any other than minor cuts and factual improvements to my account of life with Groucho in happier times.

PART ONE

1

Some years back, on my twentieth birthday, I received the following communication from my father, Groucho Marx.

'Dear Art, — Twenty years ago today you stuck your head out into the world, and I hope you're doing the same sixty years from now. This will give you a total of eighty years and when you get to my age you'll consider that plenty.'

A lot has been written about Groucho in his lifetime, but I've never read anything that sums up his philosophy of life quite so poignantly as those few lines of his own.

He's a sentimentalist, but he'd rather be found dead than have you know it. And he's a dreamer, although he likes to pass himself off as a disillusioned realist.

Why he persists in this attitude is something only he can answer.

He's lived a rich, full life, and he'll be the first to admit it. He started out at the bottom, the third son of an immigrant couple, and with his brothers — Harpo, Chico, Zeppo and Gummo — he worked his way to the top to become one of the world's best-loved comedians.

He's conquered every entertainment medium from vaudeville to television. He's had much success and very little failure, except in his early youth, and for a brief spell when he ventured forth into the field of playwriting and producing. The play, *Time for Elizabeth*, written in collaboration with Norman Krasna, folded after a week on Broadway. But that was more or less of an avocation, and, besides, it was deductible.

On his climb up the ladder he has enjoyed life to the utmost. He has shaken hands with Presidents, danced cheek to cheek with Marlene Dietrich, played baseball with Lou Gehrig, exchanged backhands with Jack Kramer, strummed guitar duets with the great Segovia, and he's insulted nearly everyone worth insulting (including two of my former employers, who promptly fired me).

He has owned expensive homes, eaten in the best restaurants, lived in the best hotels, had his clothes made by the best

17

tailors, been seasick on the best liners, and until he went to work for the Chrysler Corporation he was master of a fleet of Cadillacs.

But, unlike many show business personalities, Groucho's not at all interested in looking backward. He claims the past is something he'd just as soon forget. You'd almost think he has nothing but horrible memories of it, although I know this isn't the case.

Nevertheless, that's why I'm writing this book, and not he.

'Besides,' he's told me many times, 'when a person starts writing his memoirs, that's a sure sign he's washed up!'

Being 'washed up' is the one thing Groucho has always feared. No matter how well things are going, he's never been able to dispel the notion that it won't be very long (probably within the next day or two) before he'll be through in show business, completely destitute and a burden on society, living out his life in a home for old actors.

Since he still has seven years of a ten-year contract with NBC to serve, there seems little likelihood that this will be his fate. But, likely or not, the thought's disturbing enough to him to give him serious insomnia every night – and sometimes even in the afternoons, when it's his habit to stretch out on the couch in his study, with the radio going full blast, and take a short nap.

And he's been this way (worried, I mean – not on the couch) for as long as I can remember.

Back in the days before he and my mother were divorced, when my sister Miriam and I were still young enough to be living with our parents, the subject of 'What's Going to Become of Father?' would frequently crop up at the dinner table. It would usually be the result of something that had happened to him at the studio that day – either an argument with one of the front office executives about the script (generally culminating in threats from Groucho to quit the movie business forever) or else something that had occurred on the set.

He was never very happy when he was making a picture. The script was no good. The director was incompetent. The sound stage was draughty, and he was going to catch pneumonia. His brother Chico was too busy on the phone with a bookie to

18

memorize his dialogue. And he himself was giving a very uninspired performance. ('How can they expect you to be funny at eight in the morning?' was something he was always saying.)

Those were his standard complaints, and we learned not to pay much attention to them. But at least once during the shooting of every picture he'd come home even more downcast than usual; and, still in his frock-coat and painted black moustache (he was usually too tired to change), he'd take his place at the head of the table.

'I had a real shock today,' he'd begin in a tone so sombre you'd think something really terrible had happened – like Harpo or Chico dropping dead on the set, or at the very least that he had run over a pedestrian on his way home from the studio.

We'd wait, breathlessly, for him to drop the bomb-shell, which, for dramatic effect, he'd often hold in abeyance until after he had finished his tomato juice.

'A real shock!' he'd continue. 'I met a fellow on the set today who used to be a big star. Now he works extra for fifteen bucks a day, and he's glad to get that.'

We were always relieved to learn that it was only *that* again.

'Shows you what can happen if you don't save your money,' Groucho would go on, usually with a slight shudder. 'Here's a fellow who used to make ten thousand a week, and there wasn't even any income tax in those days. He had solid gold plumbing in his bathroom, and three swimming pools. Well, that's not going to happen to me.'

'Why should it?' Miriam, who fancied herself a comic, would ask. 'We don't even have one swimming pool.'

'No, and we're not going to. If you want to go swimming, there's a very nice pool at the tennis club. That's the mistake all these fellows make. They get their expenses up so high that when they stop working they're sunk. They think this easy money out here's going to last forever.'

The next day he would run out and buy another annuity, and that night at the dinner table he'd proudly tell us about it.

'With this new policy, when I'm fifty years old, I'll have forty bucks a week for the rest of my life – even if I never work again.'

19

'What makes you think you'll never work again?' Mother would ask, worried, probably thinking of the new car or fur coat she'd now be unable to talk him into getting her – at least for a couple of months.

'It happens to everyone,' Groucho would say with supreme confidence. 'There comes a time in show business when they just don't want you any more. And even if they do want me, I'm not so sure I can keep this up forever. I'm getting too old for slapstick. I'm tired, I've been working since I was fourteen years old. And besides, supposing I should get sick and not be able to work? Then what?'

At the time he was in his mid-forties, and had never been ill a day in his life. But he was expecting the worst – and almost welcoming it, it seemed – and he was going to be prepared for any eventuality.

Scenes of that nature would generally be followed by an economy wave, which would sweep resolutely through the Marx household, destroying everything in its path, such as charge accounts at Saks and Magnin's and the Westside Market; dinners at Romanoff's; extravagant plans for the future (new tennis rackets, bicycles, trips to Europe); and any contemplated rises in our allowance. And there would also be mild bawlings-out if anyone went out of a room without turning off the lights, or left the tap water running in the basins, or had too many shirts in the laundry, or bought something without first getting Groucho's consent, which he'd give readily if anyone bothered to ask for it.

But as a rule these economy waves would spend their fury within a couple of days; the accounts would be reopened (picking up a few new ones along the way); and everything would return to normal until the next time Groucho tangled with the top brass of MGM, or came across another destitute actor.

Since he went through this routine at least once during the making of every picture, and since each picture brought him that much closer to the termination of his contract, his anxiety about the future would increase proportionately.

Mother could never understand why he worried so.

Whenever we were in the throes of a new economy wave and she'd have to curtail her spending, she'd always predict – and with some bitterness, now that I look back on it – that Groucho Marx would never be so washed up that he'd have to seek extra work. But even she couldn't forecast that a television quiz programme called *You Bet Your Life* would eventually come along and springboard him to more fame and money than he had ever had before in his life.

Which, as you may have guessed, is exactly what happened.

Of course, he'd been considered one of America's top comedians ever since he and his brothers starred in three smash Broadway shows in a row – *I'll Say She Is, Cocoanuts,* and *Animal Crackers* – and appeared in two of the biggest-grossing comedies ever to come out of MGM – *A Night at the Opera* and *A Day at the Races.* But his name was never the household word it is today.

It's an ironic twist of fate – and a sad commentary on his judgement – that after he fortified his future with so many annuities he should be at the peak of his career at a time when the annuities are just reaching maturity.

But perhaps his almost pathological concern about the future is one of the reasons for his present popularity. Certainly it accounts for a good deal of it, for it has never allowed him to become complacent about his career or to take his ability for granted.

Whatever the reason, he's still completely astonished by his present success. And if I didn't know he was enjoying it so much, I'd be inclined to believe that he's just a little disappointed that he hasn't had to fall back on his vaultful of annuities.

2

If I've given you the impression that Groucho is a miser, I'd like to correct that notion at once. He isn't. On the contrary, he's one of the most generous men I've ever known.

If he likes you, he'll spend any amount for a present for you. If you're in need, he'll help you over the rough spots and never

21

ask for a penny of his money back. If you go out to dinner with him, he'll reach for the check, and unless you're a lot quicker and stronger than he is he'll wind up with it. And the same applies to movie tickets, caddy fees, or even a ticket at a car park.

For years he's been supporting a legion of impoverished relatives – some so distantly related that he doesn't even know them.

'And it's a good thing for them that I don't,' threatens Groucho. 'If I knew them, I wouldn't send them a penny.'

But along with his generosity he has some very peculiar quirks about money – especially his money.

To begin with, he refuses to be pushed into buying anything against his will, even if it's an item that he secretly wants. He believes that since he earned the money, he has the absolute right to decide when and how it will be spent.

And, secondly, he doesn't particularly mind how much he spends, but it hurts him to waste money, no matter how small the amount involved, and he'll go to great extremes to avoid wasting it.

Once, for example, he drove to Beverly Hills for a tin of tobacco. Beverly Hills, like a great many cities today, uses the parking meter system. The rates run from a penny for twelve minutes up to a nickel for an hour. Groucho figured that it would take him no longer than twelve minutes to make his purchase, but after he had parked in front of a meter he discovered that the only change he had in his pocket was a nickel. Now, the average person making $4,000 a week, and finding himself in a similar predicament, might throw caution to the winds and put the nickel in the slot. But not Groucho. He walked a whole block in the broiling sun – we were having a heat wave at the time – to get change of the nickel, then walked back to the meter to put the penny in, and then walked another block to the tobacco store.

On the other hand, he can be absurdly extravagant and never give it a thought. Several years ago, when he was only making $3,000 a week, he paid $1,800 to have an Inclinator installed in his house. An Inclinator is an electrically-driven contraption that carries him up and down stairs when he doesn't feel like making the journey by foot, which is never, now that he has the Inclinator.

However, he'll only stand for extravagance if he's doing the spending. If someone else – like a wife or a housekeeper – is doing the buying for him, he'll expect that person to be as frugal as Scrooge and Silas Marner put together.

I can still remember an incident that took place during the lush days immediately prior to the 1929 market crash.

We were living in a beautiful home on Long Island at the time, and Groucho was starring in *Animal Crackers* on Broadway. It was one of Broadway's biggest hits, and his net pay was about $2,000 a week. In addition to this, he was dabbling in the stock market on the side, and allegedly making a small fortune every day on Wall Street.

I was too young to play the market – I was eight, I believe – so Groucho decided to let me take riding lessons instead. But riding required riding pants, and I didn't have any. The result was that he sent Mother to New York to buy me a pair.

Mother found a likely-looking pair on sale at Macy's for $9 and sent then home COD, confident that she had made a good buy and a substantial saving. But when the delivery boy arrived with the pants and announced that it would take $9 to complete the transaction, Groucho looked at Mother aghast.

'Nine dollars for riding pants for a boy who hasn't been on a horse yet!' he exclaimed. 'That's absurd. I won't pay it.'

'They were the cheapest I could find,' said Mother. 'And it took me all day to find them at that.'

'Well, they're going right back,' roared Groucho. 'Nine dollars! I've never heard of such a thing. Why, when I was a boy you could buy a whole horse for nine dollars! Hereafter, let me do the shopping.'

The next day he took me to Abercrombie and Fitch and bought me a riding outfit that came to $41.30. On the way home he gave me a lecture on how women don't know the value of money.

When I pointed out to him that he had spent considerably more money than Mother had, he replied:

'You're darn right I did, but these are better pants. They'll outlast that cheap pair your mother bought you by at least two years.'

And as a matter of fact, they did last a long time, for he had bought them four sizes too large for me.

Groucho, of course, realizes that his spending habits are inconsistent, to say the least. And he himself isn't sure why he is constantly vacillating between a you-can't-take-it-with-you philosophy and the opposite extreme.

But in the case of the latter, he does feel that he's been greatly influenced by the impoverished days of his childhood and early youth, when money was scarce and the possibility of his ever getting any seemed remote indeed.

Minnie, Groucho's mother, had come over to America from Dornum, Germany, when she was fifteen years old and had taken a job in a straw hat factory on Manhattan's upper East Side.

His father, Sam Marx, had also migrated to New York City from the old country. Sam was an Alsatian, and a sterling patriot, who probably would have remained in his native country forever if he hadn't had to leave there abruptly to escape the French draft.

'He was only two years old at the time,' claims Groucho, 'but he was taking no chances.'

Actually, Sam was about seventeen when he strode down the gangway to take his first look at New York. And a dashing figure he was, in a green topcoat and a black stovepipe hat.

But though he was sartorially perfect, there wasn't a man in New York more ill equipped than he to earn a living and eventually support five sons. His command of the English language left much to be desired; he couldn't speak a word of it. And his French wasn't much better.

In addition to his linguistic shortcomings, he had no trade. Undaunted, however, by what some might consider serious handicaps, Sam, after finding himself a rooming house, set out to conquer the world. He immediately got a job as an instructor at a dancing school right round the corner from the straw hat factory in which Minnie had been toiling for about a year.

Finding themselves in a strange country, both Sam and Minnie knew very few people when they first came to America, and of course were extremely lonely. Although they didn't know each other at the time, both of them were whiling away their Sundays doing the same thing – riding the ferry boat to North Beach. On one of these Sunday excursions Sam, who knew a pretty girl when he saw one, finally worked up the nerve to introduce himself to Minnie, who also seemed to be without friends or even an escort. They got to talking, found that they had many things in common, and within a few months they decided to get married.

Shortly after the nuptials, Sam gave up being a dancing instructor, and decided to go into business for himself. He and Minnie opened a tailoring shop in a back room of their brownstone apartment on East 92nd Street, across from Rupert's Brewery.

Why Sam decided to become a tailor is a mystery.

'He'd had absolutely no training,' Groucho told me. 'And if you have ever seen one of his suits, you'd realize what an accurate statement that is. You see, Pop never used a tape-measure. He didn't believe in it. He said he could just look at a man and tell his size, with the result that frequently he'd make a pair of pants with one trouser leg seven or eight inches longer than the other.'

'Frenchie', as Sam was known to the family and friends, was a hard worker, but he never developed much aptitude for tailoring and the shop did not flourish. Judging by the record, he was a much better lover than tailor. In the short span of thirteen years he begot six children. One died in infancy. The five who survived turned out to be the Marx Brothers.

Listed in the order of their appearance, they were: Leonard (Chico) 1887; Arthur (Harpo) 1888; Julius (Groucho) 1890; Milton (Gummo) 1897; Herbert (Zeppo) 1901.

'Frenchie knocked off quite a few others, too,' claimed Groucho, 'but Mom never knew about those.'

With five hungry boys to feed, plus a number of unemployed relatives and assorted ne'er-do-wells also taking up residence in the Marx brownstone from time to time, there generally were more mouths to feed than food to fill them. Sam's take from the tailoring shop usually fell far short of what was needed to satisfy the grocer, the butcher and Greenbaum the landlord, whose $6 monthly rental charge did not exactly put him in a class with the robber barons of the day but who nevertheless could be pretty explosive when the Marxes didn't come up with the rent on time.

Considering such poverty, it was something of a miracle that Minnie was able to scrape together twenty-five cents every week to squander on piano lessons for Chico.

That Chico should get the lessons and not he was a sore spot with the young Groucho, for he believed that his older brother had absolutely no ear for music and that the lessons were being wasted on him. Groucho felt that he had the best ear for music in the family, and that therefore he deserved the lessons.

He never got them, however, which was no doubt the source of the intense rivalry he felt towards Chico all his life. In self-defence, Groucho eventually taught himself to play, strictly by ear, and employing an unorthodox style whereby he played the melody with his left hand on the lower register notes, and the chords with his right hand.

Money might have been scarce, but the Marxes somehow managed not to starve to death, thanks in no small part to Minnie. She was an accomplished charmer and could always talk the landlord into letting them keep the apartment, even though he knew, as well as she, that the prospect of his ever getting the rent was pretty dim.

'We never went hungry,' relates Groucho. 'At least, not *too* hungry. But there was generally some kind of a brawl at the dinner-table over who would get what. I distinctly remember one occasion when I almost lost my arm over a sweet roll.

'It was the last one on the platter, and all through dinner I had been eyeing it hungrily and trying to work up the nerve to reach for it. Finally, when I thought the other boys weren't looking, I stealthily slid my hand along the table and up on to the platter. But just as I did, Harpo picked up a meat cleaver, which he obviously had been saving for this purpose, and brought it down viciously in the general direction of my hand.

26

'I withdrew my hand just in time, but the platter was shattered into little pieces, and the cleaver went halfway through the table. What's worse, I didn't even get the roll. Uncle Julius wound up with it.'

Although Groucho was usually not averse to a little good clean fun at the family groaning board, that incident left an indelible impression on him. Poverty was not for him, he decided – not if it meant risking his life and limbs for a stale sweet roll.

Of course, there was no immediate salvation at hand. He was only twelve years old and hadn't started to work yet. But he made up his mind at the time that if he ever did get any money he would not squander it foolishly. He'd live well, but he'd salt enough money away so that, no matter what happened, he'd never have to worry about where his next sweet roll was coming from.

He never stopped worrying about it, however – even with a well-stocked deep-freeze at his disposal.

3

How my father became a comedian is a long story and one that I will touch upon just briefly, since I wasn't around to be an eyewitness in those days and can only take his word for it.

He was always an avid reader, but, despite his fascination for the printed word, he was not a born scholar. In fact, he wasn't any kind of a scholar, if his school record is any indication. He had a disdain for most of his teachers, and an unfortunate talent for being unable to solve the most elementary problems in arithmetic. These things, coupled with the fact that my grandparents couldn't really afford to support him through any more schooling, led to his decision, at the age of fourteen, to retire from the educational scene without waiting for his diploma.

But though he wasn't much of a one for academic studies, he was full of ambition. He had his heart set on becoming a doctor. Fortunately for the medical profession (and also for Harpo and Chico), there were no colleges at that time that would accept a student who had not even completed secondary school. And even if there had been, his parents wouldn't have been willing to send him.

So Sam and Minnie started looking around for a likely profession for their offspring. Harpo and Chico had already embarked on careers of their own – Chico as a piano-player in a neighbouring brothel, and Harpo as a delivery boy for a meat market. But what could Groucho do? He couldn't play the piano, and he had no desire to take up butchering as a substitute for surgery, 'although,' he contends, 'I've decided that there wouldn't have been much difference'.

Sam and Minnie looked to their family for ideas for Groucho's career. Admittedly, it was slim choosing; not many in the family have ever worked profitably. But there were some possibilities.

There was Grandpa Schoenberg, Minnie's father, who had once been a travelling magician in Germany.

There was Uncle Al Shean, Minnie's brother, who was already a star in show business and who later became internationally famous with his partner, Gallagher.

And there was Herman Schultz – a very distant relative. No one to this day is quite sure to which side of the family he belonged. But according to Marx legend, there seems little doubt Herman Schultz was the most colourful and enterprising of anyone on the family tree.

Herman Schultz was a chiropodist by trade, but when business was slack he was a professional firebug. He would go round setting fire to hotels so that their respective owners could collect the insurance money.

'His speciality was hotels in the Adirondacks – especially in the dry season,' relates Groucho. 'Herman would disappear for months at a time, and come back with a fistful of money. We didn't know he was doubling in arson at the time. All my folks knew was that he seemed very successful, and that whatever he was doing it might be a good idea for their son Julius to learn the same trade. Then one day we got a letter from Sing Sing, and my folks began to doubt the advisability of apprenticing me out to a combination chiropodist and arsonist.'

That narrowed the field right down to show business.

Groucho was hardly any better prepared for a career in the theatre than he was for one in medicine. Until then, his experience before the public had been limited to weekly appearances as a boy soprano in a local church choir. But at least a person could ad lib his way through show business and not run the risk of getting arrested for malpractice.

His first job (which he obtained by answering a newspaper ad.) was with a small-time vaudeville act called the Le May Trio. This paid him $4 a week and offered him a splendid opportunity to see the rest of the United States. It was a better opportunity to see the country than he had bargained for, however. After touring from New York to Colorado, without being enthusiastically received anywhere, the Le May Trio got cancelled in Denver, and Le May absconded with all the salary money.

Since Le May had failed to pay him for the preceding weeks as well, Groucho found himself stranded in Denver without the train fare home. In view of the circumstances, he took the only job available – piloting a horse-drawn grocery wagon over a precipitous mountain trail between Victor and Cripple Creek, Colorado.

He'd had no experience with horses before, except to give an occasional lump of sugar to the steeds being used in those days to hold up New York's mounted police force. But somehow he managed to keep the job for two months, by which time he'd saved enough money to buy a train ticket back to Manhattan.

A number of other ill-paying and short-lived theatrical jobs followed in quick succession. The high point of these was a melodrama called *The Man of Her Choice*, in which Groucho played the love interest. Evidently he played it too well, even though he was only seventeen, with just an academic knowledge of the facts of life, for his acting of the part soon got him in trouble.

It seemed that Elmer Harrison, who was producing the show and also doubling as the villain, was going steady with Rozella Keyes, the leading lady. And one night during a performance Harrison openly accused Groucho of taking on-stage liberties with his girl-friend.

'I might have been a little enthusiastic when I kissed her,' claims Groucho in defence of his behaviour at the time, 'but other than that I wasn't doing anything that Errol Flynn wouldn't be caught doing.'

At any rate, one word led to another, Groucho kicked Harrison on the shins, and a bar-room brawl ensued in front of the audience. This caused the curtain to be rung down prematurely, the act to be cancelled, and Groucho to be fired.

But at least he was in New York, not in Denver.

Harpo and Chico, meanwhile, were pursuing their own careers with varying degrees of success. Harpo was working as a bellboy in the Hotel Seville (on 28th Street, not in Spain), and Chico was song-plugging for Shapiro-Bernstein Music Publishers.

But my grandmother was not completely satisfied with the progress her 'boys' were making. And shortly after that she decided that they should have an act of their own. Chico was not available – he was still with Shapiro-Bernstein – but Harpo, Gummo and Groucho, under Minnie's prodding, were willing to take a crack at it.

The result was an act called (among other things) *The Four Nightingales*. The fourth nightingale was a fairly attractive girl whose name was Janie O'Riley. The ostensible purpose of the act was to sing harmony. Gummo and Groucho (so I've been told) were pretty good vocalists at that time, but Harpo could only sing a few discordant bass notes, and Janie always missed the high ones.

Altogether, it was a pretty untalented crew. Nevertheless, they managed to get bookings in small theatres in towns where the management wasn't too particular about the kind of entertainment it gave its patrons. Of course, each booking only lasted until the manager actually heard the Four Nightingales sing. But my grandmother was a good promoter, and whenever it was beginning to look as if they'd never get another booking, she'd always manage to pull one more out of the hat.

She couldn't keep this up indefinitely, however. Averaging one performance a theatre, it wasn't very long before they ran out of places where they could be booked. And the time eventually came when every theatre manager east of Chicago started running when he saw Minnie Marx approaching.

Unhappy, but far from discouraged, Minnie packed up the entire family, including Uncle Julius, Grandpa Schoenberg and Janie O'Riley, and settled down in Chicago. Chico, still plugging away for Shapiro-Bernstein, remained behind in New York.

Using Chicago as home base, the Four Nightingales embarked on an extensive tour of the South and Midwest. Harpo was still singing off-key, Janie O'Riley was still missing the high notes, and the act was still getting its customary lukewarm reception everywhere it played. They were frequently being cancelled by irate managers, and at least once a month they found themselves stranded without funds in some whistle-stop town.

Somewhere during all this they stopped calling themselves the Four Nightingales, and changed the name of the act to The Marx Brothers & Co. Presumably this was to hide their identity, but essentially the act was the same. They were fooling no one, and by the time they pulled into a place called Nacogdoches, Texas, they were prepared for what could have been a last-ditch stand.

Their first performance in Nacogdoches was at a matinée. It was a low-class, small-time vaudeville theatre. 'The audience was full of big ranchers in ten-gallon hats and a few small ranchers in five-gallon hats,' Groucho told me.

The first part of the performance went fairly well, but in the middle of the show the audience suddenly got up *en masse* and disappeared through the front exit. Investigation disclosed that the customers had gone outside to view a runaway mule.

Groucho and his brothers were accustomed to insults, and there was no particular reason why this one should have upset them so, but somehow or other it made them furious.

When the customers filed back into the theatre thirty minutes later, and took their seats, the show was resumed. But the Marx Brothers were no longer interested in giving a good performance, even by their low standards. All they wanted was to get even with the audience, and the only way they knew how was to

31

burlesque the kind of singing they had been doing so seriously.

This quickly evolved into a rough-house comedy bit, with the Marxes, led by Groucho, flinging insults about Texas and its inhabitants to the audience as rapidly as they could think of them.

Since this happened over thirty years ago, Groucho is not very clear about the exact phraseology of some of these insults, but he does remember calling the Texans in the audience 'Yankee spies', and throwing in a couple of lines that went something like:

> 'Nacogdoches
> Is full of roaches.'

and:

> 'The Jackass
> Is the finest
> Flower of
> Tex-ass.'

If these are samples, perhaps it's just as well that he can't remember any more of them. But at any rate they did serve to launch him on a successful career of ad libbing.

At the time, however, they were not looking for laughs; they fully expected to be tarred and feathered and run out of town on a rail. But instead the audience loved their clowning, and greeted the crudest insults and the most tired jokes with peals of raucous laughter.

And so they were suddenly comedians, with their fame travelling all the way to Denison, Texas. The manager of the theatre in Denison not only wanted to book them, but he offered to raise the salary for the whole act from $50 to $75 a week if they'd throw in an additional comedy sketch. Denison was soon to entertain a teachers' convention, and the manager expected a sell-out.

Groucho jumped at the offer, but Harpo and Gummo considered this move pure insanity. How could they promise to deliver a sketch they didn't even have?

'There's going to be a teachers' convention there,' said Groucho, 'so we'll give then a school act.'

Harpo and Gummo were still not convinced, but, having no alternative to suggest, they all put their heads together and the three of them dreamed up an act called *Fun in Hi Skule*. This was a hodge-podge of all the comedy bits they had seen and heard in other school acts, plus some original material that had been inspired by their own schooldays.

Being the most literate of the group, Groucho, of course, played the schoolmaster in the act. And to look the part he hid himself behind a black moustache, and wore for the first time his famous frock coat (which he borrowed from Uncle Julius, who was also on the trip).

'I tried to borrow the moustache from Uncle Julius, too, but he was very proud of his moustache, and wouldn't stand still long enough for me to cut it off. So I had to paste a phoney one on.'

Harpo played the part of a moronic country bumpkin – a standard character in those days – and to make sure he looked moronic he wore a wig which he improvised out of some old rope. Eventually, this became his standard stage character.

'The school act went over big for the teachers' convention,' boasts Groucho, 'and after that we were a pretty big hit everywhere else we played in Texas. I guess we could have stayed there indefinitely, but after we got ourselves reasonably solvent we decided to go back to Chicago. After all, how long can anyone stay in Texas?'

4

That was the beginning of Groucho's career as a comedian. And although it wasn't entirely inauspicious, he still wasn't very hopeful about the future. He was an extreme pessimist then, as he is now, and if anyone had predicted that he and his brothers would eventually wind up headlining a vaudeville bill at the Palace, he would have considered that person a most unreliable judge of entertainment.

He would have been wrong, however. The Marx Brothers, in

Home Again, took Chicago and New York by storm when it finally got there. In fact, their rough-house brand of humour was so popular with the sophisticated audiences at the Palace, and they were brought back for so many return engagements, that they became known as the Palace Stock Company.

Of course, it took them many years to make the transition from small-time to big-time vaudeville – years that saw a number of interesting developments in the lives of Groucho and his brothers.

For one thing, Chico gave up the song-plugging business shortly after the Texas tour, and joined forces with his brothers. Not only did he join them, but he persuaded them to abandon *Fun in Hi Skule*, and do a one-hour musical show called *The Cinderella Girl*. The book was written by Jo Swerling, one of the authors of *Guys and Dolls*, and the lyrics by the late Gus Kahn, who turned out to be one of American's most distinguished lyricists.

The Cinderella Girl was an immediate flop, and they did a number of other shows that weren't much more successful before they arrived at the Palace with *Home Again*. But *The Cinderella Girl* was a turning-point, nevertheless, for it established a pattern for their later successes. For the first time in their vaudeville careers Harpo, Chico and Groucho were a team, portraying essentially the same comedy characters that won them fame later on. And in addition to that, the new show featured Chico at the piano, and offered the customers a line-up of nine lively chorus girls. Thus sex was introduced in a Marx Brothers show for the first time (and according to reliable sources, into their personal lives as well).

And it was only fitting that Chico should be the one to introduce it. 'Chico was a real sport and a heavy spender, with the soul of a gambler and a bankroll to match,' maintains Groucho. 'When he wasn't shooting dice or playing cards, he was usually being pursued from town to town by an irate husband, or a father with a shotgun.'

Despite Chico's talent for getting himself in romantic and financial difficulties, the Marx Brothers couldn't have survived without him. His piano-playing, though not in a class with

Paderewski's, was definitely unique, and his tricks on the keyboard were a great favourite with audiences everywhere.

So much so that Harpo decided that he too would play a musical instrument in the act. This desire was hampered somewhat by the fact that there were no known instruments Harpo could play.

'That never stopped Chico,' relates Groucho, who is a little embittered on the subject after having listened to Chico's repertoire for the past forty years, 'and it didn't stop Harpo either!'

Needless to say, Harpo decided to take up the harp. He'd heard his grandmother strum one, and if she could master it, so could he — if he could get one, that is. He finally persuaded Groucho to send away for a harp, and after it caught up with him in Decatur, Illinois, where they were appearing, he buckled down to the business of learning how to play it.

Practising diligently in his dressing-room between performances, Harpo taught himself to play a few simple chords after only a week. And within two weeks he was playing duets with Chico in the act. The harp was a big hit with audiences, so it stayed in the show permanently.

Groucho, meanwhile, had bought himself a second-hand guitar, and he too was practising in his dressing-room at every opportunity. He had no desire to play it in the show, however; he simply enjoyed music. And apart from the cultural aspects of it, he had come to the understandable conclusion, after observing Chico's success with the opposite sex, that being able to play an instrument was a talent that could conceivably open many doors to romance.

In addition to trying to master the guitar, he soon found on his hands the responsibility of managing the act. Being the oldest, Chico had assumed the managership when he first joined the Marx Brothers. Part of his job was to collect the salary money from the theatre managers and distribute it among the cast.

'But we discovered very quickly that this wasn't a very practical idea,' says Groucho. 'There were substantial deficits every week, and they became more substantial as Chico's interest in the game of dice increased.'

As has been previously mentioned, Groucho is not a man who likes to see money go to waste – particularly his money. So when it became obvious that Chico would never make good the deficits, Groucho stepped in and took over the reins.

Actually, this suited Harpo and Chico fine, because one of the manager's chief functions was to get down to the theatre early in the morning and run through the musical numbers with the pit orchestra. Absolved from this responsibility, Chico and Harpo could sleep until noon, and usually did.

And any other worries concerning the show they left to Groucho, too, knowing that he was by far the most conscientious person in the company, and would ably take care of any complications that arose.

For some reason or another, he was always the most serious member of the group, and indulged in few of the pastimes that other actors found so engrossing. He hated staying up late, he drank very little, except for an occasional beer, and he disliked all forms of gambling.

Not that he disapproved; he just didn't get any kick out of that sort of thing. While his brothers were out on the town, or looking for suckers in the local pool-hall, he'd be in his hotel room, reading, or practising the guitar, or thinking up jokes for the act.

Reading was one of his favourite forms of relaxation. He devoured everything he could get his hands on, from *Variety* to political magazines to books on American history. He was a great newspaper reader, too.

One pleasure he did approve of was cigar-smoking. He was an inveterate cigar-smoker by the time he was twenty. He had picked up the habit from a tramp comedian who had tipped him off that a cigar was one of the most useful props an actor could carry with him on the stage. 'If you forget a line,' confesses Groucho, 'all you have to do is stick the cigar in your mouth and puff on it until you think of what you've forgotten.'

In those days he smoked only nickel cigars. But he had other ways of conserving money, too. While his brothers would generally end up at one of the more expensive hotels, he'd be staying at some shoddy place whose rates were in keeping with his income.

Since the entire act of twenty people was only getting $600 a week, his income wasn't very high. Nevertheless, he always managed to bank some of it, and would be constantly urging his brothers to do the same. His remonstrances, of course, were always greeted with jeering retorts – usually to the effect that he worried too much, or that he was an old grouch.

On one of their vaudeville tours through the hinterlands, Groucho and his brothers found themselves on the same bill with a monologuist named Art Fisher. Fisher's hobby was giving people nicknames. A few hours spent with my father convinced Fisher that he ought to be called Groucho. The origin of 'Harpo' is, of course, obvious. And Chico evolved from the fact that he was such a notorious lady-killer, ladies in those days being known as 'chickens'. And Gummo was so named by Fisher because he always wore 'gum-shoes', whether it was raining or not.

The new names were meant in jest, but soon the four brothers found themselves using them in place of their real ones.

It wasn't long after this historic event that the First World War came along and took Gummo, their straight man, with it.

To fill this important vacancy, my grandmother shipped Zeppo on to them. Zeppo was only sixteen at the time, but he'd had his fill of school, and was anxious to join the act.

A year of peaceful Army life was enough to convince Gummo that anything was better than being an actor, so when the war ended he stepped out of the act for good. As a result, Zeppo had a permanent job and also a permanent nickname. (There are many versions of the origin of the name Zeppo, but they are all so conflicting that the reader would do just as well to make one up himself.)

Zeppo's chief claim to fame, whenever anybody talks about the Marx Brothers, is that 'he was the good-looking one'. But actually he had talent as a comedian, too. Once, when Groucho became ill during *Animal Crackers*, Zeppo understudied for him.

'He was so good the audience couldn't even tell the

difference,' claims Groucho. 'I could have stayed out front every night, and no one would have missed me at all. And I would have, too – if I could have smoked in the audience.'

But four comedians would have been too much for one vaudeville act, so Zeppo took over the juvenile chores. By the time they scored their first big success in *Home Again* at the Palace in 1919, Zeppo was not only a first-class straight man, but an accomplished adagio dancer.

Home Again landed them in the big time for good. Oddly enough, it was written by their uncle, Al Shean, who was already an important star in vaudeville. Uncle Al didn't know whether or not his nephews had any talent, but he felt sorry for them after watching them flop in show after show. So when Minnie begged him to help her boys, he sat down in her kitchen and started writing *Home Again* on a piece of scratch paper.

Al Shean wasn't actually a writer, but he knew enough about the theatre to outline a good basic premise. With that to start from, Groucho and his brothers added some of their own inimitable jokes and comedy bits, and tried the show out in the small-time vaudeville houses around Chicago. *Home Again* caught on almost immediately, and was soon booked into the big time – the Majestic Theatre in Chicago. Two rave reviews sealed their success, and led to their being booked at the Palace in New York several months later.

Home Again's popularity in New York was evidenced by the fact that it played in the city for a solid year. By that time, the Marxes were getting $1,500 a week for the act, and eating well.

Once, when they were playing the Fifth Avenue Theatre at 29th Street, they went across the street to a restaurant between the matinée and evening performances. They lingered too long over their coffee, and didn't get back to the theatre until the curtain was going up. Having no time to paste on his phoney moustache, Groucho grabbed some black make-up, smeared on the painted moustache he made so famous, and hurried out on to the stage.

The laughs were just as numerous with the makeshift moustache, so he decided he'd stick to a painted one permanently. 'It was a lot easier to put on, and besides it didn't smell of ether like the glue from the phoney one.'

But the manager of the theatre was furious about the switch. 'Hereafter,' he said, 'I want the same moustache you gave 'em at the Palace!'

'You can have it,' said Groucho, picking the moustache up off the dressing-table and handing it to him. 'With my compliments!'

During the Marx Brothers' long stand in New York, the girl who had been dancing with Zeppo left the act.

My mother, whose name was Ruth Johnson, applied for the job and got it – probably on account of her looks more than her dancing ability. She was eighteen and strikingly pretty, and Zeppo envisaged a chance to combine business with pleasure.

He took her to dinner at Luchow's the night he hired her, and in the restaurant they ran into Groucho, who was dining with Gracie Allen. Gracie Allen, of course, hadn't married George Burns yet, and Groucho took her out quite often.

Zeppo introduced him to the new dancer, Groucho complimented him on his good taste, and then said to Ruth, 'I wish I could say the same for you.'

His opening remarks to a stranger are always a bit on the frightening side, and my mother tells me she had to fight back an impulse at the time to retreat to her native Cleveland.

The next day Zeppo escorted Ruth to the theatre for rehearsal. Back-stage they bumped into Groucho once again. He was carrying his guitar in its leather case, and he was on his way up the circular stairway leading to the dressing-rooms.

Noticing Ruth, he leaned over the iron railing, wiggled his eyebrows at her suggestively, and said in an off-hand manner, 'I ought to get married, so I'd have someone to carry my guitar!' He playfully shoved the guitar into her hand. She looked at him uncertainly for a moment, then smiled timorously and followed the brazen young star of the show up the stairs to his dressing-room.

Recalling the incident at the time of their divorce nearly a quarter of a century later, Groucho commented that that was the most costly remark he's ever made.

'It would have been cheaper to hire a porter,' he lamented miserably after the judge had just ordered him to turn over to Mother half of his $500,000 life's savings.

Perhaps because he came from a family of indigents himself, it was always one of Groucho's most fanciful ambitions to marry a rich girl.

To his way of thinking, money is more important than love – a state of mind he believes is evanescent, at best, and therefore should not be a serious consideration when choosing a wife. He always took good care to emphasize this point whenever the subject of girls and related topics came up between us in my youth.

He hasn't, however, lived by his own belief – if that, indeed, is what he truly believes. His three marriages – to women whose combined assets couldn't have kept one of them off welfare – are eloquent testimony to the fact that his cynicism about love quickly vanishes the moment he is in the company of a girl who's young, pretty and non-Jewish.

My mother's father, a Swedish immigrant named Oscar Johnson, was a journeyman carpenter. He was good at his trade, but always had to struggle to support his wife and two daughters.

No wife ever came to a husband with less of a dowry rating than Ruth Johnson. Which is probably why Groucho didn't get around to marrying her until 1920. He wanted to sock a little money away before taking on the responsibility of an additional mouth to feed. ('After all, white meat doesn't grow on trees.')

In the interim, they worked together in the same act, travelled the vaudeville circuits together, and dined together. But that's about all they did together, in spite of what Groucho might have had in mind the first time he enticed her to his dressing-room.

Ruth might have looked wanton and sexy while doing her adagio dance, but off the stage she was very proper and strait-laced.

Groucho himself could boast no great record as a conquistador of women in the towns along the Orpheum Circuit prior to meeting Ruth. Since he'd taken to the road he'd had a few fleeting sexual encounters with local hookers. And once he nearly succeeded in getting himself shot when he was caught in a hotel room with the wife of an actor on the bill with him.

But generally speaking, he never had the luck with women his brothers did. Chico, in particular, had the highest batting average of the four.

'He had a way with dames you just wouldn't believe,' Groucho recalled to me one evening with more admiration in his voice than I've ever heard him conjure up for Chico's other talents. 'He could walk into a strange theatre where there were thirty chorus girls on the bill with us. And after four days, he'd have laid half of them. He had no fear. He'd walk up to a girl – a complete stranger – give her a little squeeze on the rear end, and the next thing you'd know, they'd be in the hay. Or else he'd charm them with the piano. He was the worst goddamn piano player I ever heard. Absolutely no ear. Half the time I'd have to walk out of the theatre when he was doing his piano act. Yet he could sit down at a piano backstage and after one chorus of playing all the wrong harmonies, he'd have half a dozen great-looking broads drooling all over him. I guess today you'd call it sexual charisma.'

Why there should have been anything lacking in Groucho's own sexual charisma at that time, I can't imagine. He was thirty years old, clean-shaven, with dark wavy hair, the features of a leading man, and a well-coordinated body. In addition he was witty and entertaining, and rapidly blossoming into an intellectual. He'd been largely responsible for most of the writing in *Home Again*, to say nothing of their earlier acts, and a piece of his, published first in *Variety*, had been picked up by H. L. Mencken and reprinted in *The American Language*.

Perhaps it was the pungent aroma of those cheap cigars that were never out of his mouth or hand that kept him from being a second Rudolph Valentino. Or maybe it was his strangely ungallant way of treating the opposite sex as equals. He felt a grown woman was strong enough to open a door by herself, or to sit down at the dining-table without being helped into a chair by a man. Or possibly it was his sense of humour, which he claimed most women didn't appreciate.

However, Ruth Johnson was not to be put off capturing her man, either by Groucho's lack of gallantry or the smell of cigar smoke, which she was getting used to after their long engagement. In February 1920, while *Home Again* was playing a week's engagement at Chicago's McVicar's Theater, she and Groucho suddenly decided to get married.

Chicago seemed the appropriate spot for the ceremony. Sam and Minnie had been making the Windy City their home base for the past five years, and in addition, the bride's mother and father also had moved there from Cleveland.

The moment they announced their intentions, complications arose. They couldn't find a minister who would unite a Jewish boy with a Gentile girl — especially a couple who were in show business (which was not considered a respectable profession even as late as 1920). And the bride's mother, Josephine, was not overjoyed at the prospect of having a Jewish son-in-law.

In addition to being slightly bigoted, she was a religious kook — a jack-of-all-denominations. At various times in her spiritual life, she had been a Protestant, a Christian Scientist, a Mormon, a Baptist, a Seventh Day Adventist, and just about anything else you can think of.

And it mattered not to Josephine that Groucho wasn't a practising Jew — that he hadn't been in a synagogue since his bar mitzvah, and that the only reason he had shown up then was to get a fountain pen.

After making some frantic last minute phone calls, Joe Swerling (eventual author of *Guys and Dolls*), who was to be best man, finally solved the problem of who was to unite the lovers. He managed to find a Justice of the Peace who not only was Jewish, but also an ex-vaudevillian.

As for Josephine, she was still unwilling to accept the fact that her would-be son-in-law wasn't a member of one of her Christian denominations, but when Ruth showed her a clipping from the *Chicago Tribune*'s drama critic, Percy

Hammond, predicting stardom for the Marx Brothers, she finally consented to let the ceremony proceed.

Groucho heckled the Justice of the Peace unmercifully all through the ceremony. (Harpo could attest to this, because he was hiding behind a potted plant at the time and was moving the piece of greenery around the room, to make it appear that it was walking.) When the Justice intoned, 'We are gathered here to join this couple in holy matrimony,' Groucho interrupted him: 'It may be holy to you, Judge, but we have other ideas.'

Coming down the home stretch — pretty relieved that the ordeal was almost over — the Justice asked, 'Do you, Julius, take this woman to be your lawful wedded wife?'

'I've gone this far,' snapped Groucho. 'I might as well go through with it.'

There was no time for a honeymoon. In fact, there was barely time for a quick wedding dinner with the Brothers Marx and other members of the family before Ruth and Groucho had to hurry back to the theatre for that night's performance of *Home Again*.

I was born a year and a half later, on 21 July 1921. And to show his appreciation, my father gave my mother a box of cigars.

5

The years have blurred my earliest recollection of my father. I'm not exactly sure when or where it was that I remember seeing him for the first time.

Although it's difficult for me to differentiate between what I actually remember about Groucho in those days and what I've been told, I seem to recall seeing a man of his description hanging around when I was still in a crib. He was about thirty at the time, gaunt, bushy-haired and bespectacled, and for some reason my mother always called him 'Groucho'.

There was no such thing as a nurse or a housekeeper to look after me. For a while there wasn't even a house or, for that matter, any kind of permanent place to stay. Just hotel rooms. It seemed to me we were always travelling — for what purpose I didn't know.

The three of us usually shared one room in a hotel, and not a very good hotel at that. The Marx Brothers were working steadily, but $1,500 a week for the whole act was not really very much. Their individual salaries amounted to about $200 a week, and out of that they had to pay their own travelling expenses and hotel bills. And since Groucho now had a family, he was more determined than ever to save what money he could.

While he was not at the theatre, he seemed to spend much of his time in the bathroom. My mother had discovered soon after I was born that he enjoyed taking care of me. Not only that, he didn't even seem to mind washing nappies, so whenever it was possible she turned this chore over to him. When he wasn't washing nappies he was forced to spend most of his leisure hours in the bathroom, because it was the only place where he could read and play the guitar without waking me up.

In addition to the inconvenience of three in a hotel room, there was the question of what to do with me during the show, since my mother was still dancing in the act. Baby-sitters were unheard of in those days, and they couldn't leave me at the theatre during the performance, because most vaudeville houses didn't have individual dressing-rooms.

Groucho finally had to prevail upon a troupe of acrobats on the same bill with him to stay with me in the hotel room while the Marx Brothers were on the stage. The acrobats opened the show, and after their performance just had time to rush back to the hotel before my mother and Groucho had to leave for the theatre.

This arrangement worked out for a while, but finally Groucho had to let the acrobats go. They were conscientious baby-sitters, but they just couldn't refrain from practising their acrobatics in our hotel room. Apart from what this was doing to the furniture, the guests in the room below were constantly complaining to the manager about the disturbance overhead. The manager quite often thought it was Groucho beating up my mother, and wanted to throw us out.

The baby-sitting problem came to an end as a result of a small feud Zeppo had been carrying on with my mother ever since she had thrown him over in favour of Groucho.

For the climax of their adagio dance, my mother was supposed to do a very fancy back-bend, with Zeppo helping her up again at the finish. After they had been dancing together for some months, Zeppo discovered that my mother couldn't extricate herself from the back-bend position very gracefully under her own power. To torment her, he'd frequently let her struggle with the problem for what, on the stage, seemed like an interminable length of time before he'd condescendingly help her up. This made my mother look pretty ridiculous, and at the conclusion of their act there would always be an unpleasant scene in the wings.

But my mother liked being a part of the show, and she put up with Zeppo's unchivalrous behaviour until *On the Mezzanine* was playing in Los Angeles several years later. The incident that brought things to a head occurred one night during the performance. Zeppo, while swinging my mother round by her hands, somehow let her slip through his grasp, and she sailed into the orchestra pit, landing in the percussion section.

'The manager,' relates Groucho, 'rushed back-stage after the show and said he thought it was the greatest finish to a dance routine he'd ever seen.'

My mother, however, was not so pleased. She was pretty shaken up by the experience, and accused Zeppo of doing it deliberately. She felt he was trying to get even with her for what she had told him a few days before. She had told him that his hands were as rough as alligator skin, and that he ought to do something about them.

Zeppo's excuse for the slip during the number was that he *had* done something about them. For several days he had been using almond-cream lotion to soften his hands. He had put some on before this performance, and it had made his hands slippery.

Groucho hates family warfare of any kind, and when the problem was brought to him for arbitration, he voiced the opinion that there was justification for complaint on each side, and that the two of them ought to make more of an effort to get along, at least professionally.

But when my parents returned to our hotel room around midnight, I overheard her telling him tearfully that the Marx Brothers would have to choose between her and Zeppo. Evidently she felt that out of loyalty to his own wife he would decide in her favour. She was young and innocent, and hadn't been married to him long enough to realize that, although he'll go out of his way to be fair, he doesn't like ultimatums. Besides which, he'd been thinking for a good many months that a wife's place is in the kitchen, not in the percussion section.

'Ruth,' he said, 'we've been known as the Four Marx Brothers for a number of years now. I'm not going to change it just because you can't get along with Zep.'

'It's impossible to get along with that man,' replied Mother. 'He's much too fresh!'

'All right,' said Groucho. 'Then turn in your uniform. And tell the coach you won't be out for spring practice.'

This didn't get the laugh he'd been expecting, and when he saw the tears well up in her eyes he temporarily softened. 'Come now, Ruth. It isn't as bad as all that. Taking care of your son is a more important job than doing that bad imitation of Irene Castle.'

'It isn't that,' sniffed my mother. 'I just don't want Betty taking my place!' (Betty, Chico's wife, was also in the act, and there was some jealousy between them in those days.)

'She's turning in her uniform too,' said Groucho. 'I've already spoken to Harpo and Chico about that. No more wives in the act. Wives are a nuisance. There's only one place for a wife, and I won't go into that with a child present!'

With my mother assuming most of the baby-tending chores, Groucho volunteered for the early morning duty, which consisted of taking me to breakfast and for a walk afterwards. Even though the show kept him up late, he liked to rise early and read all the papers at the breakfast table. That way he'd be through with them by the time the noon editions came out.

At dinner-time, the three of us would generally go out to a restaurant together. One evening we were seated near a

46

prim-looking dowager at a table by herself. She was obviously quite distressed at finding herself so close to a couple with an obstreperous child in a high chair, but she was doing her best to ignore us.

I finished dinner first, and was given permission to get out of the high chair. I entertained myself by mopping up the dirty floor with a piece of toast. I was easily amused, and besides, I wasn't at all interested in Groucho's table conversation. He was a great raconteur even then, but I was too young to care much about his choice of subject matter at the dinner table. His subject would usually be inspired by an article he had read in a magazine, and whether it was politics, agriculture or medicine, he'd go on about it at great length.

I don't know what he was talking about that evening, but when I tired of pushing the toast around on the floor, I casually tossed it over my shoulder and it landed on the dowager's plate of ham and eggs.

My mother was horrified. 'Grouch,' she whispered, 'please go over and apologize to that woman.'

Rising obediently, he approached the dowager. She was glaring at him, but he maintained his composure admirably.

'Madam,' he said with a deep bow, and the proper amount of contrition in his voice, 'I'm sorry my son threw toast in your plate. And if he ever does it again, I'll have him throw the jam in with it.'

As I grew older I realized that Groucho could never quite decide whether to be a strict disciplinarian or a pretty soft touch. I think he felt that, for our own good, a little discipline was necessary. And our own good was always uppermost in his mind. But whenever he was on the point of meting out punishment, his sense of humour would get the better of him.

He didn't believe in spankings, and if Mother dared lay a hand on us, no matter how justified she was, he'd become furious. He used to say that grown-ups didn't have the right to 'slug' children who were too small to defend themselves. And besides, he felt, it wasn't safe. When the children grew up and were large enough, they might hit him. He always took the long-range view of things.

If my sister or I did something really bad — like lying or breaking a piece of furniture — he'd put us to bed and threaten to make us go without dinner. He claimed this was more effective than spankings. I don't know how effective it was, but it was certainly more pleasant, especially since, in all the years I was growing up, he never once carried out the threat about no dinner.

After I'd been incarcerated in the bedroom for a while, he'd open the door and say in a grim tone, 'Do you think you can behave yourself from now on?'

I'd, of course, answer 'Yes', and he'd reply, 'All right. Put your clothes on and come down to dinner. I don't know why I should have to eat that dinner, and not you.'

He punched hard to cover up his soft spots. He didn't have the heart to make anyone go hungry. Besides, he liked having his children around him at the table, and if it came down to a choice he preferred children's company to that of the grown-ups. This was always a source of contention whenever he and my mother were having ten or twelve people in to dinner. Mother believed that we should eat early on those occasions, and be packed off to our rooms before the company arrived.

But Groucho would have none of that. 'I don't see the kids all day. When am I going to see them if I can't eat with them?' he'd ask, even if he'd been around the house steadily for the past two weeks.

At the dinner table, he was always very conscious of whether we were eating or not. Frequently he'd interrupt his stories to bark out, 'If you don't drink all that milk, you're not going to get any dessert.'

If that didn't work, he'd try another tack. 'Don't you know that milk is good for you? It builds bones. It's good for your teeth. I always drank my milk when I was a boy, and look at my teeth — filled with cavities.'

Often his exhortations at the dinner table varied in accordance with what the medical writers were currently saying. One night he might admonish you for concealing your helping of spinach beneath an empty baked potato skin, and a couple of meals later he'd say to my mother, 'Don't force them to eat if they don't want to, Ruth. I read a long article by a doctor in *Harpers* today who thinks spinach is absolutely worthless — maybe even injurious. Leave them alone. Children are like animals — they'll eat when they're hungry.'

A couple of months after he first told me spinach was worthless, I tried leaving the spinach on my plate untouched. Glancing at my plate as the housekeeper took it away, he shook his head ominously and said, 'No spinach, no dessert.'

I reminded him that he had told me spinach was worthless.

'That'll teach you not to believe everything your father tells you,' he replied, handing me the cake platter.

It was a pretty confusing atmosphere in which to grow up. You never knew from one day to the next just what his views were on spinach. Or on anything else, for that matter.

He went through a long period once when his sole purpose in life, it seemed, was to keep me from putting too much sugar on my breakfast cereal. This phase reached a climax when we were still on the road with *Home Again*.

Because the four Marx Brothers frequently stayed at the theatre after their nightly stint, smoothing out the rough spots in the show and devising new routines, it was usually late when Groucho returned to the hotel. Consequently he wouldn't feel like getting up early to take me to breakfast in the mornings.

To spare my mother the pleasure, he bribed Ed Metcalf, one of the bit players in the show, to get me up every morning and take me to breakfast. Metcalf was a burly, red-faced Irishman who played the part of the detective in Harpo's renowned knife-stealing scene.

Groucho warned Metcalf not to let me pour the whole bowl of sugar over my oatmeal, but Metcalf construed it to mean no sugar at all. Every morning, for four successive days, he foiled my attempts to get the sugar bowl. By the fifth day I was getting pretty sick of him, and when he still refused to allow me even one small spoonful, I blew my three-year-old top and said, 'Pass the sugar, you son-of-a-bitch!'

Metcalf didn't quite know how to handle the situation. His first impulse, of course, was to wallop me, but, not knowing how Groucho might feel about it, he refrained from using brute force, and escorted me back to the hotel, remarking along the way that my father would undoubtedly give me a sound thrashing.

After Metcalf had departed, Groucho sat me down and shook his head in silent disapproval. After what seemed like hours, he finally said, 'Arthur, I'm surprised at you treating Mr Metcalf that way.'

'Well, he wouldn't let me have any sugar,' I complained.

'That's no way to get it,' said Groucho patiently. 'If you expect him to be nice to you, you should first say, "*Please* pass the sugar." Then if you want to spice it up with "you son-of-a-bitch", that's okay!'

6

The hard times that Groucho had been predicting – almost welcoming, it seemed – finally befell the Marx Brothers when I was barely out of nappies.

It came on the heels of an apparent windfall.

While Groucho and his brothers were sitting around during their summer lay-off in 1922, Abe Lastfogel, their agent, came up with an offer to play their new act, *On The Mezzanine*, at the Coliseum Theatre in London, England, for three weeks.

Naturally, they leaped at the opportunity. The pay was good, the job wouldn't interfere with any future bookings coming up on the Keith/Albee vaudeville circuit, and it would give them and their families a chance to see something of the world.

They left for England with high expectations. Now the whole world was going to be their stage – not just the United States.

But the trip seemed to have a jinx on it.

On The Mezzanine was an enormous flop in London. Jokes that had been killing the people in New York got boos and jeers from the English audience.

About half-way through the show came the crowning insult. The audience started lobbing pennies on the stage. In those days that was the Londoner's way of saying, 'Yankee, go home!'

Groucho, feeling that all was lost anyway, stepped to the

footlights, held up his hand for silence and announced in sombre tones, 'If you people are going to throw coins, I wish to hell you'd throw something a little more substantial — like shillings and guineas.'

This brought down the house, and although it didn't prevent the management from cancelling the act immediately after the performance, it changed what had promised to be a complete rout into a minor victory. Groucho's wisecrack on the brink of defeat not only won him the sympathy of the audience, but the line was quoted all over London, and it resulted in the act being booked by a rival theatre chain.

For their second attempt at what Groucho calls 'licking the Redcoats', the Marx Brothers discarded *On The Mezzanine* and resurrected *Home Again*. Its humour was dated, but apparently that's what the English music-hall audiences wanted.

Home Again was a huge success in London, and afterwards it toured the provinces for months before returning to the United States.

The Marx Brothers should have stayed in London.

When they returned to New York, they discovered that E. F. Albee, who was the head of the vaudeville circuit and an absolute tyrant, was furious with them for accepting an engagement in London without his permission. Although they hadn't been aware of it, one of the small-print clauses in their contract stipulated that it was strictly up to Albee whether or not they could accept employment elsewhere, even if he had no work for them on his own circuit.

The Marxes claimed that they didn't know those were the rules. And besides, what difference did it make? Their trip to Europe hadn't interfered with any jobs Albee had for them, had it?

Albee glowered and said that wasn't the point. He then slapped them with a large fine.

The Marxes countered by calling Albee a dictator, setting fire to his wastebasket, and refusing to pay the fine.

Understanding, warm-hearted man with a great sense of humour that he was, Albee tore up their contract and said he'd fix it so they'd never work in vaudeville again.

The Marx Brothers scoffed at Albee's blustering threat. They'd already been offered a contract by the Schubert chain, at more money, and now they were free to take it.

But the Schubert chain folded after a few months, taking the Marx Brothers' careers in big-time vaudeville down with it. There was nothing left but to start touring the sticks again. But they soon discovered they weren't getting many jobs in small-time vaudeville either. And, after a while, none. Albee, who was pulling strings in the background, was making his threat a reality.

The small theatre owners were afraid to book the Marx Brothers for fear of reprisal action by the vaudeville tzar. Unfortunately for the Marx Brothers, the smaller circuits were dependent on the overflow from Albee's circuit for their talent. If they crossed Albee in any way, he would see to it that their supply of talent was cut off, forcing their theatres to close.

So who needed the Marx Brothers?

The famine went on for several months, with things looking more and more desperate. Groucho had just about exhausted his savings buying bread for the three of us, and he was even considering going into another line of work (except no other line of work would have him), when Chico turned up with an offer to do a legitimate show.

It was one of the weirdest offers in the history of the legitimate theatre. A thumbnail history of it goes something like this:

A shoe-string producer, Joseph M. Gaites, had produced a flop called *Love for Sale*, with a libretto by Will Johnstone, cartoonist of the *New York Evening World*, and music by his brother, Tom. Gaites walked away from the disaster with no money – just a warehouseful of expensive scenery and props.

Shortly afterwards, Gaites met a man named James P. Beury, who was a successful coal dealer from Allentown, Pennsylvania. Beury not only had plenty of money, but he also owned the Walnut Street Theater in Philadelphia. The theatre was dark, but with the summer tourist season approaching, Beury wanted desperately to put a show in it.

Gaites, smelling a sucker, promptly suggested that he build a musical show around his left-over scenery. The idea appealed to Beury, so Gaites quickly contacted Will Johnstone and asked him if he had any ideas.

Johnstone had none, until he bumped into Chico one afternoon standing forlornly in front of the Palace Theater.

'What are you doing?' asked Johnstone.

'Nothing,' replied Chico, 'and I don't even think I'm allowed to stand here.'

Without any coaxing, Chico recounted the sad saga of the Marxes. Johnstone, who had seen them at the Palace, and been impressed, grabbed Chico by the arm and dragged him up to Gaites's office.

Gaites liked the idea of building a musical around the Four Marx Brothers and his leftover scenery, but not realizing their fortunes had sunk as low as they had, was fearful he couldn't offer them enough salary to make the venture worth their while.

Chico, on the other hand, was afraid to ask for too large a salary for fear of blowing the deal, so he said, 'We don't want any salary. Just give us ten per cent of the gross.'

Groucho was furious with Chico for offering to work without salary, but it turned out to be the smartest deal they ever made.

The show, hastily slapped together in three weeks, with Groucho and Will Johnstone collaborating on the book, was a hodge-podge of some new material and many sure-fire gags and routines the Marx Brothers had been killing audiences with for years. It opened at the Walnut Street Theater in Philadelphia under the misleading title of *I'll Say She Is*. Nobody knows the exact origin of the name, but it must have had some kind of magic, for the show was an immediate success, both with audience and critics, and it played seventeen capacity weeks in Philadelphia before running out of customers.

At that point, they had to make a decision: did they want to risk New York and a possible lambasting by the toughest critics of them all, which could mean folding? Or should they stay on the road and milk the less sophisticated towns, where their rough-house type of comedy was more certain to be appreciated?

The producer decided on the latter course. Why should they kill a sure thing just because of a little vanity? So *I'll Say She Is* toured the United States for nearly a year. By then the show was solid as the Chase Manhattan Bank. Every joke and comedy routine had been honed to perfection.

There was only one trouble. After a year, there weren't any other legitimate theatre towns to play. It was either take *I'll Say She Is* to New York, or close the show.

Faced with being unemployed again, the Marxes had no choice but to risk going up against Alexander Woollcott and the rest of the New York critics, who no doubt were already sharpening their stilettos in anticipation.

I'll Say She Is opened at the Casino Theater in New York City on 19 May 1924. It came in so completely unheralded that *The New York Times* hadn't even planned on sending Woollcott to cover it. They assigned their second-string critic to attend the Marx Brothers opening. But at the last minute, another show – the one Woollcott was supposed to cover – postponed its opening, so Woollcott changed his plans and deigned to see *I'll Say She Is* instead.

Groucho has always felt that that was the biggest break in the Marx Brothers' careers. Woollcott, at the time, occupied a pedestal of unparalleled importance in theatrical reviewing. 'If he liked you, you were made.'

He liked them.

Woollcott not only gave them a good review, he wrote a rave. The one he raved most about was Harpo. He wrote:

'There should be dancing in the streets when a great clown comes to town, and this man is a great clown.'

Singling Harpo out for such an encomium didn't exactly thrill Groucho. Harpo may have been his favourite brother, but Groucho has always believed that the word – either spoken or written – deserves more praise than a few funny faces and some well-timed honks on a rubber horn.

But if he was a wee bit envious of Harpo, he didn't let it spoil his enjoyment of seeing, the next morning, a line at the box office that wound clear around the block and up Broadway.

*

Minnie Marx's faith in her four sons had finally been vindicated.

Only one thing marred Minnie's complete enjoyment of her boys' triumphant return to Broadway's Great White Way. On opening night, she was getting dressed to go to the theatre, and while reaching for her hat, she fell off a stool and broke her leg.

But Minnie didn't let little things like a cast on her leg or the fact that she was in great pain keep her away from the Casino Theater that May night so long ago.

She insisted on being driven to the theatre in an ambulance. There she was carried down the aisle to her front-row seat by two white-coated attendants – just as the curtain was going up. And she remained in her seat, with her cast-encased leg propped up on the brass rail of the orchestra pit, beaming with maternal pride every time one of her boys socked over a joke, until the final cheer-laden curtain call.

Sam Marx, my grandfather, was as proud of his boys as Minnie – even though his grasp of the English language was pathetically small, and he didn't understand what half the jokes were about. Remaining in his seat during the interval, Sam overheard a couple in the adjacent row arguing about whether the Marx Brothers were real brothers.

The argument became pretty heated, with the wife stating that they were, and the husband insisting that they were 'fakes'.

The argument naturally piqued Sam's interest, and finally he tapped the husband on the shoulder and said, 'Oh, Mister, I think you are wrong. I know for sure the boys are brothers.'

The man looked at Sam sceptically. 'You know that for sure, do you?'

Sam nodded confidently.

'Want to make a little bet on it?' asked the stranger, taking out a handful of bills.

Sam considered the proposition a moment, then said, 'Vot odds will you giff me?'

As for me, I was too young to attend the opening at the Casino Theater and personally witness the Marx Brothers' transformation from just another rough-house comedy act into internationally-known stars who, from that evening forward, were never out of the spotlight. However, once the excitement of being in a New York hit wore off, Groucho would take me to the theatre on matinée days and let me view the performance from the wings. I regret that I was really too young to appreciate the comedy (and also the scantily-clad chorus girls who were milling around me in the wings), but I vividly recall two of the most celebated routines in the show.

One was the sketch where the detective (Ed Metcalf) was congratulating Harpo on his honesty. As Metcalf shook Harpo's hand vigorously, silverware began to fall clatteringly to the floor from Harpo's sleeve. The detective couldn't believe that he'd been deceived so completely, and shook hands with him again. More silverware rained on the floor. They kept this up for a good fifteen minutes, by which time the audience was paralysed from laughing so hard.

The other scene I remember was the one where Groucho, as Napoleon, was bidding farewell to Josephine before he departed for the battlefield. He made love to her passionately, and whispered sweet words in her ear, such as, 'Your eyes shine like the pants of a blue serge suit.' And after he had caught her with another man, 'Jo, you're as true as a $3 cornet.'

It was a little disturbing seeing him make such ardent love to a woman who was not my mother, but after I'd seen the show a few times I grew accustomed to it and accepted his explanation that it was all part of a day's work.

With the success of *I'll Say She Is*, our nomadic existence came to an end. We settled down in a spacious but not very luxurious apartment on Riverside Drive.

Not long after the opening, Groucho made his first extravagant purchase. He bought a seven-passenger Lincoln sedan for $6,000. The car seemed as tall as it was long, it had a window separating the driver's compartment from the back seat, and it was loaded down with all kinds of nickel-plated trimmings.

The Lincoln was delivered at the stage door of the Casino Theater one Wednesday afternoon during the matinée. Groucho was pretty excited about it. At one stage of his vaudeville career he and his brothers had all owned motor-cycles, and had travelled from town to town on them, sometimes transporting chorus girls on the handlebars. But this was his first full-sized motor vehicle.

Chico was on the stage doing his piano solo when the Lincoln arrived, and the Napoleon sketch was to follow. But Groucho couldn't wait for the show to be over before trying out his new car. Figuring Chico would be on for another ten minutes, he hopped into the Lincoln, and, dressed as Napoleon, went for a spin round the block.

The Lincoln performed smoothly, but Groucho had not counted upon the traffic being so heavy, nor had he taken the one-way streets into consideration. About the time the Napoleon sketch was to start, he was wedged in between two trucks three blocks from the theatre, and he was still trying to find a street where he could make a left turn.

'Chico had to play fourteen encores,' he contends. 'And this was pretty difficult, since he only knew ten numbers.'

In his desperation to get back to the theatre he made an illegal left turn, and of course a policeman stopped him. One look at Groucho dressed as Napoleon was enough to convince the gendarme that he was a refugee from Bellevue's psychiatric ward.

'But I tell you I'm one of the Marx Brothers,' insisted Groucho. 'And I'm due on stage right this minute.'

'If you're one of the Marx Brothers,' said the sceptical cop, 'let's hear you say something funny.'

'If you're a policeman, let's see you arrest somebody!' retorted Groucho.

There was no reason why that line shouldn't have landed him in the nearest jail, but evidently the policeman felt that only a Marx Brother would have the nerve to say such a thing, and he not only let him go, but escorted him back to the theatre.

The following Sunday Groucho, sportingly dressed in a pair of long pants, said, 'Ruth, let's go for a spin in our new car.' It was a beautiful spring day, and my mother and I were looking forward to an outing in the country as we climbed in the front seat.

But we got no farther than Central Park. There Groucho

parked the Lincoln under a tree and alighted.

'Why are we parking here?' asked my mother. 'I thought we were going for a ride.'

'Riding on Sunday is for yokels,' he answered.

He forthwith produced a duster, a jar of car polish and some rags. 'I have to polish the car. You and Arthur can sit on the grass and play.'

Stripping down to his undershirt, he laboured for the next three hours, and even polished the nickel plating. Passers-by must have thought we were the chauffeur and his family out for a jaunt while the Master was away at Southampton or Glen Cove for the weekend. After the car was as shiny as Groucho could make it, we piled in again and went back to the apartment.

That was how we spent every Sunday for the first year we owned the car.

Though you wouldn't suspect it from the way he spent his Sundays, Groucho was the toast of New York in those days. All the famous wits of that era – Dorothy Parker, Bob Benchley, George Kaufman, Heywood Broun, F. P. Adams, Harold Ross, George Jean Nathan and Alexander Woollcott – took the Marx Brothers to their bosoms and were fighting for their company. They were being quoted in all the columns, and wined and dined by the Long Island social set.

Suddenly finding himself accepted by Manhattan's brightest intellectuals was an enjoyable novelty, but Groucho didn't revel in it the way his brothers did.

He has never been a very gregarious fellow. Beneath his confident and caustic exterior lurks an enormous inferiority complex, largely born out of his limited formal education. He hates large gatherings of any kind. He has many close friends, most of whom are writers, but he prefers to see them individually or in small groups. And sometimes he prefers not to see them at all, or even his family.

'I'm a born hermit,' he once told me. 'My idea of a good time is to lock myself in my room with a big Havana and read the *New Yorker*.'

Harpo, Chico and Zeppo, however, were born mixers, the

life of any party. They gambled for high stakes, they were expert bridge and croquet players, they could do card tricks and they could entertain musically. Groucho might sing a song or two if he were in an exceptionally amiable mood, but generally he had to rely on conversation to make himself noticed. And for this he felt hopelessly inadequate alongside the likes of Kaufman, Benchley, Woollcott, Parker and the rest of the crowd. They could speak intelligently on every subject, and they tossed off big words with consummate ease.

Frequently he wasn't quite sure what they were talking about, but, feeling that he might not get another invitation if he remained too quiet, he took to breaking into the conversation by twisting their pontifical statements around into jokes, or making outrageous puns from their big words. Today he considers pun-making on a par with wearing lampshades and women's hats, but in the Roaring Twenties it was not only an acceptable form of humour, but, more important, it enabled him to enter into the most intellectual discussion without running the risk of revealing his ignorance.

'They never caught on to me,' he confesses proudly. 'They thought I was a great wit.'

Along with his joking he knew when to listen, and he learned a great deal from his new friends. He read the books he heard them discussing, saw the plays they recommended, and even started doing some writing of his own. Before long he was a frequent contributor to F. P. Adams's *Conning Tower*, and he was also beginning to get his humorous articles published in all the national magazines.

Today he's one of the few entertainers I know of who doesn't have to have his articles 'ghosted' but because he's in such a high income bracket it's almost impossible to get him to write anything. Over the years, however, he has published two books, *Beds* and *Many Happy Returns*, and they are still very funny. But as far as he's concerned, the high point of his literary career was when H. L. Mencken printed an excerpt from one of his articles in *The American Language*.

His self-education was pretty rapid because of his association with the literary set, and ever since he's been partial to writers as friends. Not out of any desire to be highbrow, but simply because he'd been hanging around the theatre all his life, and with the possible exceptions of George Jessel and Fred Allen (his favourite comedians, by the way) the companionship of other actors didn't amuse or interest him greatly.

He might have been the toast of New York when we were living on Riverside Drive, but I wasn't aware of it. All I knew was that the other children on the block had fathers who went to work every morning and came home at six o'clock. Mine hung around the apartment all day, like a bum, and read or played the guitar, or took me for long walks in the park. Finally, I went to him and told him that my playmates wanted to know why he didn't go to work in the daytime, like the rest of the fathers.

'You go back and ask them what their fathers do at night while I'm at the theatre,' he advised me. 'On second thought, maybe you'd better not. It's an unfair question.'

Actually, there were a great many advantages, I discovered, to having a father who was available during the day (except, of course, on Wednesdays and Saturdays, when he played matinées). And I think the other children in the neighbourhood appreciated having him around, too.

Groucho loved children – he still does – and was never so busy that he couldn't take time out to entertain them. He'd sing and play the guitar for us, he'd participate in our games, he'd treat the neighbourhood to ice-cream cones, and he loved to engage in long conversations with my friends. One of his favourite pastimes was story-telling. If other children were around, they could get in on it, too. But always, before leaving for the theatre in the evenings, he made it a point to sit down in the massive chair in front of the fake fireplace, light up a cigar, and tell me a special bedtime story.

Generally he'd stick to the tried and true classics, but they weren't very true when he got through with them. He'd keep the same story structure of the original, but it would be so full of jokes you'd hardly recognize it. It would be part Robert Benchley, part Ring Lardner, and part (a big part) Groucho Marx.

I was pretty young to appreciate the humour in his stories,

but what difference did that make? He told them well, and he could always manage to stretch a ten-minute story into an hour. And when bedtime is fast approaching, that's more important than actual content.

The other children who heard his stories were a litle mystified by them, too, but they seemed to enjoy them just the same. They liked being with him. And it wasn't because he was a celebrity, because I don't believe many of the children (or even the grown-ups) in the neighbourhood realized he was a star. (I know I didn't.) Riverside Drive and 161st Street wasn't a very theatre-conscious community, and besides, he wasn't easily recognizable in those days. He didn't wear a moustache in private life, and only his close friends and people in theatrical circles knew him as Groucho Marx.

Outside the theatre he still clung to the name of Julius H. Marx (he didn't change it offically to Groucho until years later), and from appearances he could have been an ordinary young businessman, except, as I say, that to most people he apparently had no business. His glasses and his habitual intense expression gave him a studious look; he lived modestly, displayed no theatrical mannerisms, and he stayed in the background as much as possible.

He enjoyed going unrecognized; it gave him an opportunity to converse with non-show people, like the butcher or the grocer, on their own level. He liked to get their views on things. Frequently, he'd kid them along at the same time, but if he did they never knew they were being ridiculed, he did it so subtly. He still indulges in that sort of thing when he can, but he wears a real moustache full-time now, and his television programme has made him so nationally known that it's almost impossible for him to play an anonymous role. Occasionally, however, it's his luck to come across some poor soul who doesn't have access to a television receiver, or who lives in an area where reception is bad or where there is no television at all.

I was with him the last time he met such a person. It was in Phoenix, Arizona, where we had gone to watch the Giants in spring training.

One morning, dressed in blue jeans and rumpled polo shirt,

he strayed over to a combination curio shop and fruit-stand that was across the street from the resort where we were staying.

'I'd like some fruit,' he said to the proprietor.

The proprietor was a mousy-looking woman, who obviously didn't recognize him, but she was terribly anxious to please.

'Certainly,' she said. 'What kind of fruit?'

'Do you have any wax fruit?' he asked.

She shook her head.

'I'm sorry to hear that,' he said, feigning disappointment.

'Why do you want wax fruit?' she asked, puzzled.

'I'd like to put some in my room,' he explained.

'What for?'

'Well, supposing some company drops in, I should have some fruit around, if I'm any kind of a host.'

'Why don't you get some real fruit?' she asked. 'We have lots of real fruit, and it's pretty cheap at this time of year.'

'No; I don't want real fruit,' he said, shaking his head solemnly. 'It rots, and then the first thing you know you're stuck with it. But wax fruit will last you a lifetime. You don't have to run out every time company's coming and buy more.'

'But what good is wax fruit?' asked the woman.

'I'll tell you what's good about it,' explained Groucho. 'Wax fruit looks better than real fruit.'

'But you can't eat it.'

'No; but it looks nice. And besides, I don't want my company coming over and eating my fruit. If they want to eat fruit, let them eat fruit at their own house.'

'I'm afraid I can't help you,' she said.

'For your own good you ought to put in a line of it,' he advised her. 'I'll bet you'd clean up with a good line of wax fruit here.'

She looked doubtful; there wasn't another customer in the store.

'How's business?' asked Groucho.

'Terrible!'

'How come?'

'Well, the curio shop down the street gets all the business.'

'Do they have wax fruit?'

'No. They have a wooden Indian out front, and people stop to have their picture taken with it, and then they drift into the store.'

'Why don't you get a wooden Indian?'

'Can't afford it.'

'What about a real Indian?'

'Can't afford that either. A real Indian would cost me about $8 a day.'

'How much can you afford?'

She thought it over for a moment. 'Well, no more than $1 a day.'

'I couldn't work for that,' said Groucho.

'Are you an Indian?'

'No; but I used to watch Jim Thorpe play football, and I once passed through the depot at Albuquerque. I know how they act. But I couldn't do it for $1 a day. Ten years ago, perhaps, but not with the inflated dollar today. It would hardly pay for my gas back and forth to Los Angeles.'

'You couldn't commute from Los Angeles,' she said.

'Why not? It's only 400 miles. I really hit it up when I'm on the road.'

'You just couldn't,' she said. 'You'd have to live here.'

'That's out of the question. My brothers wouldn't stand for it.'

'Your brothers?'

'Yes. Jimmy and Al Ritz. That's Jimmy over there' – he pointed to me – 'and I'm Harry Ritz. We're a night-club act but we don't work much. I thought maybe I could fill in as an Indian when we're not working. But I guess I'll have to forget it.'

Before we left, he thought he'd make up for wasting her time, so he bought a bag of real apples. Just as we were leaving the store, he took an apple from the bag and bit into it crunchingly. 'Say, this is quite good!' he exclaimed to the bewildered proprietor. 'Are you sure it isn't wax?'

The lady was still shaking her head as we crossed the street.

7

My mother never quite understood Groucho's sense of humour. And since his sense of humour motivates a good deal of what he says and does, it naturally follows that she never quite understood him either.

Most women don't, for that matter. He's a man's man, and a children's man, and possibly even a dog's man. But his behaviour in general is entirely too individualistic, and his attitude toward the female sex a little too bizarre, for him to be fully appreciated by women.

My mother realized, of course, that she was married to an extremely funny individual. And at times he could make her laugh as heartily as anyone. But she was a shy and retiring person and could never get used to the way he would openly defy convention, simply, it seemed, to see how many people he could shock.

By 'shock' I don't mean that he was vulgar, for I know of very few men who shy away from dirty stories and ribald speech more than he does. He considers smut the 'easy laugh department'. He never used it on the stage, believing it to be in extremely poor taste, and he rarely uses it in private life.

He doesn't mind ordinary cursing (though believes it symptomatic of an impoverished vocabulary). He'll tell an off-colour story occasionally, and even a very dirty one, if it's funny as well as dirty and only men are present. But he won't use obscene language just for the sake of being obscene. And above all, he won't resort to it in mixed company.

In this respect he's somewhat of a puritan. Not only does he refrain from telling obscene jokes himself in mixed company, but he deplores the use of them by anyone else. And he cringes with embarrassment when obscenities come out of the mouths of women.

Actually it was not so much *what* he said that annoyed my mother. Her chief complaint was that he didn't know when to be funny and when to act like a normal human being. He knew, of course; but, as I said before, he's an individualist, and sometimes he just can't control his impulses to do something that'll get a laugh. And the more solemn the occasion, the more difficult it is for him to control these impulses.

Groucho's behaviour at his wedding ceremony was a case in point. Very few women would stand for that sort of thing, much less think it funny. My mother put up with it for twenty-one years — a record, I'm sure — but it never ceased to embarrass her.

What was even more disconcerting to her was that at an occasion when an air of jocularity was necessary — like a party they were throwing — he might sit in a corner all evening, gloomily discussing the world situation.

And if she made an attempt to prod him into livening things up he'd retreat even further into his shell, start yawning at eleven o'clock, and shoo all the guests out of the house by eleven-thirty. Or if it was at someone else's house, he'd announce that he was coming down with a cold and that he had to get home and take a sleeping pill. He never actually does catch a cold. He gets what he now refers to as a 'grippy feeling', the symptoms of which are cold feet and the fact that his pipe doesn't taste good. This usually comes on about a week before he has to submit to an ordeal he isn't particularly looking forward to — like a big party, or the starting date of a picture, or a benefit where he has to make a speech, or sometimes it's even noticeable the night before his television programme is filmed. As soon as the ordeal is over, however, he's in perfect shape until the next one looms up on the horizon. And since he's pretty much in demand, both professionally and socially, he goes through one 'grippy feeling' after another.

But he never had a 'grippy feeling' when he took the family out to dinner at a restaurant. On these occasions, Mother could always count on him for big jokes, especially if the restaurant was crowded, and he hadn't made a reservation, and the head waiter didn't recognize him.

'Name, sir? There'll be a short wait.'

'Jackson,' Groucho would usually reply. 'Sam Jackson. And this is Mrs Jackson, and these are all the little Jacksons.'

Jackson was his favourite *nom de plume*, and Mother would always do a slow burn whenever he used it at a time like this. She knew that if he'd give the head waiter his real name we'd probably get a table immediately.

'Groucho!' she would whisper. 'Tell them who you are.'

'Why should I?' he'd reply. 'If I can't get in under the name of Jackson, then I don't want to eat here. I don't like restaurants where you have to be a celebrity in order to get in.'

'Then you should have made a reservation,' she'd say. 'You just can't walk into a restaurant on a Thursday night without a reservation, and expect to get seated right away if you don't tell them who you are.'

At this point we'd either leave for another restaurant, or else he'd appear to give in to her request and tap the head waiter on the arm. 'My wife wants me to tell you who I am,' he'd say. 'My name's not really Jackson. It's Schwartz, and I'm in the whole-sale plumbing supply business. And this is Mrs Schwartz, and all the little Schwartzes.'

If the head waiter thought he was peculiar, the waitress, when we'd finally be seated, would consider him completely mad.

'Miss,' he might begin, glancing up from the menu, 'do you have frog's legs?'

'I'll ask the chef,' she'd reply.

'No; you're not supposed to say that,' Groucho would explain in a patient tone. 'When I say, "Do you have frog's legs?" you're supposed to answer, "No, rheumatism makes me walk this way."'

She'd nod, bewildered, and he'd say, 'Okay. Now let's try it again. Miss, do you have frog's legs?'

Her face would go blank. 'It isn't on the menu. I'll have to ask the chef.'

He'd shake his head. 'Now you've spoiled it. We'll have to start all over aga—'

'Grouch,' my mother would interrupt. 'This girl is busy. Why do you waste her time with such foolishness?'

'It's not foolishness. It might come in very handy for her some day. Supposing vaudeville comes back and she wants to get up an act. Look at the shape she'd be in with this sure-fire material. She wouldn't have to run around trying to find someone to write some stuff for her at the last minute. She'd have it right on the tip of her tongue.'

He had many variations of this routine, all stemming from old and tired vaudeville jokes, and none of them ever failed to infuriate my mother. She used to say that if he wanted to make himself look ridiculous that was his business, but she wished he wouldn't do it when he was with her.

This was like asking Ben Hogan to stop playing golf. He couldn't – he got too much fun out of it, especially if he thought it amused me or a close friend of his who happened to be along. Besides, and at the risk of sounding traitorous, I suspect that it was really a way of drawing attention to himself without actually revealing his true identity. For a number of years he had a fixation about not wanting to get any special privileges just because he was a celebrity. He couldn't bring himself to walk into a restaurant and say 'I'm Groucho Marx.' But at the same time he couldn't completely reconcile himself to being unrecognized. So he took the reverse tack, making himself conspicuous by other methods.

He was never at a loss for other methods. Just when my mother would think he was going to behave himself for a change, he'd come up with some fiendish new scheme.

My father hates sight-seeing, for instance, but once when we were on a trip to Salt Lake City with him, Mother talked him into going on a guided tour through the Mormon Tabernacle. My father's deportment was admirable through most of the proceedings, and he even seemed to be interested when the guide stopped the group in the main auditorium and started to lecture us about the fine acoustics in the building.

This is the high point of the tour through the Tabernacle, and the guide always finishes his talk by announcing that the acoustics are so amazing that you can 'actually hear a pin drop. To prove it, ladies and gentlemen, I'm going to drop a pin, and I want you to be very quiet and listen to it drop.'

A rapt silence settled over the group as the guide took a pin from his coat pocket, held it in the air dramatically for a moment, and then let it fall to the floor. You couldn't hear the pin drop, but the people, obviously mesmerized by the ritual, imagined that they did, and nodded their approval.

'I see you all heard it,' said the pleased guide, ready to move on to another point of interest.

'I couldn't hear a thing,' answered Groucho in a loud tone from the rear of the group. 'Would you mind dropping it again? And use a bigger pin this time – a bowling pin. I'm a little hard of hearing!'

A burly guide approached him from the rear and tapped him on the shoulder. 'We don't want any wise guys around here, mister. We'd like you to leave now, without giving us any trouble.'

'I'm not a wise guy. But I paid my money, and I think I'm entitled to hear a pin drop.'

'Would you like us to call the police?'

'You can't arrest me. Do you know who I am?'

My father was aroused, and my mother, though annoyed, was at least pleased that he was going to abandon his mantle of anonymity, to save us from complete disgrace.

'No. Who are you?' asked the guide. He still didn't know my father, but there must have been a spark of recognition, for his tone had softened somewhat.

'My name's Jackson,' said my father. 'Sam Jackson. And this is Mrs Jackson, of the Stonewall Jacksons.'

The Jacksons were promptly expelled from the Mormon Tabernacle, and my mother and father didn't speak for the remainder of the trip.

8

Groucho never wanted to play Hamlet. But during the First World War he had dreams of becoming a farmer.

So compelling was this idea that he talked his brothers into pooling their financial resources with his and purchasing a 5-acre farm in La Grange, Illinois. They were going to raise chickens and grow vegetables for the war effort.

Since La Grange was within easy commuting distance of Chicago, they figured they'd be able to attend to the farm chores in the forenoon before leaving for any vaudeville engagements they might be fortunate enough to have.

It seemed like a practical arrangement, and anyone but the Marx Brothers probably could have made it work.

Unfortunately the Marx Brothers didn't know anything about chickens, and the chickens didn't know anything about the Marx Brothers.

Like good farmers, they rose at five o'clock the first morning and attended to the chores.

'By the second morning we weren't so enthusiastic,' recalls Groucho. 'We didn't get up until six. By the third morning we were getting up at seven. And by the end of the week we were getting up just in time to have a leisurely breakfast around eleven o'clock, and then, if we were lucky, we had to leave for the city to go to work.'

Needless to say, a rigorous schedule like that left them little time for caring for the needs of a thousand hungry chickens and for ploughing the fields.

Even when they weren't working they refused to hang around the farm. They'd find other reasons to go to the city.

While they were pursuing their various interests, the farm would be left in Sam and Minnie's care. Sam knew even less about chickens then he did about tailoring. As a result, the chickens were dying off rapidly and the five acres were going to seed.

The Marx Brothers didn't care. They were embittered on the subject of chickens by the time they had owned the farm for a couple of months. The chickens weren't laying. Not only weren't the Marxes getting fresh eggs, but they were afraid they'd lose their draft exemptions if they couldn't prove to the agricultural inspectors the government sent out that they were producing enough food to make a dent in war-time shortages. But the Marx Brothers were an ingenious, never-say-die lot. They overcame this problem by buying eggs at the grocery store and planting them under the hens whenever they got word that the government officials were coming out to inspect the place.

'We fooled them for quite a while,' Groucho admitted to me once, 'but they finally caught on to us when we made the mistake of putting brown-shelled eggs from Long Island Reds under our hens, whose eggs were supposed to have white shells.

'Fortunately, we all flunked our draft physicals because of bad eyesight. So we sold the farm immediately and moved back into the city.'

After this experience, Groucho realized that he wasn't cut out to be a farmer. But like most boys born and brought up in the city, he still had dreams of owning a house in the country.

Being the cautious type, he didn't buy his house until after *Cocoanuts* – a satire on the Florida land boom written by George Kaufman and Irving Berlin – was firmly established as a Broadway hit in 1926.

He could have afforded a house before that if he had been willing to buy it through the time-honoured mortgage plan. But apparently all the melodramas he had seen in the past, in which leering villains foreclosed mercilessly on destitute heroes and heroines, had left their mark on him. He refused to let himself be put into such a vulnerable position, and wouldn't buy a home until he could pay all cash for it.

Our first house was in Great Neck, Long Island, and my parents found it on one of the few Sundays Groucho spent driving our Lincoln instead of polishing it. It was made of brown stucco, and it had three storeys, ten rooms, a steep-pitched slate roof, and an even steeper bluestone gravel drive-way that washed down to the street corner in every rainstorm. After each storm, Groucho could be seen rushing down to the corner with shovel and a wheelbarrow and hauling the expensive bluestone back to our driveway.

Great Neck was just rural enough for his tastes. It was forty-five minutes from Broadway, and the closest chicken was in the poultry market in what was then a very tiny suburban village.

In those days, before it became overpopulated, Great Neck was more or less a show business colony. Some of our neighbours whom I can remember were Al Jolson, Ruby Keeler, Eddie Cantor, Jane Cowl, Sam Harris (who produced *Cocoanuts*), Larry Schwab (another Broadway producer), cartoonist Rube Goldberg, *Saturday Evening Post* writer Sam Hellman, F. Scott Fitzgerald and his wife Zelda, Ring Lardner, and Bobby North (also a Broadway producer). In addition to the fact that he was friendly with most of this crowd, Groucho liked Great Neck because it enabled him to live the life of a country gentleman. No one was better suited to being a country gentleman than Groucho.

He was a very enthusiastic and conscientious young home-owner. If anything, he was a little too conscientious to suit my mother. She felt, and often said so, that it was a woman's job to run the house, and a man's job to earn a living. He agreed with her in principle, but since his job enabled him to do both, he frequently did, whether she fully appreciated his interference or not.

He couldn't help it. He'd been living in hotels, apartments and boarding houses all his life, and when he finally became a home-owner, nothing could allay his enthusiasm for getting deeply involved in its management.

At first, he was mainly concerned with the care of the grounds and the planting of a fruit orchard. His idea of a perfect dessert is a bowl of fruit, and he had wild dreams of stepping out of the back door some day and being able to pick apples, pears, peaches, cherries and plums right off his own trees.

It never happened this way, because we had to move away before the trees reached a fruit-bearing age.

'The story of my life,' insists Groucho. 'I've spent a fortune buying fruit trees and raising them. And every time they reach the stage when they're about to bear fruit I move to another house.'

At the time, however, he had no idea that this would be their fate – or rather, his fate. He treated them with tender care, and spent many an hour at the nursery in the village of Great Neck trying to find out why they weren't already bearing.

'What's the matter with those crooked fruit trees you sold me?' he'd ask the man at the nursery. 'They're not doing anything.'

'But Mr Marx – they're baby trees. Give them time.'

'I don't want to give them time. I'm not getting any younger, you know. Pretty soon I'll be too old to eat. And in the mean-time I'm spending a small fortune for fruit at the market.'

To appease him, the nurseryman would stick him with $30 or $40 worth of the latest gardening equipment, and send him home believing that he was a natural-born horticulturalist.

This he wasn't. He was fair when it came to pulling out weeds, he could mow a lawn adequately, he could clip a privet hedge very unevenly, and he could tell the difference between roses and lilacs. But Luther Burbank had nothing to fear from him.

Eventually he realized this, and broke down and hired a gardener. But his interest in his fruit trees never waned.

He watched their progress closely from day to day; and if one of them became diseased and looked as if it were going to die he'd feel as depressed over this as he would over the illness of a good friend.

Back he'd go to the nursery, sometimes accompanied by the gardener, but more often with me, and there would be a long conference with the nurseryman about insect sprays, plant food and fertilizers.

When he wasn't trying to prod his fruit trees into growing faster, he'd be chopping down other trees. He likes a lot of light in his houses, and we had a number of stately shade trees on the premises that kept our rooms continually dark during the day.

So he bought a two-handled lumberjack's saw, and, with me assisting, starting hacking away at the tall timber and cutting the trees up into logs for the fireplace. In addition to being a frustrated farmer, he must have been a frustrated lumberjack in those days, because even after there were no more trees blocking the light he still kept on chopping down the timber with a Paul Bunyanesque fury.

At any rate, we soon had plenty of daylight in the house — just as we had an abundance of lamplight at night. He wouldn't stand any lamps or wall brackets that weren't practical enough to take 100-watt bulbs. If Mother brought home a lamp purely for decorative purposes, he would make her take it right back.

He's still that way. When he goes on a trip, he carries a couple of 100-watt bulbs in his suitcase, just as a precaution.

'I've spent too many nights groping my way around hotel rooms and going blind trying to read by those dim yellow lights they give you,' he says.

In Great Neck, Groucho wasn't just concerned with growing fruit and keeping the house light. The first summer that we had moved into our new home he decided that we ought to join a beach club. After investigating a number of them, he drove us over to the Sands Point Bath and Sun Club, filled out an application and handed it to the manager.

'Are you Jewish?' asked the manager, not at all impressed that the applicant was a celebrity enjoying huge success on Broadway.

'Not a practising one,' replied Groucho. 'Actually, I'm an American.'

'Well, we're very sorry, Mr Marx,' said the manager, 'but we don't allow Jews to swim at our beach.'

'What about my son?' retorted Groucho. 'He's only half-Jewish. Would it be all right if he went into the water up to his knees?'

However, Groucho was allowed to join Lakeville Country Club – at the time, perhaps the finest golfing layout on Long Island's North Shore. The initiation fee was five thousand dollars, which was a lot of money for the way Groucho played golf, but Eddie Cantor, Al Jolson and Ruby Keeler (who was married to Jolson at the time) were all members, and he enjoyed their company, so he splurged. Besides, there was no reason for Groucho to believe he couldn't become a scratch shooter if he applied himself. He already had a hole-in-one to his credit – made at the Brae Burn Country Club in Boston a couple of years earlier. It had been quite an exciting experience for him, too.

Because he was a world-famous comedian, news of his feat made the front page of *The Boston Globe*'s sport section the morning after it happened, along with a picture of Groucho in a little box. The box was flanked on one side by a picture of Bobby Jones and on the other by Walter Hagen. The caption read simply 'Groucho joins the immortals.'

That afternoon, when Groucho arrived at Brae Burn to take

his daily exercise, he found he was being trailed by a phalanx of newspaper reporters and photographers.

Under that kind of pressure, he took a twenty-two on the same hole where he'd previously scored the ace, and about a hundred and twenty-two for the entire round.

The next morning the sports page ran the same illustration, with one change. There was a blank space in the box where Groucho's picture had been. And underneath it, the caption read 'Groucho leaves the immortals.'

The longer Groucho was a home-owner, the more he became interested in all phases of running the house – even the shopping. Mother was a good shopper, but Groucho didn't trust her judgement entirely. He had to go along.

First of all, it gave him the opportunity to wander through the grocery store gossiping with the assistants and some of the pretty housewives. And secondly – and more importantly – there was then no chance of the wrong kind of rye bread or pumpernickel being smuggled into our house. Groucho has always been particular when it comes to rye bread and pumpernickel.

If Mother was busy at home, Groucho would frequently do the shopping for her. And even though she didn't particularly like his interfering with the running of the house, there were certain advantages to his doing the shopping. He'd usually go to the most expensive food speciality shop in town – the one he had warned her not to patronize – and he'd come home loaded down with all kinds of imported delicacies and out-of-season fruits and vegetables.

'Why don't you buy this kind of cheese when you go shopping?' he'd say smugly. 'That cheese you bring home tastes as if it was made in a soap factory.'

'Because they only have processed package cheese in the regular markets. And you told me not to go to the one you just went to. You said they were highway robbers.'

'They are. But they have good stuff. Even their meats and vegetables are better, if you want to know the truth.'

'Do you want me to go there from now on? I will if you want me to.'

'Yeah. Why don't you try it for a while?' he'd say. 'I don't know that they are so much more expensive, at that. At least you get something for your money. Not like that roast we had the other night that was all fat.'

But as soon as Mother would start patronizing an 'extra fancy' market on her own, and the bills rolled in, Groucho would become furious.

'I don't know why it costs us so much for meat this month,' he'd say, riffling through the bills. 'Why, the average family could live all year on what it cost us for meat this month.'

'The average family doesn't buy their meat at Kleinhardt's.'

'Then why are we buying our meat there? I'm sure the stuff is just as good at the A and P.'

'You told me to go there.'

'Well, you're the woman of the house. You should know better.'

If you could say nothing else about Groucho, at least he was inconsistent. And that always kept things from being dull around the house.

I think he did it deliberately. He'd rather be unreasonable than dull or trite, with the result that it's practically impossible to win an argument from him. No matter how justified you are he'll twist things around so that it's your fault. It's a defence mechanism he resorts to rather than have to admit he's wrong.

He'd rather do anything than admit he's wrong – even if it means risking his life.

I know of no better example than the time back in 1927 when his stubbornness was nearly responsible for wiping out the entire Marx family and a Swedish nurse named Sadie.

It was on the day we were bringing my mother, our new baby, Miriam, and the nurse home from the hospital in New York City, where Miriam was born.

Groucho, in his anxiety to get Miriam home safely, was driving very slowly and cautiously, even for him. And when we approached the railroad crossing in Great Neck, he slowed the Lincoln to such a snail's pace that it stalled – right on the tracks.

He stepped on the starter several times, but the engine wouldn't respond. At that moment we heard the familiar tooting of a Long Island Railroad train approaching from around the bend.

'The 3.02 is right on time,' remarked Groucho, glancing calmly at his wrist watch.

'My baby!' screamed Mother. 'Let's get out of here.'

'And leave a $6,000 dollar car on the tracks?' replied Groucho. 'Not I. These cars don't grow on trees, you know.'

'I don't give a damn about the car,' said Mother hysterically.

'Well, I do,' replied Groucho. 'She's got a lot of miles in her yet. She just flooded, but I'll get her started. Just be calm, everybody – be calm.'

But nobody was calm, and he *couldn't* get the engine started. And when the train came into view, Mother grabbed Miriam from out of the arms of the nurse, alighted from the car and urged the rest of us to run for our lives, too. Sadie and I did, but Groucho remained at his post, refusing to be swayed by female hysterics.

As the train drew closer, Groucho suddenly shouted out of the window, 'Hey, Ruth – in case I get killed, the key to the vault is behind *The Works of Shakespeare* in my study!'

Mother shuddered and refused to look. Groucho was quite pale himself, but as I mentioned before he's a pretty stubborn fellow. He sat there, grimly trying the starter, and out of the corner of his eye watching the train come closer and closer.

I often wonder what would have happened if the train hadn't turned out to be a local that had already started to slow down for Great Neck Station before it ever rounded the bend.

Fortunately it was, and it came to a grinding halt just ten feet short of the Lincoln.

'Damn!' said Groucho, as we all piled back in the car. 'Now I have to find a new hiding place for the vault key!'

Mother was furious with him during the rest of the ride home, but he insisted that he had done the only thing possible under the circumstances.

'After all,' he said righteously, 'would a captain desert his sinking ship? Would Lord Nelson quit the Battle of Trafalgar?'

9

I don't know whether or not the incident at the railroad crossing had anything to do with it, but soon after that Groucho hired a chauffeur named Otto.

Having a chauffeur to drive him to and from the theatre, while he sat in the back seat puffing importantly on a large cigar, was the fulfilment of a boyhood dream.

But Otto was not with us for long – Groucho never had much luck with chauffeurs. Either they talked too much while he was in the back seat trying to think up new ad libs for the show, or else he just didn't approve of their driving. It was usually the latter.

He's one of those people who hate to drive themselves, but who trust very few others behind the wheel of an automobile – especially his automobile. He'd deny that he's a back-seat driver – and I'd be the last person in the world to accuse him of it – but God help you if you don't keep your eye on the road every second, obey all the traffic laws, and follow his directions on how to get somewhere, which will usually land you eight or ten miles from your destination.

Apart from the fact that he considered his own driving superior to that of most chauffeurs (which will give you a slight inkling of the calibre of man in our employ in Great Neck), there was another reason why he eventually abandoned the idea of having a driver.

Chauffeurs always doubled in butlering – at least the ones who worked for us did – and Groucho didn't approve of fancy service at the dinner table. All he asked for was good, simple cooking. It angered him to have to wait for the meat, the potatoes, and the vegetables to be brought in one at a time on separate platters and passed slowly round the table by the butler.

'What became of the potatoes?' he'd bellow impatiently after he'd helped himself to the meat and the butler had disappeared inside the kitchen for a moment. 'Has that guy got lost or something?'

'Give him time, Grouch. He probably had to wait for Hazel to dish them out.'

Groucho would give him another ten seconds, during which

time he'd be glowering at the meat on his plate. If the butler hadn't returned by then, there would be another explosion.

'This is a hell of a way to have to eat,' he'd say in a loud tone. 'By the time I get the potatoes and vegetables, my *meat*'ll be ice cold. Why can't we just put all the food on the table at once and help ourselves? That's the way we did it when we were kids.'

'No one does it that way any more.'

'Why not?'

'It just isn't done.'

'Well, what about the families where they don't have anyone else to pass the food? I'll bet *they* get the meat and vegetables at the same time.'

'That's different. But if you're going to have someone to do the serving, you might as well do it right.'

'Who cares what's right? I'd rather be poor if I have to go through life getting my vegetables fifteen minutes after my meat. Who are we trying to impress, anyway?'

My mother came from humble beginnings herself, and wasn't trying to impress anybody. But Great Neck was a wealthy community, and she knew that if she served boarding-house style, some of the more catty wives would criticize her housekeeping abilities. She didn't want that. Not with her husband one of the leading lights on Broadway.

They finally reached a compromise when they discovered that they could buy a silver serving platter that was divided into three compartments: one for potatoes, one for vegetables, and one for meat.

Even with the new dish, Groucho would have preferred having all the food on the table at once, but in those days he was still pliable enough to make certain concessions to the female sex which he wouldn't dream of making today.

One of the many concessions he wouldn't make was eating by candlelight. My mother, like many women, felt that candles added a soothing, romantic atmosphere to a dining-room. Groucho felt they were something for the Dark Ages.

It was quite a shock to Mother to see his reaction the first time she tried lighting our dining-room in Great Neck with candles only.

'What's this — a coal mine?' he said, walking straight to the electric light and flipping it on. 'I have to see what I eat. Candles are for tea-rooms and gigolos.'

If they had company, he'd allow my mother to have the candelabras lit until the guests entered the dining-room and were seated. Then he'd announce, 'If you've all seen the candles we'll dispense with them immediately. We just want you to know we have them.'

The chances are that he wouldn't even leave the candelabras on the table. He'd put them on the sideboard. He hated to have anything obstructing his view of the person across the table from him. Table floral displays were also an anathema to him, particularly if they were tall. 'Who's buried under there?' he'd remark, and soon the flowers would be on the sideboard alongside the candlesticks.

In addition to the fact that he insisted on the dining-room being as brightly lit as a movie set, he had — and still has — some pretty eccentric eating habits. In the thirty-two years I've known him, I don't believe he's ever sat through an entire meal without complaining about the food, the service, or both.

And he'll complain no matter where he happens to be eating — at your house, his house, or in his favourite restaurant. He's not at all biased that way.

Another thing Groucho always insisted on at home was eating at a 'reasonable' hour. Nothing upsets him like having to wait until eight-thirty or nine for his dinner (even if he isn't a bit hungry before then).

When he and my mother were giving a dinner party, he'd wait until the guests had had time for one drink, and then he'd start asking, 'Hey, Ruth — when are we going to eat?'

If she told him that dinner wouldn't be ready for perhaps another twenty minutes, and that he should help himself to some *hors d'oeuvres* if he was hungry, he'd say, 'I don't want to get filled up on all that tea-room fodder. Why isn't dinner ready?'

'You know how it is when you have roast beef, Groucho. It's better to let the people wait than have the roast well done.'

'That's the cook's look-out. What's she been doing in that

79

kitchen all day that she can't have the dinner ready on time? I'll have to give her a talking to.'

Before the next dinner, he'd instruct the cook to have dinner ready at seven-thirty and no later. That was certain to be the night that Max Gordon, a well-known Broadway producer (who was usually an hour early), or some other of his friends, would show up late, and the roast would be well done.

'I don't know why it's so hard to get the roast beef the way I like it,' he'd say to my mother the following morning.

When she'd point out to him that the well-done roast beef was the usual result of putting the roast in the oven too early, he'd shake his head sadly and mutter, 'Amateur cooks – the world is full of amateur cooks!'

If he discovered, after several dinners at someone else's house, that his hosts were habitual late eaters, he'd make a mental note of it. The next time he was invited there he'd have his dinner at home first, despite my mother's protests that it was impolite and that he wouldn't like anyone to do that to him.

'No one has the right,' he'd tell her, 'to invite you to dinner at seven o'clock and make you wait until ten before giving you something to eat.'

If he found that a couple he knew were habitual late arrivers, he had his own way of curing them of the habit. He'd start dinner without them the next time it happened. Coming into a dining-room and finding dinner half over was sure to embarrass people and teach them to be more punctual in the future.

Mother thought this was impolite, too, but Groucho said, 'When I tell people seven o'clock, I don't see how they can misunderstand me to mean a quarter to eight. My diction isn't that bad. I can be heard in the last row of the balcony.'

He also expects guests to leave at a reasonable hour. He doesn't like to have them hanging around until three or four in the morning. He wants to go to bed.

He'll never tell anyone to leave, however. If his guests persist in ignoring his yawns, he'll stand up and make the announcement that he's tired and going to bed. 'You people stay as late as you like. You know where the liquor is – enjoy yourselves.'

'You'd be surprised,' he once told me, 'how many people

stay and have a hell of a time after I go to bed. One of these days I'm going to throw a party and never come out of my room at all. I think it'll be a smashing success.'

This isn't a new practice with him. He was doing it when we were still living in Great Neck. I think he learned it from an experience he had with Ring Lardner, who was a frequent visitor to our house in those days. Lardner was one of his best friends and favourite authors, and he loved to come to our house and discuss show business with Groucho over a glass of brandy. Groucho enjoyed his company immensely, except for one thing – Lardner would never go home.

After staying up until 4 am with him on several occasions, Groucho decided that he was getting too old for keeping such late hours. (He was thirty-six at the time.) He'd have to teach him a lesson. So the next time Lardner visited us and seemed disinclined to leave by midnight, Groucho stood up and said, 'I don't know what your plans are, Ring, but I'm going to bed.'

Lardner told him to go right ahead, and when Groucho came down to breakfast at nine o'clock the following morning his guest was sitting in the same chair, staring into space, drunk.

'I thought you were going to bed,' said Lardner. 'Don't let me keep you.'

Groucho imagined Lardner was playing a practical joke on him, but the same thing happened whenever he came over after that.

'I never did cure Ring of staying late,' recalls Groucho. 'But it taught me one thing – never let a guest tell *you* when to go to bed. I'll gladly pay for the liquor, but they'll have to drink it in their own time.'

Much as he likes to sound inhospitable, Groucho has always been a very soft-hearted host. He could never say 'No' to anyone who called up at the last minute and wanted to bring an extra friend or two. And if none of his guests imposed upon his hospitality in this way, he'd usually think of someone *he* wanted to invite at the last minute.

After many years my mother became hardened to this sort of thing, but when she first set up housekeeping she was a very nervous and inexperienced hostess, and the slightest change in plans would upset her terribly and was almost certain to precipitate an argument.

It started with the very first dinner party they gave in the new house in Great Neck.

I don't remember what the occasion was, but they were having ten people in to a sit-down dinner: the George Kaufmans, the Max Gordons, the Sam Harrises, the Bobby Norths, and the Bill Parkses, some wealthy non-show business neighbours of ours.

My mother, of course, was extremely apprehensive. Not only because they had never attempted to entertain ten guests before, but because the Parkses were coming. Parks was not part of the show business crowd. He was a wealthy manufacturer who lived across the street in a house that made ours look like a squatter's shanty. But he had become friendly with my mother and Groucho because they were neighbours, and he had had them to dinner a couple of weeks before. They had come home awed by the fact that the Parkses had had five servants to wait on four people in the dining-room.

They couldn't hope to compete with that kind of class – and I'm sure the Parkses didn't expect them to – but nevertheless my mother was pretty jittery about returning the invitation, and she went to great pains to make her dinner as nice as possible.

We had a couple working for us, but Mother hired an extra serving girl so that the vegetables wouldn't be late coming in. And she must have spent at least a week arranging and rearranging the table settings. This was the most difficult part of all, for our dining-room was not especially large, and when the table was extended with extra leaves there was barely room to walk round it. And even with the extra leaves it was going to be a tight squeeze getting all the place settings at the table, and still have room enough for the candelabras and a rather large bowl of flowers.

But somehow she managed, and by the time the party was only an hour away our dining-room looked like a picture layout in *House Beautiful*, and my mother, in a new hostess gown, was beginning to feel confident that she had nothing to fear.

Then the phone rang and Groucho answered it. 'Sure,

George, bring him along. This is Liberty Hall. Always room for one more.'

Hanging up, he turned to my mother and said quite casually, 'Put on another plate, Ruth. That was Kaufman, and he's bringing Morrie Ryskind along. Ryskind's his new collaborator. He's a lot of fun.'

My mother turned white. 'Oh, my God,' she cried as though she'd been mortally wounded. 'How could you do such a thing to me?'

'What's wrong?' asked Groucho calmly. 'We have plenty to eat, haven't we?'

'Of course we have. It isn't that. There isn't any more room at the table.'

'Don't be ridiculous. We can always make room for one extra person.'

'But we can't. There's barely enough room at the table as it is.'

Groucho looked unconcerned. 'Then we'll set up a card table.'

'And spoil the looks of everything? Besides, there won't be room enough to get round to serve.'

'I'm sure we can manage. Just set up the table.'

'Isn't it going to look awfully strange having one person at a card table?'

'Then let Arthur sit at the table with him. He wanted to stay up with the company, anyway. Now there'll be room for him.'

'But Groucho – grown-ups don't want children around.'

'Oh, stop making such a big issue out of one extra person. My mother used to cook for eleven people every night, and you never heard a squawk out of her. And if she could do it alone I don't see why we can't – with three servants to help!'

That settled it. A card table for four was set up in a corner of the dining-room. It was to accommodate not only Morrie Ryskind and me, but two others whom my mother had decided to move over from the main table. She had made this strategic move at the last minute, figuring that since the card table had to be in the way of everything, anyway, she might as well load it to capacity. For with two fewer people at the main table she could make it smaller by removing one of its leaves, and there would be more space in the dining-room for the servants to get round.

Everything probably would have proceeded smoothly and according to plan after that if Morrie Ryskind hadn't shown up with two extra uninvited guests himself.

'Mr and Mrs Harry Ruby,' he said, introducing the songwriter and his wife to my mother and father. 'I hope you don't mind, but the Rubys didn't have anything else to do tonight either, and I thought you might need someone to play the piano.'

'Don't give it a thought,' said Groucho in a hearty voice. 'This is Liberty Hall. No trouble at all.'

Mother would have been glad to argue this point with him if she hadn't been so busy helping the maid put the leaf back in the dining-table again, and the two place settings that had been removed earlier back on. By the time this was done, the domestics were in a state of complete bewilderment, from which they didn't emerge for the remainder of the evening.

It turned out to be a real Alice Adams party, with everything, of course, going wrong.

The first thing that happened was that the serving girl arrived drunk. In her first and last appearance of the evening, she came swaying through the living-room with a plate of hot *hors d'oeuvres* and dropped them in Mrs Parks's lap.

'She couldn't have dropped them on Ryskind,' commented Groucho. 'She had to drop them on one of the invited guests.'

The serving girl was paid off and on her way home in a taxi by the time dinner was announced.

When the roast beef came in for the first time it was practically raw, and Groucho had to send it back to the oven for another thirty minutes. During the interval, the guests adjourned to the living-room for another round of cocktails made of bootlegged gin and orange juice.

Promptly upon our return to the dining-room, Groucho removed the candles and the flowers from the table and put them on the sideboard.

'Isn't that better?' he said. 'At least we can all see each

other. At least, I hope we can all see each other. If we can't I'm going to get another bootlegger.'

The roast beef was finally pronounced fit by a board of experts consisting of Harry Ruby, George Kaufman and Groucho. But when it took the butler five minutes to serve three people, I could see that Father was already getting annoyed.

'Can't he leave the meat, and we'll pass it?' he asked Mother. 'Then he can go and get the potatoes and the vegetables.'

Mother gave him a silencing stare and went back to talking with Millie Gordon. Groucho went back to staring balefully at the lonely slice of beef on his plate, then got to his feet and stormed into the kitchen. He returned a moment later with the mashed potatoes and a gravy boat and ladle, and handed them to the dignified-looking Mrs Parks.

'Here, girlie,' he said. 'Help yourself, and pass them around!'

Mother was horrified, as Mrs Parks smiled without conviction and helped herself to the mashed potatoes. But Mr Parks laughed heartily and said to Mrs Parks, 'Groucho's got the right idea, Emily. Why can't we do the same when *we* have company?'

That was all the encouragement Groucho needed. Jumping up, he rushed back to the kitchen, came out in a moment with the peas and carrots, and started them around the table family style.

'Now will you please sit down and eat your dinner?' demanded my mother. 'Clarence can do the rest.'

'Clarence is a *schlemiel*,' said Groucho. Clarence was in the kitchen out of earshot by then, and Groucho was happy at last. He had his meat, potatoes and vegetables on his plate all at the same time.

'Marx,' said Max Gordon, 'you really know how to live! If I tried that at home, Millie would bash my head in.'

'Give me time,' said Groucho. 'The evening's not over yet.'

And it wasn't. The worst was yet to come.

The dinner itself was considered a success. The food, for

some odd reason, was good, and everyone had two and three helpings.

It was after the table had been cleared and the coffee was about to be served that it happened.

When Clarence came in with the first cup of coffee and set it down at my mother's place, Groucho said, 'You mean to say you're going to have to make fifteen trips back and forth to the kitchen just to serve coffee?'

Clarence nodded.

'Put it all on a big tray,' suggested Groucho. 'It'll save you some work, and we'll be able to have the coffee *with* our dessert.'

Clarence disappeared inside the kitchen, and returned five minutes later with fourteen cups of coffee on a huge tray.

'That's more like it,' said Groucho, getting up. 'And I'll get the cream and sugar!'

He was crazed with success. He was confident, as he dashed into the kitchen, that he had found the perfect formula for good service at home. He was not so confident as he dashed out again with the cream and sugar and collided with Clarence, who at that moment was passing in front of the swinging door with the tray of coffee cups.

All hell broke loose as the two of them crumpled to the floor amidst the clattering of falling china and silverware.

In an instant my mother was in the kitchen and out again with an armful of dish towels, and the cook was right behind her flailing a mop.

Groucho still hadn't had time to pick himself up. He was lying on the carpet in a puddle of lukewarm coffee, with broken cups all around him. But there was one cup that hadn't broken. It was standing right side up, with a few drops of coffee still in it.

Raising himself up on one elbow, Groucho lifted the cup with his free hand and drank from it.

'Are you all right?' asked the cook, bending over him.

'Of course I'm all right,' said Groucho amiably. 'It was a splendid dinner all around. There's just one thing I want to know! Why isn't the music playing?'

10

Actually, our life in Great Neck wasn't very social. It couldn't be – not with Groucho playing in a show six nights a week and doing matinées on Wednesdays and Saturdays.

Sunday was his only night off, and that was usually when ne and Mother would have company, or else go to dinner at the homes of friends. Occasionally they'd make dates for other nights of the week, but it would have to be with the proviso that their friends would be willing to go their own way after dinner, or else accompany Groucho to the theatre and see the show.

This wasn't a very practical arrangement, since a good many of their friends lived and worked in the city, and couldn't always get to a dinner in Great Neck as early as Groucho had to eat in order to make an eight-thirty curtain. He could have met them in the city, of course, and sometimes he did, but he preferred to dine at home, because he had had his fill of eating out when he was in vaudeville.

Sunday night was also the only night of the week when he could see a show other than his own. And because it was such a rare treat for him to be in the audience instead of on the stage, he was usually in a very good mood when he went to see someone else perform.

One Sunday evening he took Mother to the Wintergarden, where the great Houdini was appearing. During his act, Houdini announced that he was going to do his famous needle-threading trick. He would put some thread and a dozen sewing needles in his mouth, and the needles would come out on the thread. And to prove to the audience that he didn't have some needles already threaded concealed beneath his tongue, Houdini asked for a volunteer from the audience to come up on stage and examine his mouth.

Groucho volunteered and took his place on the stage beside Houdini.

'Very well, sir,' said Houdini. 'Now, before I do this trick, I want you to examine my mouth very carefully and tell the audience whether or not you see anything in there.'

Houdini opened his mouth wide, and Groucho peered in.

'I see something,' he said.

'You do?' said the surprised Houdini. 'What do you see?'

'Pyorrhoea!' answered Groucho, and he returned to his seat.

Most nights, Groucho, Mother and I (and Miriam, when she reached the age of two) would have a six-thirty dinner by ourselves, and then Groucho would leave for the theatre alone. Sometimes Mother would go with him, but only if she didn't have to see the show.

She had seen *Cocoanuts* and *Animal Crackers* performed every night during their Boston and Philadelphia try-outs, and many times more after they had opened in New York, and an alarmed look would cross her face at the mere suggestion that she should sit through either one of them again.

'I don't blame you,' Groucho would say. 'If I were in your shoes, I wouldn't see it either. And I wish I were in your shoes. I'm getting pretty sick of this turkey myself. I'd like to stay at home once in a while, too.'

Mother wasn't too fond of staying at home alone. Great Neck wasn't very built up in those days, it was especially lonely at night, and the house seemed large and frightening to her.

There was nothing that Groucho could do about that, but to make Mother feel a little more secure he bought a .32 calibre pistol and kept it in the top drawer of his dresser, where it would be easily accessible in case anyone tried to break into the house while he was gone.

A week after he bought the gun, Mother came into the bedroom and found Miriam, who was a toddler by then, standing on a chair in front of the dresser, with the gun in her hand.

She retrieved the gun before Miriam could do any damage, but when Groucho came home she told him what had nearly happened and ordered him to get rid of the gun immediately.

He turned pale, but he said, 'Why get rid of it? I paid a lot of money for that gun. We'll just have to find a place where Miriam can't get hold of it.'

For about an hour he went through every corner of the house looking for a safe place to hide the gun. Finally, his expression brightened, and he walked to the wall safe in their bedroom and opened it up.

'Why didn't I think of this before?' he said, putting the gun in the safe, closing the heavy iron door and twirling the dial. 'Miriam will never get at it in here.'

'But, Grouch,' protested Mother, 'the safe's the first place a burglar will go to. How will I ever get the gun out if I need it?'

'We won't use that gun for burglars,' replied Groucho. 'We'll get another gun to keep in a handy place!'

He was joking, of course, about getting a second gun, but the original gun remained locked in the safe from that day on.

Fortunately, Mother never had any need for it, but she was always a little unhappy whenever she was in the house by herself.

Groucho was very understanding about these matters. He realized that being the wife of a legitimate stage actor could be an awfully frustrating experience six nights a week, if she didn't go out once in a while without him. So generally he was pretty co-operative about what she wanted to do while he was at the theatre. And if she didn't have any ideas, he'd more than likely suggest something himself.

If Mother didn't want to go out by herself, it would be perfectly all right with Groucho if one of his bachelor friends, like Sam Behrman or Morrie Ryskind, took her to a show – or even to a night-club.

It wasn't any problem getting escorts for Mother in those days, even on a platonic basis. She was one of the prettiest women around Manhattan, and no one could do the Charleston better than she, nor was anyone more willing.

Groucho didn't mind a bit – just as long as *he* didn't have to do the Charleston. He hated any kind of night life himself, and if he could get his friends to take her dancing it relieved him of the duty.

On Wednesdays and Saturdays Groucho stayed in town after the matinée, and Mother, whether she had any after-dinner plans or not, always drove in and ate with him at Moore's or Sardi's between performances. It was usually Moore's, because in addition to having good food and being handy for the theatre it was the most brightly lit restaurant in New York.

Sometimes, at Groucho's suggestion, I would go along and have dinner with them. I always considered this a great treat — not only because he would take me backstage before the performance and let me play with the props and scenery, but because it was fun eating in Moore's even for a child of six.

A good many prominent personalities ate there in those days, and Groucho would point them out to me as they came in.

'There's Jack Dempsey,' he'd say. 'He's Champion of the World. You'd better behave yourself at the table tonight, or I'll have Jack come over here and knock you out.'

Or, 'You see that fellow over there? That's Will Rogers. I taught him to play the guitar when we were on the bill together in Grand Rapids.'

Groucho knew everyone, from Eddie Cantor to Mae West, and at some point during the evening he'd table-hop and take me along, and then I'd know everyone.

But the main reason I liked to eat with him after the matinée was because I'd get a chance to see my uncles.

Almost always Harpo, Chico, Zeppo and their wives would be at the table with us, and I enjoyed that immensely, because no child could have more doting uncles than they were. They'd shower me with expensive toys, slip $10 bills in my pockets when Groucho (who disapproved) wasn't looking, and spoil me in every way possible.

Apart from presents, the Marxes were a hilarious group when they were together. They were loud, raucous, and never took anything seriously. The jokes would fly back and forth across the table so rapidly you couldn't keep up with them. And all the brothers but my father were accomplished at the art of doing table tricks. They'd be springboarding silverware into glasses of water, making rabbits out of napkins, pulling cards from their sleeves, and perhaps shooting dice with the sugar cubes.

It was that way whenever they'd get together, which in those days was still fairly often. Usually they'd come to our house – in addition to the restaurant gatherings – because Groucho was the only one of the brothers who owned a house. And besides, we had a pool table, and they still loved to play. But sometimes we'd go to their apartments in New York, and about once a week there would be a family gathering at Sam and Minnie's house in Little Neck.

My grandparents were in their middle sixties then, and Minnie's health was failing rapidly, but they were happy at last in the reflected glory of their famous sons, who were doing everything possible to make them comfortable.

They bought them a house, gave them a car and a chauffeur, and saw to it that they'd never again have another financial worry. In return for this, Sam and Minnie were always anxious to cook a Stuffed Miltz for them, or some other German dish from their past that they were constantly getting cravings for.

Undoubtedly it was Minnie, whom they loved dearly and who unquestionably was responsible for some of their success, who kept the brothers together as a social group. Because it wasn't very many years after she died in 1928 that they started to drift apart.

Of course, they still saw a good deal of one another, since they worked together and were constantly being thrown into one another's company whether they had any desire for it or not. And as individuals it wasn't unusual – and still isn't – for one Marx Brother to entertain one of the other brothers. But it's been at least fifteen years since I've seen the five of them assembled round the same dinner table. I've often regretted this, because not only did they seem to have fun whenever they were together, but it was fun being with them.

Their growing apart was inevitable, I suppose. To begin with, they saw so much of one another when they were in vaudeville and in legitimate shows that when they got the opportunity to see new faces it was the natural thing to want to do. And, secondly, outside their careers they've always had completely divergent interests and ideas of how they wanted to live.

Chico and Zeppo, for instance, have been heavy gamblers from the day they first started making the kind of money that permitted them to wager $2,000 and $3,000 on everything from the turn of a card to the outcome of a girls' softball game.

Chico and Zeppo have tapered off somewhat in the last few years, but basically they're still the same. If you want their company at dinner and you're not a gambling man yourself, you can get them, but immediately after the meal they'll excuse themselves and head for the nearest card game. Not only card games, but any place where they can go and stand a reasonably good chance of losing their money.

Harpo was a gambler, too, but of a different sort. With him it was an avocation. For many years he was a bachelor, and he went around with a group of bachelors who idolized the late Alexander Woollcott, their unofficial leader. This was a more sporting group. They played expert croquet, no-limit poker, and championship bridge for a dollar a point. Occasionally Harpo and Chico would team up together at bridge, and when they did they were a formidable combination.

Since his marriage to Susan Fleming in the mid-thirties, Harpo has done practically no gambling at all. Age and four children have mellowed him and curbed his gambling instincts. But when the Marx Brothers were playing on Broadway Harpo, too, travelled in a crowd that had very little in common with Groucho.

Groucho was a family man who could play neither bridge nor croquet, and whose main interests were his children, his work, his books, his guitar and a small coterie of close friends.

The only time he was willing to make an exception was when he'd get an invitation to play poker with the crowd who, in the mid-twenties, used to congregate at the Hotel Algonquin: Dorothy Parker, Heywood Broun, Woollcott, Benchley, F. P. Adams, George Kaufman, Harold Ross and Robert Sherwood. But he was never very good at the game, nor was he especially interested. He merely used it as a device to be with these people, who were such poker-addicts themselves that frequently the only way he could spend any time with them was to participate in their card games.

'And besides,' adds Groucho, 'that group was fun to be with *in spite* of the fact that they took their cards seriously.'

Once, after we moved to California, Groucho, in an unwitting moment, let Norman Krasna talk him into taking bridge lessons. Krasna couldn't play either, and he thought it would be nice for the two of them to learn together. So they hired a bridge teacher, who came to our house in Beverly Hills one evening after dinner.

The teacher was a prim, middle-aged woman whose name was Cynthia Jones. She sat down at the table with Krasna and my mother and father, and started out by saying, 'Now, the first thing we do is to deal thirteen cards to each person.' She dealt the cards. 'Now we arrange the cards in our hands according to suits – hearts, spades, and so on.'

'What does a spade look like?' asked Groucho, completely deadpan.

Very patiently, Miss Jones explained to him abut the different suits.

'Why do we have to call a spade a spade?' asked Groucho. 'Why can't we call a diamond a spade for a change? That's the trouble with this game. It's too reactionary. What this game needs is young blood!'

Miss Jones cleared her throat. 'As I was saying, the first thing we do is arrange the cards according to suits.'

'Why do we have to do that?' asked Groucho.

'Because that's how you play the game.'

'That's how *you* play the game, you mean.'

'No; but those are the rules.'

'Whose rules?'

'Well, we're going to play the Culbertson system.'

'What right does he have to dictate to me how we're going to play bridge?' asked Groucho indignantly. 'This is my house. Let him play the Culbertson system in *his* house if he wants.'

'Grouch,' urged Mother, 'We're paying this woman for lessons. Let's listen.'

'How much are we paying?' asked Groucho suspiciously.

'Five dollars an hour,' announced Miss Jones.

'It's too much,' said Groucho. 'We could have bought Culbertson's book for a buck and a quarter.'

After about an hour of suffering through his interruptions, Miss Jones thought they knew enough of the fundamentals to try playing a hand. At this point they recessed, while Mother went into the kitchen to get a pitcher of ice-water and Krasna excused himself to go to the washroom.

Alone with the teacher, Groucho leaned over to her and said, 'Miss Jones, how about you and me blowing this joint and heading south over the border? I know a nice little hotel in Tijuana. Of course, we won't have enough people for bridge, but we can play two-handed strip-poker.'

Miss Jones promptly collected her things, streaked for the door, and was never heard of again.

11

When he was in a show, Groucho's free nights were too precious to waste on indoor sports he wasn't interested in.

There were too many books he hadn't read, too many authors he was just discovering: Priestley, H. G. Wells, Somerset Maugham, Arnold Bennett, Huxley, and even Tolstoy.

He read most of their complete works, and everything else that was in the rather large library he was swiftly accumulating in Great Neck. He was even interested in the children's books which he had bought for me, but which he hadn't had the opportunity to read when he was a child.

He was particularly delighted, if I remember correctly, with the Winnie-the-Pooh stories of A. A. Milne and *The Swiss Family Robinson*.

After he had read me the first chapter of *Swiss Family Robinson* one Sunday night he sent me to bed, and stayed up until dawn finishing the book. The next time he was going to read aloud to me I brought out *Swiss Family Robinson* again. But Groucho returned it to the shelf and selected *Jack the Giant Killer*.

When I asked why, he said, 'I've already finished *Swiss Family Robinson*. I'll tell you how it comes out. You wouldn't like the middle part, anyway. It's too good for children.'

So he gave me a quick synopsis of it, and we were on to *Jack the Giant Killer*. He didn't have time to waste reading the same book twice.

He could do some reading, of course, in his dressing-room

between acts, and occasionally, if Chico was in the throes of a long musical number, Groucho would wander into his dressing-room in the midst of the show and read a few lines from *War and Peace* or the *Journals of Arnold Bennett*.

But that wasn't the most satisfactory way of keeping up with what was going on in the world of literature.

It wasn't too satisfactory for me, either, because even though he read to me as often as he could he didn't have as much time for bedtime stories now that we were living in Great Neck.

Broadway was a good hour away by automobile, and Groucho, being a nervous performer, liked to leave himself plenty of time to eat and make the drive into town. Not only because he opened the show and had a fear of being stuck in a traffic jam on the 59th Street Bridge when the curtain was going up, but because he felt too dull and sleepy to give a good performance if he went on the stage immediately after a heavy meal.

He preferred to be made up and in costume by eight o'clock at the latest. In that way he could spent a quiet half-hour on the cot in his dressing-room, napping or reading until the boy knocked on the door and yelled, 'Overture!'

The revelation that the show was about to begin never failed to send a shiver up and down his spine and give him a momentary sick feeling in the pit of his stomach.

He just couldn't be casual about it – even after twenty years in the theatre, and while enjoying the reputation of being one of America's top comics. Every time he walked out on the stage, he told me, he was firmly convinced that he was going to forget all his lines, and that this particular performance was going to lay a big egg.

He was never to overcome this fear completely. Many years after *Cocoanuts*, while I was a student at Beverly Hills High School, the principal asked me if I wouldn't talk him into making a funny speech at one of our assemblies.

I knew he didn't particularly relish the idea of appearing in public (especially when he wasn't getting paid), but I didn't think he'd mind making a few funny remarks for a group of schoolchildren. After all, he was a professional entertainer, and Beverly High *wasn't* the Palace. But when I mentioned it to him he immediately changed the subject, and when I brought it up again he said, 'Maybe next year. I'm busy now.'

However, I kept after him for about a week, because the Principal was hounding me, and besides, I figured that if he did make the appearance it would do a lot for my personal prestige on the campus.

He remained stubborn to the last, and finally it became necessary for me to bring out my ace-in-the-hole. 'Well, Eddie Cantor made a speech at school when Marilyn asked him to,' I said one evening, after he had just turned me down for the seventeenth time.

'He would,' said Groucho. 'He'll go any place where he can make a speech – even if no one asks him to.'

I don't know whether or not mentioning Eddie Cantor made him change his mind, but about two days later he came to me and said, 'I'll make a deal with you. If you paint the porch furniture, I'll give a talk at your school.'

He probably didn't think I would paint the porch furniture, but I did, and there was no way of his escaping now.

He worked on the speech for days. He had trouble finding a suitable topic, he had trouble writing it, and he had more trouble memorizing it. Finally, on the night before his appearance at high school, he emerged from his study, looking worn and haggard, and gripping a manuscript that had so many pencil notations on it that you couldn't read the typing.

'I'm worried about this speech,' he said. 'I don't know if it's right for a high school audience. And I don't know it very well, either. Do you think it would be all right if I *read* it tomorrow?'

'Eddie Cantor didn't read his,' I told him.

'I'm sure of that,' replied Groucho. 'He probably sang twelve songs besides.'

'No; he only sang three!'

'Okay,' said Groucho in a doomed voice. 'I won't read it. I'll stumble through it the best I can.

On the morning of the speech, while the Principal was announcing to the assembly that 'Beverly Hills High was fortunate in having an honoured guest with us,' he stood in the wings looking as pale and nervous as he must have appeared the night *I'll Say She Is* opened in New York.

I was sure he would do the speech badly, that the students wouldn't understand his humour, and that he would be hooted off the stage amidst the shouts of 'We want Eddie Cantor back.' But he came through like a professional, didn't forget a word and, needless to say, was a big hit.

According to him, it isn't uncommon for an actor to get a sinking feeling before he goes on the stage, 'particularly if he's any good'. But I believe he is more apprehensive about facing an audience than most actors. Certainly more so than Harpo, Chico or Zeppo ever were. Frequently they'd show up at the theatre at the very last minute, coming directly there from various card games around town, slap on their costumes and make-up without even looking in the mirror, and stroll out on to the stage as unconcerned as if they were entering someone's parlour.

On several occasions their nonchalance was responsible for some pretty embarrassing moments. One incident in particular was, I'm sure, the most embarrassing of all. It happened during the first act of *Animal Crackers*, one night after the show had been playing on Broadway for about a year, and the cast was getting pretty sloppy, anyway.

The scene was in the palatial home of wealthy Mrs Ritten-house (Margaret Dumont), who was giving a formal reception in honour of Captain Spaulding (Groucho), the great African explorer. As each guest arrived at the top of the marble staircase in Mrs Rittenhouse's living-room, the butler would take his or her coat, and the guest would be announced and proceed down the stairs to the reception. When Harpo was announced, the butler was to whisk off his cape, revealing that he had nothing on underneath but a pair of swimming trunks.

That's how Kaufman and Ryskind wrote it, and it usually turned out that way, but one evening Harpo was detained and didn't arrive at the theatre until the curtain had already gone up.

He hurriedly undressed and donned his cape and red wig, but in the excitement of trying to make his first cue he completely forgot about putting on his trunks. The result was that when the butler relieved him of his cape, Harpo found himself in full view of the audience with nothing on but a very skimpy G-string.

Harpo was not easily embarrassed or flustered, but he was that night, and with a shriek he fled into the wings. As he left the stage, Groucho turned to the audience and said, 'Tomorrow night he's not going to wear anything, so get your tickets early!'

Once the curtain rose Groucho's nervousness disappeared completely. He was as relaxed on the stage as he was at home in his study, and as uninhibited as the worst extrovert. He rarely forgot a line or a piece of business, and he was never at a loss for a funny ad lib to cope with an unexpected development on the stage. And if there were no unexpected developments, he would frequently stray from the original manuscript anyway, just to break the monotony of saying the same lines night after night.

The monotony was the only thing that occasionally tripped up Groucho. After playing the same show for two or three hundred performances the lines would come so automatically to him that he wouldn't have to think about them. When he did think about them he'd get into trouble. His mind would go blank for a moment.

'Would you mind giving me that cue again?' he'd have to say to Chico, if it happened while the two of them were doing a scene together. 'I seem to have lost my place.'

'No trouble at all,' Chico might reply. 'You said to me, "Do you know what an *auction* is?" and I said, "Sure, I came over to this country on the Atlantic auction." Now do you know where you are?'

By that time he would know, of course, but frequently he'd pretend that he didn't, just to confuse Chico.

'No, I don't know where I am,' he'd say. 'But I've seen you some place before. Say, you aren't by any chance related to that red-headed moron I've seen running around here tonight, are you?'

'Sure; he's your brother!'

'Well, if he's my brother,' Groucho would say, switching to a Jolsonesque southern accent, 'how come you're an Italian and I'm from the deep South?'

While Chico was thinking that one over, Groucho would slip back into the show dialogue. 'We have a quota at this hotel.'

'Now I don't know where *I* am,' Chico would reply. 'Give me that line again.'

'Oh, no,' Groucho would answer. 'You're getting the same cut out of the show that I am. You figure it out.'

Eventually they'd get back into the dialogue and the show would proceed. But it was rarely the identical show twice. They were all constantly striving for new lines and better pieces of business.

And it's a good thing for their shows and careers that they were so adept at this; because no authors, not even Kaufman and Ryskind, who had no peers when it came to writing Marx Brothers material, could sit down at a typewriter and knock off a perfect piece of material for them. Their humour was entirely unique and individualized.

Chico played an Italian; Harpo played a deaf-and-dumb sex fiend; and Groucho played a brash, wise-cracking charlatan who never stopped talking.

If an author would write Italian dialect material, the chances were he couldn't write for Groucho. If he could write Groucho's dialogue, then he might not be good for Chico. And if he could write for both of them, he couldn't write for Harpo. No one, for that matter, could write for Harpo.

'How can you write for Harpo?' George Kaufman once complained when they were in the throes of putting *Cocoanuts* together. 'What do you put down on paper? All you can say is, "Harpo enters". From that point on, he's on his own!'

Harpo, more than anyone, had to know how to devise his own material. It was either that or have no part when the show opened. And frequently he didn't have much of a part when a show of theirs opened out of town for the try-outs. All he'd have would be a trunkful of props, his harp and his puckish sense of humour. It would be entirely up to him to experiment with these ingredients in front of a live audience and find out what was funny and what wasn't.

As a result, their out-of-town openings were usually a shambles, with none of the brothers, authors or producers knowing what was going to come next. *Cocoanuts* and *Animal Crackers* died torturous deaths in Philadelphia and Boston. They were over length and unfunny, and appeared destined for failure in New York. But by the time they arrived on Broadway they were transformed, as if by magic, into hilarious vehicles. The dialogue would be sharp, the situations airtight, and even Harpo would have a fat part.

It's a show business axiom that any show can be greatly improved by a few weeks on the road. But once it's a hit on Broadway the people connected with it are content to leave it alone.

The Marx Brothers, however, never stopped tinkering with the material from opening night until the show closed – perhaps two years later. By the end of its run the show would barely be recognizable – even to its authors.

One night, during the last few weeks of *Cocoanuts*' two-year run on Broadway, George Kaufman and Heywood Broun were watching the performance from the standing-room section. They weren't watching; they were just killing time by talking. But at one point Broun noticed that Kaufman was ignoring his conversation, and in an annoyed tone asked, 'What's the matter with you?'

Kaufman, whose attention had been directed towards the stage for the past several seconds, turned back to Broun and said, 'I may be wrong, but I thought I just heard one of the original lines!'

Many people would be so fascinated by the flexibility of the Marx Brothers' performances that they would come back and see the show half-a dozen times or more. Still others would return to catch the parts of the show they missed the first time because the audience's laughter had drowned out so much of the dialogue.

Bobby Jones, the golfer, once visited Groucho in his dressing-room after the performance, and said, 'I just had to come back and meet you, Groucho. This is the twelfth time I've seen *Cocoanuts*.'

Groucho was always particularly delighted if an outstanding figure in some other field dropped by his dressing-room after the show to pay him a compliment. And there were a number of them, including Calvin Coolidge, Al Smith, Jimmy Walker and even the Prince of Wales (later to become the Duke of Windsor).

He would deny he was ever impressed with meeting that kind of person. But he was, nevertheless. I remember him coming home and telling me with great enthusiasm that he had spent an hour with the Prince of Wales in his dressing-room, that they had got along famously, and that the Prince had invited Groucho to drop in on him at Buckingham Palace if he was ever in the neighbourhood. (Groucho attempted to take him up on this, too, but that comes later, when we were in London.)

The Marx Brothers were great favourites with politicians and royalty alike – probably because it was a refreshing change for them to meet someone like Groucho, who showed them anything but proper respect. If he knew, for instance, that an important personage was in the audience, you could count on him, at some point in the performance, to throw in a few impudent ad libs especially for that person's benefit.

'I see we have the Honourable Mayor Walker with us,' he announced to Chico while they were giving a show one election eve. 'I wonder why he isn't at home stuffing ballot boxes.'

The night Calvin Coolidge came to see *Cocoanuts* Groucho stepped to the footlights, eyed the President for a moment, and then said, 'Aren't you up past your bedtime, Calvin?'

But of all the people who saw *Cocoanuts*, the one who made the greatest impression on him was Herman Schroeder.

He and Schroeder had been school chums back in the days when the Marx clan was hiding from the landlord on 93rd Street. But twenty years had elapsed since then, and Groucho barely remembered his old playmate when he presented himself at his dressing-room door one night after the show.

Schroeder had always been a stodgy, humourless fellow, even as a child, but now he appeared stodgier than ever.

'I saw the show tonight, Julius,' he said. 'I thought you were quite good.'

'Glad you liked it,' said Groucho, starting to remove his black moustache with cold cream and a towel. 'What are you doing these days?'

'I'm doing very well,' said Herman, clearing his throat in a stuffy manner. 'I'm a lawyer now. I'm a junior partner with Handel, Grossmeyer and Handel.'

'Glad to hear it,' said Groucho politely.

'My annual income is $9,000,' announced Herman. 'And in two years, when they make me a senior partner, it will be $12,000 a year.'

'That's nice,' said Groucho.

'I also have $1,900 in the bank and a $20,000 endowment policy for the wife and kids, and we live in a nice apartment up in the Bronx. Yes, sir, I'm really doing well.'

'Herman – I'm proud of you,' said Groucho, playing it perfectly straight. 'I always knew you'd come through.'

Herman beamed. 'It's just as my mother used to tell me. If you work hard and go to church, a person's bound to be successful. Do you go to church, Julius?'

'Well, I haven't been yet today,' replied Groucho.

'Maybe that's your trouble,' said Herman.

'Trouble?' Groucho looked at him curiously. 'What kind of trouble?'

'Well – the reason *you're* not doing any better.'

'I thought you liked the show,' said Groucho. 'Didn't you just finish telling me how good I am in it?'

'I meant no reflection on your ability as an actor,' said Herman. 'What I mean is, this is no way for a man of your age to have to earn a living – smearing black grease-paint on your face and cavorting around the stage every night like a lunatic.'

'No; it isn't very dignified,' admitted Groucho.

'You're not a boy any longer,' pointed out Herman. 'It's about time you settled down.'

'Do you really think so?'

'I certainly do. Besides, what can a job like this pay? Not very much, I don't suppose.'

'Oh, the pay's pretty good,' said Groucho. At the time, his share of the profits amounted to approximately $2,000 a week.

'Tell me, Julius, what *do* you make in a job like this?'

'Well, at the moment I'm getting fifty a week. But when my

102

brothers make me a full partner, I'm going to get raised to fifty-five.'

'That's what I mean,' said Herman. 'This is no business to be in.'

'What do you suggest I do?' asked Groucho.

'I'd start looking around for another line of work,' Herman advised him. 'Before you're too old to get into anything else.'

'Herman Schroeder,' said Groucho, 'you're perfectly right. But what kind of work do you advise me to get into? I don't know anything but show business. I didn't even finish grammar school.'

'You could go to night school until you get your diploma.'

'How could I live?'

'You could get a temporary job in the daytime.'

Groucho shook his head. 'No; if I'm going to make a change, I'd like to get into something where I could make some money right away.'

'Have you ever considered selling?' Herman asked. 'You're a glib talker. You'd probably make a good salesman.'

'I've considered it,' replied Groucho, 'but I don't think it would work out. You see, most actors steal, and I'm afraid I'd always have my hand in the till.'

'Not really!' exclaimed Herman.

'I wouldn't kid you,' said Groucho, taking his gold watch off the dressing-table and holding it up. 'You see this watch? I stole it at the Ritz-Carlton in Boston. And that trunk over there in the corner? I picked it up right from under a Red Cap's nose at the Union Depot in Philly.'

Herman stared at him open-mouthed.

'As a matter of fact, I wouldn't get too close to me,' Groucho went on. 'I might steal *your* watch. And that gold chain, too! I've always wanted a gold chain.'

'I'd better be going,' said Herman, backing toward the door.

'So soon? We haven't decided on a business for me yet.'

'I'm afraid it's getting late.'

'Say — I've got an idea!' exclaimed Groucho. 'How about taking me in with you and those partners of yours? I could be a junior partner, with a little practice.'

'Oh, we couldn't take in any more partners,' said Herman nervously.

'Why not? I wouldn't ask for much at first. Say five thousand a year and all I can steal.'

'I'm afraid not,' said Herman, turning to go. 'Goodbye, Julius.'

'Goodbye, Herman.'

At the door Herman turned round again. 'Julius,' he said, 'you used to be a good boy. It's not too late to mend your ways. Think over what I told you. And do me a favour. Don't steal any more.'

'I wish I could stop,' said Groucho sadly, 'but unfortunately, it's the only way I can make both ends meet.'

12

Although it would have taken a good deal more than a Herman Schroeder to make Groucho quit the theatre, he was never so enamoured of the life of a legitimate actor that it would have broken his heart to give it up.

Of course, he liked the money and the prestige that went with being a Broadway star – especially the money. And I doubt if he would have been happy, or even successful, in the pants business, for example. But you could never say of him, as you can of so many actors, that he has grease-paint in his blood.

Many actors – especially comedians – live for that moment when they can be on the stage in front of an audience. Hearing laughter and applause gives them a lift that nothing else can give them. For Groucho, all those needs are fulfilled in a once-a-week, two-hour work-out in front of a very much alive television audience. Then it's an ice-cream soda at Wil Wright's, and home in semi-seclusion until the next week.

About once every ten years since he quit Broadway he'll get a yen to return to the stage. In 1940 he read a book called *Franklin Street*, which he thought could be turned into a very fine stage vehicle for himself. He suggested it to George Kaufman and Arthur Sheekman, another old friend of his, and the two of them excitedly agreed to collaborate on it – if Groucho would promise to appear in it. He gave his word, but after they completed it he bowed out of the production, saying he didn't think it was 'right' for him. He probably had a premonition of disaster, because *Franklin Street* folded in Baltimore. But even if it had been the finest play written since *Hamlet*, he would have found something wrong with it. Because when the chips are down, his yen for the bright lights of Broadway suddenly disappears.

It was the same thing with *Time for Elizabeth*, the play he wrote in collaboration with Norman Krasna. It was his original idea to do a play about a businessman who retires and then finds out that a life of idleness isn't so much fun. It was also his idea to play the leading role himself. He figured he'd be perfect for the part, since he had tried retiring for about six months and discovered that he didn't like it at all.

This intrigued Krasna, and the two of them set to work on the play in the spring of 1941, and brought the completed manuscript to New York in the autumn. By this time Groucho had had his fill of New York. He let several people read *Time for Elizabeth*, and he was advised by Kaufman, Max Gordon and Pulitzer prize-winning playwright Owen Davis not to let it go into production as it was. It needed more work, they said.

So Groucho and Krasna flew back to the coast and decided to do another draft on *Time for Elizabeth*. They had just completed it when Pearl Harbor came. That ended the venture for the time being. It wouldn't be very patriotic, they felt, to do a play about a man retiring to escape income taxes when we were in the midst of a war.

After the war they did three more versions of the play, and in 1948 finally decided that they had a draft that they were satisfied with.

'Who do you think would be good to play the lead?' Groucho asked his collaborator the day they finished the play.

'What do you mean?' asked Krasna, shocked. 'I thought we wrote this for *you*.'

'Well, we did,' said Groucho, 'but any good actor can play the part. Why don't we try to get someone else? As a matter of fact, it might be better with a straight actor in it. If I'm in it, the critics will expect a Marx Brothers comedy, and they'll be disappointed.'

'What's the matter?' asked Krasna suspiciously. 'Don't you think it's any good? Do you think it'll be a flop? If that's your attitude, let's just put it in a drawer and forget about it.'

'I think it's very good,' said Groucho. 'I think it'll be a big hit. That's the trouble.'

'What do you mean by that?'

'Well, if it's a hit,' replied Groucho, 'that'll mean that I'll probably have to spend a couple of years in New York — walking around in the slush in the winters, working every night, and living in that stifling heat in the summers. I don't want to do that any more. I'm very comfortable here.'

As it turned out, he could have played the part himself and been back in his home in Beverly Hills the following week. *Time for Elizabeth* closed after eight performances.

'If I only could have been assured of that,' claimed Groucho, 'I should have been glad to take on that part myself.'

Groucho never believed that *Time for Elizabeth* was a great play, but he felt, after listening to the audience's reaction on opening night and also during the try-outs in San Francisco and Los Angeles, that it could have been a popular one if the critics had treated it with a little more kindness and if *he* had played the leading role instead of Otto Kruger. Just to find out for his own satisfaction, he tackled *Time for Elizabeth* himself at La Jolla Playhouse in the summer of 1953, five years after the Broadway disaster. His one-week engagement there was the outstanding success of La Jolla's summer stock season. The management had to schedule two extra matinées to cater for all the customers who had been turned away from the regular performances.

Time for Elizabeth could have played to capacity all summer if other shows hadn't been booked previously into the theatre, and if Groucho had been willing, which he wasn't. He also received several offers to bring the show to Broadway again, with him in it, of course, but he turned these down, too.

I realized why, after watching him do the show every night in La Jolla.

On opening night he was keyed up and razor sharp. He was going to prove to everyone that he could make it a good play, or at any rate a very entertaining one. And he did.

On Thursday night his performance was no longer exactly sparkling or inspired.

And on closing night – Saturday – he looked as if he could take *Time for Elizabeth* or leave it – preferably the latter. At one spot in the third act the action called for him to stretch out on the couch, say a few lines, and then stand up again. He managed to lie down on the couch without any trouble, but when the cue came for him to get up again he didn't budge. In fact he remained on the couch for about five extra pages of dialogue, and for a moment I thought perhaps he was planning to finish the act flat on his back.

He finally made it to his feet, and the play proceeded without any serious harm done to it, but I knew then that he'd had his fill. He'd proved his point, and now he wished he were home on his own couch.

That's what I mean about him not having grease-paint in his blood.

13

In his Broadway days, of course, Groucho gave an energetic performance every night – and at one point in 1928 he was not only appearing in *Animal Crackers* on the stage, but also making the moving picture version of *Cocoanuts* at the same time.

But he was young then, and anxious to hasten the day when he would have so much money in the bank that he would never have to work again if he didn't feel like it.

Cocoanuts was one of the first sound movies ever to be made. It was also the first of five pictures the Marx Brothers had signed to do with Paramount, which, very conveniently, had a studio in Astoria, Long Island, in addition to their Hollywood plant.

Astoria was on the way to New York from Great Neck. Groucho would leave for the studio early in the morning, shoot until six or seven in the evening, and after a hasty meal with his brothers would go straight to the theatre. It was hard work, for picture-making then was even more arduous than it is now.

The technicians were as unfamiliar with working with sound as were the actors. The equipment was crude and constantly breaking down in the middle of a scene. Simple scenes had to be shot over as many as twenty and thirty times. The slightest noise two blocks away could ruin a take. That's why it took them five months to shoot their first picture. That plus the fact that on matinée days they couldn't work on the picture at all – except in the mornings.

'Sometimes I'd get so punchy,' Groucho told me, 'that I'd find myself spouting the dialogue from *Animal Crackers* in a scene I was doing in *Cocoanuts*, and vice versa.'

But *Cocoanuts* couldn't have been made otherwise – at least not at the time. The Marx Brothers had a run-of-the-show commitment with Sam Harris, the producer of *Animal Crackers*. There was no telling how long *Animal Crackers* would be running on Broadway, and Paramount wasn't willing to wait. The picture studio wanted the Marx Brothers while they were hot. (After all, how long could comedians last?)

No one could have been hotter than they were after the opening of *Animal Crackers*. The critics' attitude seemed to be that the Marx Brothers could do no wrong, and evidently the theatre-going public thought so, too.

Animal Crackers was a bigger hit than any of its predecessors, and the Marx Brothers were in their prime as a team. The book, by George S. Kaufman and Morrie Ryslind, was full of lines that are still being quoted; and the score, by Bert Kalmar and Harry Ruby, contained a comedy number that has since become a sort of classic. It was called 'Hooray for Captain Spaulding,' and Groucho sang it and did an eccentric dance to it after his first entrance – his arrival at the Park Avenue reception Mrs Rittenhouse was throwing for him (the same scene I described earlier, when Harpo forgot to wear his trunks).

Dressed in boots, riding pants and a pith helmet, he was supposed to be a famous explorer who had just returned from the wilds of Africa. He was carried into the reception on an

African sedan chair, hoisted by four husky Nubian slaves. After alighting from the chair, he reached into his pocket for his wallet and said to one of the slaves, 'How much do I owe you?'

The slave mumbled the price and Groucho replied, 'That's an outrage. I could have got a Yellow Cab for a buck and a quarter. I *told* you not to go through the Park.'

After disposing of the slaves, Groucho turned to the assembled guests and sang 'Hooray for Captain Spaulding', which started out with:

> 'Hello, I must be going.
> I cannot stay, I only
> Came to say,
> I must be going.
> I'll stay a week or two,
> I'll stay the summer through,
> But I am telling you,
> I must be going.'

Finally persuaded to stay, he gave a résumé of the Spartan life he had led in Africa:

'Up at six, breakfast at six-thirty, and back to bed at seven ... One morning I shot an elephant in my pyjamas. How he got in my pyjamas I don't know.'

I remember *Animal Crackers* more vividly than I do their other shows – partly because I was older by then and could appreciate what was taking place on the stage, and partly because I was in it a few times myself.

I didn't have any illusions about becoming an actor, but I enjoyed watching the show from the wings, and I'd frequently be standing there when Groucho would be getting into his sedan chair.

To give me a thrill, if he was in a good mood he would sometimes say, 'Hop in, and take a ride with me,' and then he'd pull me into the chair with him.

I'd ride out on to the stage and have to sit there while he went through his routine with the Nubian slaves. Much to the audience's bewilderment, the routine would contain no reference to the little boy in short pants, who remained in the sedan chair, gaping worriedly out into the sea of faces, until he was carried back into the safety of the wings again.

Miriam received the same kind of treatment as soon as she was old enough to walk. In London, in 1931, I remember Groucho interrupting Harpo in the midst of his harp number to have Miriam, who was then three, with Shirley Temple curls and blue eyes, sing 'Show Me the Way to Go Home'.

He didn't inflict this sort of thing on audiences very often, but sometimes he just had no will-power.

The odd part about it was that whenever one of us finished a stint on the stage he'd say, 'Well, how do you like being an actor?'

If I said I didn't particularly like it, he'd scold me for being too diffident, and if I said I liked it, he'd say:

'Well, don't ever let me catch you wanting to be an actor. You can be anything else – a doctor or a lawyer or even a garbage man – but if I catch you getting any ideas about the stage, I'll beat your brains out.'

Despite his insistence that his life as an actor was a pretty horrible one, I wasn't quite convinced. And I don't think he was either.

Things had never been so good for him – especially as 1928 progressed into the boom days of 1929.

Not only was he in a smash show on Broadway, but *Cocoanuts* was as big a hit with the nation's moviegoers as it had been on the stage, and *Beds* was being serialized in *College Humour* and about to be published in book form. Money was pouring in from everywhere, and there was no income tax to speak of.

On the home front everything was going well, too. Except for a few typical husband-and-wife arguments, all was serene between him and my mother, and if there was a hint of serious trouble ahead it was not noticed at the time. He had always wanted two children – a boy he could play baseball with, and a girl he could cuddle – and he had them. And his prized orchard was at last showing some signs of life. An apple was beginning to sprout on the cherry tree.

It was a crazy, wonderful era. Babe Ruth, Bobby Jones, and

110

Bill Tilden were still the Big Three of sports. Rudy Vallee, in *The Vagabond Lover*, was causing women across the nation to swoon. People were making gin in their bath-tubs, and Anaconda Copper was selling for $175 a share.

Getting in the spirit of the times, Groucho exchanged the staid Lincoln sedan for a very flashy convertible Packard, with red wire wheels and a rumble seat; he bought my mother a long sleek Cord – the first model put out; and, as I mentioned earlier, he paid $5,000 to become a member of the exclusive Lakeville Country Club in Great Neck.

Determined to master the sport, he played eighteen holes every day when he didn't have a matinée.

But in his case determination was not enough, and his golf game never improved; in fact, if anything it grew steadily worse – which is odd because he's a pretty good natural athlete.

His main trouble seemed to be that the sight of a golf ball unnerved him. He had a perfect practice swing. No golf professional could ever find a flaw in it. But as soon as you put a ball down in front of him his game fell apart.

Once he missed a 2-foot putt on the eighteenth hole. He was so furious that he hurled his putter to the green, embedding it about one foot deep in the velvety green turf that had been brought over to Lakeville from Scotland.

Needless to say, the Greens Committee was not pleased, and instigated a movement to have this ordinarily mild-mannered actor tossed out of the club immediately. But they did give him a chance to defend himself at the expulsion proceedings.

'Sure, I have a terrible temper,' he confessed, 'and I wouldn't blame you no matter what you decide. But I don't think throwing me out is the answer. That's no punishment. Look how happy you'll make me. I won't have to play this confounded game any more.'

In view of his testimony, the Committee reconsidered and let him remain a member. To show his gratitude, Groucho, while playing the water hole the next day, killed one of the club's prized swans with a wild No. 2 iron shot.

With his golf game in such desperate straits, he was constantly on the look-out for some magic cure-all to lift him out of the ranks of mediocrity. He was beyond the stage where he thought lessons could help him. He was now spending his free time poring over all the how-to-play books by the world's best professionals, and devouring anything in the newspapers that might contain a hint on how to lower his score.

As a result, he didn't have to stick to any one method of playing. He had a number of different swings at his command.

On the first tee, he might start out by making an announcement like, 'I think I'll use the *World-Telegram* swing today.' And then he'd take a vicious cut at the ball. If by some miracle it went straight and far down the fairway, he'd stick with the *World-Telegram* until he dubbed a shot, which would be almost immediately.

At this point he'd switch to another swing – perhaps something he had read in Gene Sarazen's book. With Groucho doing it, Sarazen's swing looked exactly like the *World-Telegram* swing, which in turn resembled all the rest of his assortment of swings.

Even if the swings had been different, he never would stick with one long enough to find out whether or not it was practical. And sometimes he'd combine two or three of his favourite swings. For instance, 'Today I'm going to try the *Evening Sun* swing on the back-swing, the Gene Sarazen on the down-swing, let the clubhead do all the work like Walter Hagan, and after I hit the ball spit on the ground to keep my head down. Angus McTavish at the St Louis Country Club told me I should try the spitting.'

In any case, he can only concentrate on the game for a few holes. Once he has used up all his swings and he realizes that the whole thing is pretty hopeless – at least for the remainder of the day – the match quickly degenerates into a deliberate comedy of errors.

Anyone intent on breaking par will do everything possible not to get mixed up in a game with him. For his attitude – in fact, his whole game – is very contagious, and pretty soon everyone else in his foursome, threesome or twosome will be playing just as badly as he.

To give you an idea of what a devastating effect his game has on other people — he once played golf with Ben Hogan in Palm Springs. On one hole, Hogan got a fourteen.

'I do it deliberately,' claims Groucho. 'How else could I beat a fellow like Hogan?'

But although he still plays occasionally — he's using the Tommy Armour swing now — he actually retired from serious golf in 1935. The match that hurried this decision took place on the famous Pebble Beach course in Monterey, California.

His opponent was Ed Sullivan, the well-known columnist and television personality. It was a close match, with Groucho only seventeen down, when they arrived at the famous windswept 18th hole. The 18th is bordered on the left by the Pacific Ocean and some steep cliffs, which you must stay clear of when you tee off or suffer the consequences.

Groucho teed up breezily, and with hardly any effort hooked five new balls into the Pacific Ocean. But after many years of golf-playing he had learned to control his temper on a course. Very calmly, he removed the remaining balls from his bag and, stepping over to the edge of the cliff, dropped them into the ocean one by one. Then he hurled his bag of clubs over the cliff and returned to the hotel, as lighthearted as if he had just been reprieved from the gallows.

14

Although 1929 was a period of carefree living and spending, Groucho was not being too reckless with his money.

Other people could own yachts and strings of polo ponies or go off for extended vacations on the French Riviera. But, except for the $5,000 he had parted with to join Lakeville, Groucho was playing things very conservatively. He was preparing for that well-known rainy day.

By the autumn of 1929 he had accumulated a nest-egg of roughly $250,000, and he was keeping it in a nice safe place — the stock market.

Knowing how wary he has always been of schemes where you can make money without working for it, I'm amazed that he ever let himself get sucked into Wall Street.

As I've mentioned previously, he has no gambling instincts, and never — even in the most prosperous times — did he stop looking for ways of keeping unnecessary expenses down around the house. He was as conscious of the price of pumpernickel in 1929 as he had been before *I'll Say She Is* put him in the high income bracket.

Yet when it came to tips on the stock market he was as gullible as everyone else. He'd accept without question the word of a total stranger, and invest thousands of dollars in a stock that he knew absolutely nothing about.

It would be an understatement to say that he didn't realize playing the market was so risky. He was in it because, like everyone else, he was convinced that it was a sound investment. You were in partnership with big business. Financiers had been on to this for years. Did J. P. Morgan, the Whitneys and the DuPonts bury their money in banks that only paid two or three per cent interest? Of course not. They put their money to work for them. That's why they could afford luxury yachts.

It was amazingly simple. Groucho could never get over the wonder of it.

Every morning, after he had eaten breakfast and read the newspapers, he would get in his car and drive down to Newman Brothers & Worms, his Wall Street representatives, who had a branch brokerage office on Great Neck's main street. There he would solemnly study the ticker tapes and watch the boy marking the latest quotations on the huge board.

He would sit in the office by the hour, watching his stocks go up and up and gloating over his good fortune. He was not alone: he'd meet all his friends and neighbours and the local tradesmen in the place, and they would exchange tips and discuss the latest financial trends as if they really knew what they were talking about.

Very often, if I wasn't at school, he'd take me with him, promising he wouldn't bore me with it for long.

'I'll just take a quick look,' he'd say, 'and then we'll go home and play baseball.'

His quick look would usually last for a couple of hours, by

114

which time I had given up trying to persuade him to leave and walked home.

Or if we were driving through the village on our way to the beach or some other place, he'd have to park the car and dash into his broker's 'just for a minute', to see how things were going.

'What an easy racket,' he'd exclaim jubilantly, when he returned to the car – if he returned. 'RCA went up seven points since this morning. I just made myself $7,000.'

Although there was no one less qualified than Groucho to analyse the strength of the nation's economy, he must have had a premonition of disaster.

One day, in early October 1929, he found himself standing in front of the ticker tape machine with Mr Green, who managed this particular branch of Newman Brothers & Worms.

'Wonderful times we're living in,' commented Mr Green, pulling off a piece of tape and showing it to Groucho. 'Look at this, will you? RCA is up to $535 a share. Have you ever seen anything like it?'

Groucho agreed that he hadn't, and then added: 'There's just one thing I don't understand, Mr Green. I own RCA, too. But how can it be selling for $535 a share and never declare a dividend? If a company's sound and making money, it should declare a dividend once in a while. Doesn't that seem strange to you?'

Mr Green shook his head sagely. 'Mr Marx,' he said reassuringly, 'it's difficult for the average man not schooled in high finance to comprehend what is going on today. But I can tell you this. Wall Street is no longer localized. We're now in a world-wide market. It's going to keep going up and up and up. Is that clear?'

'Well, I think I know what you're talking about,' replied Groucho, 'but I still don't understand why RCA doesn't declare any dividends.'

'Look, Mr Marx, this thing is bigger than both of us. Don't fight it. Just be assured that you're going to wind up a very wealthy man. And I know what I'm talking about. I'm in the market myself. I'm a family man, and I wouldn't take the risk if

I didn't know the market is sound. I've invested my whole life savings in it — $8,000. It's the only sure way to become a millionaire.'

If Groucho had had any real doubts about the wisdom of entrusting his fortune to the financial geniuses of Wall Street, they were dispelled by his conversation with Mr Green.

The next day — it wasn't really the next day, but it makes a better story — the stock market began its historic collapse.

At nine in the morning Groucho was wakened from a sound sleep by an urgent call from his broker.

'There's been a slight break in the market, Mr Marx. You'd better get down here with some cash to cover your margin.'

'I thought I was covered.'

'Not enough for the way things are going. We'll need more. And you'd better hurry!'

All was bedlam at Newman Brothers & Worms when he arrived there. Ticker tape was knee deep on the floor, people were shouting orders to sell, and others were frantically scribbling cheques in vain efforts to save their original investments.

Father joined the latter group, but it was hopeless. He was in much too deep. He quickly went through his cash that wasn't tied up in stocks, and then he left to borrow more.

In the next two days he borrowed money from the bank, he borrowed money on his insurance, and he even mortgaged the house. But soon all that was gone, too.

Three days after that first call from his broker he knew the worst. Not only was he penniless, but he was in debt, besides.

15

The picture wasn't as bleak for Groucho after the crash as it was for some.

He was still making $2,000 a week in *Animal Crackers*, which continued to play to capacity business for some months to come. Following its Broadway run, the show had a long and successful tour on the road. And after it finally closed, in the summer of 1930, the Marx Brothers still had four more pictures to make for Paramount, at $200,000 a picture for the team.

Groucho was in far worse shape mentally than he was financially. All his life he had been striving for complete financial security, and berating others – principally his brother Chico – for spending their money on ridiculous luxuries, instead of putting some away for the future, as he was doing. *He* had known the value of money. He had invested it – wisely, he thought.

Now it was gone. Those who had squandered their money foolishly were just as well off as he. Probably better off, because at least they had had the fun of spending it.

'There's no justice,' he announced at the dinner table one night shortly after the crash. 'Chico's got the right idea. He has no money either, but meanwhile he's had a hell of a time for himself – dames, gambling, the best hotel suites, private schools for his daughter. Well, from now on I'm going to live by his philosophy – eat, drink and make merry. Ruth, run out and find me a girl named Mary!'

We knew better than to take this kind of talk seriously. He had said this same thing many times before the crash, but when it came to putting it into practice it never lasted for more than a couple of hours. He just didn't have it in his nature to live 'dangerously', or to shrug off the loss of $250,000.

While people all around him were selling their yachts and jumping out of windows, Groucho was worrying himself to the brink of a nervous breakdown. He never actually had a breakdown, but he was in a state of severe depression for many months afterwards.

'I've given some unfunny performances in my time,' he recalls, 'but the one I gave the night of the crash would have depressed an undertaker. I just didn't feel like making people laugh. I wanted to cry.'

The next night he was in even worse shape. He sat brooding silently in the dressing-room before the performance, and when it was time for him to make his first appearance on the stage he wouldn't move. He had never done anything like this before, and Harpo, Chico and Zeppo were sick with fear as they frantically ad libbed in front of the audience for fifteen minutes, while everyone, from the Assistant Stage manager up to Sam Harris, tried in vain to get Groucho out of his dressing-room.

Fortunately Harry Ruby, the show's composer, was backstage that evening, and when he heard what was going on he rushed into Groucho's dressing-room.

'Listen. You can't do this,' said Harry. 'The audience is out there waiting for you. They paid to see you, and you've got to give them a show.'

'What for?' asked Groucho. 'What's the use of working and making money? I'll only lose it again.'

'If you don't get out there,' threatened Ruby, 'I'll play the part myself.'

He sat down at the dressing-table and started to paint a black moustache on himself.

'Okay. You win,' said Groucho, grabbing his pith helmet from the hook and striding towards the door. 'No audience deserves to have to look at you for a whole evening.'

If his brothers were apprehensive about the kind of performance he was going to give, they must have felt reassured by the first ad lib after alighting from the sedan chair. Indicating the sedan chair with his hand, he said to one of the carriers, 'Take this out and sell it. I just got word from my broker that he wants more margin.'

After that, he kept up a running fire of jokes about the crash that had the audience rocking. Many of the lines were so good that they stayed in the show permanently.

At home, he was not so funny. He was more obsessed than ever with the idea of living economically. These were trying times, and the budget just had to be cut.

Unfortunately, it wasn't easy to cut our budget, for we didn't have any major extravagances to eliminate. Nevertheless, the order of the day – every day – was to 'conserve'.

'We're spending too much money,' began Groucho's first fireside speech after the crash. 'We're going to have to eliminate every unnecessary expense around the house. Hereafter I don't want anyone to spend a nickel without first consulting me.'

'All right,' said Mother agreeably. 'Where do you want to start economizing first? In the kitchen?'

'Yes; let's start in the kitchen.'

'Well, we can let the cook go,' suggested Mother. 'That'll save a hundred and fifty a month.'

'No; we can't do that,' replied Groucho. 'I like Mary's cooking. Let's save somewhere else. What about food-buying?'

'Well, we could buy hamburger instead of ground sirloin.'

'I don't like it as well. It's too fatty.'

And so it went, with Groucho overruling every cut that Mother suggested. They couldn't let the nurse go because cooking and taking care of the children would be too much work for Mary, and she might quit. They couldn't let the gardener go, because then Groucho might have to do the gardening, and that would leave him no time for golf. And if he couldn't play golf, then it would be a waste of money to belong to the country club. And he couldn't resign from the country club, because then he'd have no choice but to do the gardening.

As a result, he had to be content with ferreting out the smaller, inconsequential items – electricity, water, oil for the oil-burner, even tooth-paste – and issuing daily ultimatums to conserve on them.

Sometimes he had to go to even more ridiculous extremes than that to make himself believe he was being economical.

My grandmother used napkin rings at her table, and from her Groucho got the idea of doing the same at our house. If each person used a napkin for a whole week, the laundry bills would be smaller.

So he bought four of the most expensive sterling silver napkin rings you could buy, and had our names engraved on them. This came to $113, but in the long run he figured it would be worth it.

In twenty years, he probably would have saved at least $7 by using napkin rings, but we didn't keep them twenty years. In fact, the napkin ring régime lasted only until the third night, when he unrolled his napkin and was shocked to find food-stains on it.

'What's this?' he exclaimed indignantly. 'Can't a person get a clean napkin around here?'

'Next Monday you'll get one,' said Mother, 'unless we have company before then.'

'I want a clean napkin,' he demanded.

'Grouch,' Mother pointed out, 'there's no use having napkin rings if you're going to use a clean napkin every night.'

'Then let's get rid of the napkin rings,' was Groucho's solution. 'I don't like them. They're old-fashioned. Whose idea were they, anyway?'

But apart from the fact that his warnings to economize were a little more frequent after the crash than they had been before (though no more effective), there wasn't the slightest change in our mode of living, with the possible exception that we no longer had any friends who could afford yachts.

In short we were a long way from the poorhouse, as Mother used to remind Groucho whenever his complaints about the bills became too unbearable to her.

But this was small consolation to a habitual worrier like Groucho. Maybe we weren't in the poorhouse *yet*, but with his savings gone, what was going to become of all of us when he was eighty years old and too sick and feeble to work any more? Or supposing Paramount went under? Or supposing the public suddenly didn't want the Marx Brothers any more? Or supposing the government collapsed, and the money he was making turned out to be worthless?

He'd ponder the pros and cons of these questions every night after he had gone to bed. And at six o'clock in the morning he'd still be awake, thinking about them.

Thus began his introduction to insomnia, and they've been constant companions ever since.

Even before the crash he was an exceptionally light sleeper. If a car backfired in Little Neck, it would wake him instantly. Ordinary household noises while he was still in bed in the morning – a pan dropping in the kitchen, Miriam or I raising our voices, the stairs creaking under someone's weight – would put him in a foul humour for the rest of the day.

After the crash, while he was suffering from insomnia as well, these same noises would send him forth from his room, ready to commit mayhem – even if he was just lying in bed wide awake at the moment he heard them.

'For heaven's sake,' he'd yell, if he was in one of his milder moods, 'can't a man get a little sleep around here without you kids raising the roof? Now shut up or I'm going to take your bicycles away from you.'

Retreating to his room, he'd slam the door and lock it. When he finally emerged for breakfast, dressed in a long bath-robe, he'd be scowling at everyone – even those who had nothing to do with waking him.

'We're going to have to do something about those kids screaming when I'm trying to sleep,' he'd say to Mother omin-ously. 'I can't work all night and not be able to sleep in the morning. I'll ruin my health. I won't be able to work.'

'I don't know what I can do about it,' Mother would reply hotly. 'The children are not being especially noisy. But this is not the most well-built house in the world. Every noise carries – you know that.'

'I don't know what the solution is, but we're going to have to do something – or I'm going to start staying in town and sleeping in a Turkish bath!'

He never quite reached the point where he carried this threat out; but occasionally, if we made enough noise, he'd forbid Miriam and me to get out of bed in the mornings before he did (school days excluded, of course). This would usually last for one morning, by which time he'd realize that it wasn't our fault that he had insomnia, and the restriction would be lifted.

'But try and be a little quiet from now on,' he'd say, and for the next few mornings we'd all be tiptoeing around the house in mortal fear of making the slightest sound.

We couldn't keep it up indefinitely, however, and eventually the cook would drop another pan in the kitchen, or I would yell out of the window of my room to the boy next door, and Groucho's harangues would begin all over again.

In the first month he was afflicted with insomnia, he used up all the conventional cures.

He tried reading himself to sleep, but that only made him more wide awake.

121

He'd try drinking a glass of beer before he went to bed, and when that didn't work he switched to hot Ovaltine.

He read all the books on how not to worry, but of course there's never been a book written that could stop him worrying.

He tried sleeping on his back, on his stomach, on his right side, on his left side; with one pillow, two pillows, three pillows, no pillows; with the windows open, with them shut; with the lights on, with them off; alone, not alone; sitting up in a chair; lying on the floor; with the radio on, with it off; with pyjamas, with no pyjamas; and with a night-coat.

He finally settled for the bed, one pillow, a night-coat and bed-socks. (He had heard that no one could hope to fall asleep with cold feet, but in his case it didn't make any difference.)

After the bed-socks failed to do anything more than keep his feet warm, he was feeling pretty despondent about the whole situation. And one night, at a party with the late Bob Benchley, he said glumly, 'If I don't get some sleep soon, I think I'll kill myself.'

An expert on insomnia himself, Benchley suggested to Groucho that he try taking a hot bath scented with pine needles every night before turning in.

Willing to grasp at any straw, Groucho bought a bottle of the pine needle solution on the way home, and tried it in a hot bath before going to bed. This appeared to be the answer. Almost immediately, the soaking and the smell of the pine needles relaxed him. Within fifteen minutes his eyelids started to feel heavy, he became drowsier and drowsier, and finally he fell asleep in the tub.

When Mother heard a gurgling sound coming from the bathroom, she rushed in, pulled his head out of the water before he could drown, and helped resuscitate him.

'What happened?' he asked groggily.

'You nearly drowned,' said Mother. 'Don't you ever try this again.'

'No matter,' he said. 'At least I'm sleepy. Hand me a towel and my night-coat. Quickly! I want to get to bed before I wake up.'

But by the time he dried off and got into bed he was wide awake.

'That's a fine insomnia cure,' he told Benchley the next time he saw him. 'I fell asleep in the tub and almost drowned.'

'Who said it was an insomnia cure?' exclaimed Benchley. 'You said if you didn't get some sleep you wanted to kill yourself. Well, I was just expediting things.'

In desperation, Groucho started taking aspirins before retiring, and finally graduated to sleeping pills. The pills worked for a few nights, but as soon as his system got used to them they were no longer effective. Since he was afraid of becoming a drug addict if he leaned too heavily on sleeping pills, he decided to stop trying to cure himself and began looking around for a doctor who could help him.

On a friend's recommendation, he consulted Dr Richard Hoffman, a psychiatrist who had a lavish suite of offices on Park Avenue. Hoffman was supposed to be an expert on insomnia. His method of dealing with an insomniac was to get him to relax. He'd do this by telling him that 'nobody ever died of not sleeping. So stay awake.' This may have worked with your average insomniac, but not with Groucho. A year after his first consultation he was still lying awake half the night. But at least Hoffman had helped him to acquire a certain philosophy about his sleeplessness that made the dark hours of the night seem a little less torturous.

Today he is one of the best-adjusted insomniacs I know. He's completely resigned to the fact that he's never going to sleep like a child, that when he goes to bed at night he's going to lie awake for a couple of hours or maybe three, and that he will probably wake up at five or six in the morning. He's so resigned to this that occasionally he relaxes enough in bed to get a good night's sleep.

In addition to the fact that insomnia is something he can complain about, which is in its favour these days when he has very little else to complain about, he makes a game of it. While he's lying awake, he has all sorts of time-passers which he has devised to keep him from fretting about the fact that he isn't sleeping.

For example, one night he might run through the whole alphabet trying to think of a baseball player's name beginning with each letter. When the baseball season is over, he switches to playing the alphabet game with football players. And in the spring and early summer he does it with golfers and tennis players.

'It keeps me from getting stale,' he says.

Besides making up new games to play while he's trying to get to sleep, he keeps his bedroom well equipped with all the latest sleeping gadgets.

His greatest source of delight is his electric blanket, because with it he doesn't need any other covering. He can't stand the weight of two ordinary blankets on him, no matter how light they are.

'They make me feel as if I'm in an iron lung,' he claims.

He also wears a mask to keep out the light, puts wax in his ears so that he won't hear any noises, and keeps a B.B. gun next to his bed so that he can take pot-shots at the neighbours' dogs if they start barking in the middle of the night. Since he is an even worse marksman than a golfer, the dogs are perfectly safe.

When he is ready for bed, dressed in his sleeping coat and black mask and gripping his B.B. gun, he resembles a man from outer space.

He doesn't take his electric blanket with him when he travels, but he never goes anywhere without his mask and ear-plugs.

Last year he took a trip to Palm Springs with his friend Irwin Allen, the producer of the movie version of *The Sea Around Us*. They didn't go to a hotel, but instead rented a small bungalow near the Tamarask Golf Club, a new club which Groucho and his brothers and a group of his friends had invested money in. The purpose of the trip, as a matter of fact, was to celebrate the opening of Tamarask, and on their first night in Palm Springs Groucho and Allen went to a party at the club.

As usual, Groucho got tired of the festivities by around eleven o'clock, and had a yearning to get back to the bungalow and the latest copy of the *New Yorker*. Irwin Allen had no such yearning, however, and at Groucho's suggestion decided to stay at the party.

Taking the only key, Groucho returned to the bungalow, read in bed for a little while, then carefully stuffed the wax plugs into his ears and turned out the lights. But he had forgotten to leave the door unlocked.

When Allen returned a couple of hours later he practically knocked the door down pounding on it, but he got no response. Thinking perhaps that Groucho had gone out again, he peeked in the window, which was also locked, and saw him in bed, sleeping blissfully. Allen yelled at him and banged on the glass, but it was no use. Groucho didn't stir. The ear-plugs were working like a charm, and Allen had to spend the night sleeping in his car.

'That'll teach you to make a trip with a man who wears ear-plugs,' said Groucho when a bleary-eyed and bedraggled-looking Irwin Allen presented himself at the door the next morning.

'Why didn't you come looking for me?' asked Allen, annoyed. 'Didn't you think it strange when I didn't come back to the bungalow by morning?'

'Strange? Not a bit,' replied Groucho. 'With all those pretty girls at the party, why would you ever want to come back to little old me?'

16

Travelling with Groucho, with or without ear-plugs, has always been somewhat of an ordeal, though a pleasant one.

One of the things that make it an ordeal is that there is no known method of transportation that he doesn't have a strong aversion to. Ships make him seasick. He isn't afraid of flying, but he can't stand the food served on aeroplanes. Trains are out of the question, because he can't sleep at all in a Pullman berth. He claims that Pullman blankets are made in an iron-factory. And travelling by automobile is too slow, and usually very uncomfortable and tiring.

Secondly, he's highly suspicious of hotel managers, room clerks and anyone else who has anything to do with establishing room rates. He somehow seems to feel that all people in the hotel business, from the keeper of the smallest roadside motel to the manager of the Savoy in London, have banded together in a common conspiracy to bilk him of his last dollar.

As a result, his relations with these people are generally pretty stormy. Once, for example, when he was contemplating a trip to New York, he phoned up the Hampshire House from his home in Beverly Hills, and told the room reservations clerk that he wanted a small suite consisting of a bedroom and sitting-room. He was told that such a suite would cost him $50 a day.

'Fifty dollars a day!' he exclaimed. 'That's a lot of money just for a place to sleep.'

'Those are our rates,' said the clerk in a supercilious tone. 'And it's really not very much considering what a lovely view the suite has of the park.'

'Would *you* pay $50 a day just for a place to sleep?' countered Groucho.

'No,' admitted the clerk.

'Well, neither will I,' said Groucho, banging the receiver down in its cradle.

When Miriam and I were in our teens, he and Mother took us on a number of week-end trips around Los Angeles — to Palm Springs, Lake Arrowhead, Coronado and other resorts. The pattern for these trips would always be the same.

None of these places is more than three hours away for the average driver. But with Groucho driving it always took us six, partly because we made so many stops for drinks, rest-rooms and flat tyres, and partly because he would never heed Mother's warnings that he was on the wrong road.

We never seemed to arrive at a resort until dinner-time. This is a sort of drop dead hour for Groucho, anyway. He's nervous, irritable and in need of that one drink he usually has before dinner. After a six-hour drive, he'd be even more irritable because he wouldn't have had his afternoon nap.

But no matter what time we arrived, or how many times

previously he had stopped at this hotel, he'd always be surprised by the rates – even if they had been quoted to him when he made his reservation by phone.

'Too much,' he'd say. And then we'd pile our mountain of luggage and weary bodies back into the car, and we'd drive all over town, while he checked the rates at each hotel and inspected the rooms.

And we'd always wind up slinking back into the lobby of the hotel where he had originally made his reservations, and he'd have to say to the room clerk, 'I've changed my mind. Do you still have those rooms?'

The first major trip I remember taking with Groucho saw the four Marx Brothers and their wives bound for London during Christmas week 1930.

It was a combination business and pleasure trip. *Animal Crackers* had finished touring the country and had been made into a hit picture by the autumn of 1930. The Marxes' next picture for Paramount – no one as yet knew what it would be – was not scheduled to go before the cameras until the following spring, in Hollywood, which they had decided to make their home, since they had no further plans for any stage productions on Broadway.

In the meantime, since they were technically unemployed, they allowed themselves to be booked into London's Coliseum for a six weeks' vaudeville engagement, starting the first week in January.

But though it was business that took Groucho to London, I don't think he would have accepted the engagement if he hadn't been in dire need of a change of scene and some relaxation. Despite the fact that he hadn't suffered any actual hardships as a result of the stock market crash, the past year had been a strain on him in other ways. His mother Minnie had died of a heart attack very unexpectedly, and it had been a severe blow to him as well as to his brothers.

At first, Groucho and Mother planned to go to Europe without Miriam and me. And at first Groucho seemed quite enthusiastic about making the trip. But as their sailing date approached he became more and more sullen, as though he wasn't really looking forward to it for some reason.

Then one night at the dinner table he turned to me and said, 'How would you like to go to Europe?'

I, of course, was delighted. But Mother was a little more reserved in her enthusiasm.

'I thought this was going to be a pleasure trip,' she said.

'It is,' replied Groucho. 'But I can't have a good time if I have to be away all that time without seeing the children.'

'Children?' Mother was horrified. 'Don't tell me you want to take Miriam, too?'

'Of course. We can't take Arthur and leave Miriam behind. It would be unfair.'

'Chico and Betty aren't taking Maxine,' said Mother, referring to my fourteen-year-old cousin.

'That's their business,' said Groucho. 'I like to be around my children.'

'I like being around them, too,' said Mother. 'But I'm going to be the one who'll wind up sitting in a hotel room with them nights, while you're out seeing the sights.'

'I've thought of that,' said Groucho. 'We'll take the nurse along, too.'

'What about Arthur's school?' asked Mother. 'You can't just yank him out of school in the middle of the year.'

'Why not? Going to Europe will do him as much good as sleeping in a classroom.'

'I know, Grouch, but he'll get behind the other children in his studies.'

'Tell his teacher about the trip,' Groucho advised her. 'She can give you some school work for him to take along. You and I can tutor him.'

'It's going to be awfully expensive taking five people to Europe,' she reminded him. It was an unfair blow, hitting him in the pocket-book, but she saw her chances of a vacation without children slipping away, and she was willing to try anything.

But Groucho was not vulnerable. 'Who cares how expensive it is?' he said. 'What good is money if you don't spend it?'

'Are you sure you're feeling all right?' asked Mother.

Groucho's mother, Minnie Marx, at the age of 25.

Groucho's father, Sam Marx, the tailor, *c.* 1890.

Groucho, aged 15, about to embark on his theatrical career.

Groucho, the young vaudevillian, enjoying some afternoon recreation on the baseball diamond.

Groucho enjoying one of his first cigars.

The four Marx Brothers, on their farm in La Grange, Illinois, 1917. They were doing their bit to help the war effort by raising chickens.

...th, Groucho, the author, sister
...riam and Uncle Harpo on the
...ramount lot during the shooting of
...ck Soup, 1932.

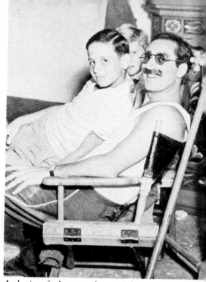

A doting father on the set of
Duck Soup, 1932.

...e Marx Brothers on the set of
...ck Soup.

Groucho, Miriam and Ruth on the lot of Paramount studios, Hollywood, 1933.

Ruth and Groucho resting on their rackets, 1933. (*Paul Wesolowski Collection*)

The family that plays together, stays together – or so we're led to believe. Groucho on guitar leads Miriam, the author and Ruth in family songfest.

e three Marx Brothers, after Zeppo left the act to become an agent, 1935.

ntemplative Groucho at home in
erly Hills, *c.* 1935.

Chico and Groucho courting Carole
Lombard after her guest appearance
on *The Kellogg Hour*, a radio show,
in 1939. (*Paul Wesolowski
Collection*)

A rare get-together of all five Marx Brothers. L to R: Gummo, Groucho, Harpo, Chico and Zeppo, at Groucho's house in Beverly Hills, *c.* 1938.

One last chorus with Groucho and Miriam before the author, in Coast Guard dress blues, sets sail for the South Pacific in 1944.

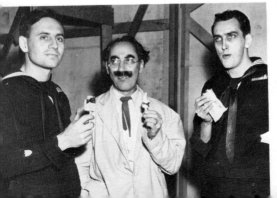

The author and shipmate Bob Howard visit Groucho on the set of *A Night in Casablanca*, the day of their discharge from the service after the Second World War.

oucho giving his second wife, Kay,
ne instruction in the game of
:ket billiards.

Groucho assisting the New York
Giants baseball team, at their spring
training headquarters in Phoenix,
Arizona, 1951.

oucho handling the ball in a
kyard basketball game with the
hor, 1954.

Groucho's daughter and grandson –
Melinda with the author's son, Steve,
1956.

Groucho and his third wife, Eden Hartford, dancing – one of his least favourite activities. (*Paul Wesolowski Collection*)

Groucho dancing with Audrey Hepburn, on one of the rare occasions when he agreed to put on a tux.

Eden, Melinda and Groucho at the première of *Carousel* in Hollywood, 1956. (*Paul Wesolowski Collection*)

Groucho *c*. 1960.

says he isn't as funny at home as
on stage? Groucho with the
or.

Groucho and grandson – the author's
son, Andy, with his grandfather's
cigar in his hand, 1968.

R: Groucho, humourist Sid Perelman, and critic Kenneth Tynan in a
lon hotel, *c.* 1970. (*Paul Wesolowski Collection*)

Groucho with his daughter-in-law, Lois, and Elsie the poodle.

The inimitable Groucho.

Erin Fleming and Groucho outside the theatre where he received his honorary Academy Award Oscar, 1974. (*Paul Wesolowski Collection*)

'I'm feeling fine now that the kids are going along.'

Groucho was the champion of children's rights. He believed that children were not born to be left out of things. He felt just as strongly in favour of our going on all trips with him and my mother as he did about having us at the dinner table with them.

Whether or not we should accompany them on trips was always a good starting-place for an argument, for, devoted a parent as my mother was, she usually preferred to leave us at home. After all, since she was the mother, much of the responsibility of looking after us fell on her. With us along, she couldn't be as carefree and relaxed on a trip as she would have liked.

Now that *I'm* a parent I can see her point, but when Miriam and I were children we naturally looked at it selfishly and were always on the sidelines rooting for Groucho in these arguments. He usually won out, just as he did about the trip to Europe.

In this case he made it up to her – not only by taking along a nurse, but by booking the most luxurious steamship accommodation the French liner, the *Paris*, had to offer. We had the Royal Suite, which consisted of three bedrooms, two baths, a dining-room, a butler's pantry, and a large living-room complete with gold-inlaid upright piano.

Our accommodation was the envy of the rest of the Marx family, who had to make the voyage in ordinary staterooms, without pianos. No one could understand why Groucho, of all people, and in the midst of the depression, had suddenly turned into a Diamond Jim Brady-type spender. Had he really stopped worrying about money, or was he a little bit off his rocker from having insomnia night after night? But there was no explanation. It was just another example of his inconsistent spending habits.

We sailed from New York on 23 December, a wintry white day with a wind of gale proportions howling off the Hudson River.

The *bon voyage* party for the Marxes was held in our suite because of the lavishness of it. A great many of Groucho's

129

friends came down to see us off, including Harry Ruby and the whole New York Giants football team. The team presented him with an autographed football, which he promptly gave to me as soon as they departed. Dozens of people were milling around, the champagne was flowing, and I remember a great many choruses on the piano of Harry Ruby's latest hit song, 'Three Little Words'.

In the midst of the festivities Sam Harris shouted, 'Where's Groucho? We can't let him go without a chorus of "Captain Spaulding".'

It was then noticed that he had disappeared. A search party was sent out for him, but they came back without him. Finally, about fifteen minutes before sailing time, the door to one of the bathrooms opened up and out he staggered, his face absolutely green.

'What's the matter?' asked Mother, rushing up to him.

'I'm not sure,' he moaned, holding his stomach, 'but I think I'm getting seasick.'

And we hadn't even left the dock yet!

17

My parents made three ocean trips together during their marriage, and on none of these voyages were they on speaking terms by the time they reached their destination.

Shipboard life represented all the things that Groucho hated and Mother loved: gay parties, with the women in long dresses and the men in white dinner jackets; dancing until the late hours; convivial companionship; and organized play.

Added to this was the fact that Groucho never felt physically up to par with the unsteady motion of a deck beneath him. He'd only be in bed, actually seasick, for a day or two, but even after he was up and about he'd always be on the verge of seasickness, and that would keep him in a continually grumpy mood.

As for the *Paris*, she was carrying very little freight in her holds when we crossed on her, and consequently had no ballast to speak of. As a result, every time she rolled to one side on the mountainous seas she'd lie there for several sickening moments, while everyone on board wondered whether she would ever right herself again. Then, with a convulsive groan, she'd start back, and the same thing would be repeated on the other side. Groucho had put himself to bed even before the *bon voyage* party had broken up.

Christmas on the *Paris* wasn't too unlike our previous ones, except that we had no tree of our own, and we had to hang our stockings from a porthole instead of on the fireplace. There was a mammoth Christmas tree in the main lounge, however, and Mother and Groucho had come aboard well supplied with presents.

Miriam and I ripped open our packages in record time, with Mother and Groucho looking on, and opening a few of their own. With each present he opened, Groucho would exclaim, 'Just what I needed!' and toss it carelessly back in the box.

'Did you like the presents I gave you?' Mother asked him after the last package had been opened.

'Very much,' said Groucho. 'There's just one thing that worries me. How am I going to take them back and exchange them if we're in the middle of the Atlantic Ocean?'

Groucho's attitude to Christmas has always been the same – on land or on sea. He believes that the Christmas spirit is commendable, but that the holiday itself has become much too commercialized.

'Only children should get presents,' he has contended every year at Christmas-time for as long as I can remember. 'This business of grown-ups exchanging presents is ridiculous – a racket foisted on the public by the greedy shopkeepers of America. Just as Father's Day and Mother's Day are all very lucrative rackets.'

However, he accepts Christmas with good-humoured resignation, and he was always a very generous Santa Claus. But at Christmas-time the most thankless job I can think of is trying to buy him a present that he won't exchange on the following day.

One year my wife and I and our two children ate Christmas Eve dinner with him, and afterwards he opened his presents.

131

He received seven pairs of cuff-links from various people around town. After he had opened his packages, he remained sitting in front of the Christmas tree, looking extremely despondent.

'Why so glum?' I asked.

'You'd be glum, too,' he answered, 'if you had to spend all day tomorrow going from store to store, exchanging cuff-links.'

One year I managed to give him a present which he kept and was actually pleased about. It was a plum tree, and it's growing in his back-yard today. But how many plum trees can a man use?

On the *Paris*, of course, he was stuck. There was absolutely nothing he could do with his presents but keep them. 'It was the most frustrating Christmas I've ever spent,' he recalls.

But, frustrating or not, the Christmas spirit was maintained to the bitter end. The final offering of the day was the reading by Groucho of *The Night Before Christmas*. It was his own version, and I don't remember all of it, but the first two stanzas went like this:

''Twas the night before Christmas
And all through the house,
Not a customer was stirring,
Not even a louse.
Because Christmas week has always
Been a drop dead week in the theatre.

'The stockings were hung on
The chorus girls with care,
In hopes that some rich playboys
Soon would be there.
The children were home,
Fast asleep in their beds,
With visions of B.B. guns (with which to maim their parents)
Dancing round in their heads.
Mother, of course, was fast asleep, too,
Dreaming of mink coats that she wanted to come true.
But poor old Father was still wide awake,
Thinking of the bills and getting a bad stomach-ache.'

And so ended a typical old-fashioned white Christmas with Groucho.

Once on the trip across, Groucho decided that it was about time I did some studying, despite my protests that it was still technically Christmas vacation.

'You're getting enough vacation,' he said. 'Bring your arithmetic book. I'll tutor you.'

Reluctantly, I dug out my maths book and handed it to him. He opened the book at the first lesson. 'I'll start you out with an easy problem,' he said. 'If you have five apples, and ten people to eat them, how would you divide them so that everyone could have the same amount?'

Even I knew that. 'I'd cut them in half so there would be ten pieces,' I said.

Groucho shook his head gravely.

'What's the matter?' I asked. 'I know that's the right answer. I can show it to you in the book.'

'I don't care what the book says,' he replied. 'The right answer is – you'd make apple sauce. I know that because we had the same problem in *Fun In Hi Skule*.'

Much to my relief, the rest of his tutoring on our trip to Europe was of the same calibre, so there was no danger of my learning anything, or getting bored.

A group of English newspapermen and women boarded the ship when we arrived at Southampton, and before we disembarked there was a welcoming party for the Marx Brothers. The champagne must have been pretty strong, because Groucho gave out interviews and entertainment to the ladies and gentlemen of the press as if they were old friends.

He generally isn't available for interviews until he has arrived at his hotel and has had a night's sleep. Even then he won't be too co-operative, but if a reporter is persistent enough, in a polite way, of course, he will finally give in and talk freely.

At any rate, he was exceptionally co-operative with the English press. Mother was so pleased to see him being garrulous that she made up with him – they hadn't been on speaking terms for two days – and by the time we boarded the train for London they were as friendly as man and wife.

In London, we stopped at the Savoy. We didn't arrive there until two in the morning, but, except for the fact that we were very tired, everything appeared to be going smoothly – until the room clerk quoted the price of our accommodation, that is.

I don't remember what price he quoted, but I do know that Groucho considered the room rates 'outrageous'. His first thought, naturally, was to tell off the management and go hunting for a cheaper hotel. But because we were in a foreign city, and he was unfamiliar with the hotel situation, Mother was able to persuade him that it would be foolish to spend the rest of the night tramping the streets of London, in a very heavy fog, in order to save a few dollars.

'All right,' he said, after giving it considerable thought. 'We'll stay here tonight, but tomorrow we're going to find an honest hotel – one where they don't charge you according to *who* you are.'

But once we were settled in our rooms, he was so pleased with them that he wouldn't dream of moving. We stayed there the entire six weeks we were in London.

However, to make up for the fact that the room rates were high, he forbade us the use of 'room service' in the mornings. In fact, he wouldn't let us eat breakfast in the hotel at all, and insisted that Sadie take Miriam and me to breakfast at Slater's, a cheap lunchroom across the street.

The vaudeville show that the Marx Brothers presented at the Coliseum Theatre was a sort of potpourri of the best comedy routines they had done in the past. It was very popular with English audiences, and this time there were no penny-throwing incidents.

Groucho was very much impressed with London – much more so than he was with Paris – I suppose because London really is a man's city, as they say.

He liked the English people and their customs, the men's shops and even the sight-seeing. 'There's only one thing wrong with England,' he said. 'You can't get a decent cup of coffee. But I suppose I shouldn't complain about that. I can't get a decent cup of coffee at home either.'

Except for their coffee, he felt that the British were a more civilized people on the whole than Americans.

To him this has always been exemplified by an incident that took place one morning in Hyde Park, where we had gone to play two-handed soccer.

Groucho and I usually played some kind of ball game together whenever we were travelling, and since he was so enthusiastic about England he had bought a soccer ball.

There was only one trouble with soccer, as we found out. It was an unhandy game to play in an alley behind the hotel. Groucho looked around for a better playing field, and finally hit upon what he thought was the perfect solution – Hyde Park. So we went there one morning and started kicking the ball around on a grassy spot beside a flock of grazing sheep.

We had been there about five minutes, when Groucho kicked the ball with a little too much gusto, and it landed in the sheep flock, frightening the animals and causing them to scatter. At that moment a bobby happened along, and hurried over to us.

'I'm awfully sorry, sir, but football isn't permitted here,' he told us.

'This isn't really football,' replied Groucho. 'We're not even keeping score.'

'It's against the rules and regulations to play football here,' said the bobby. 'This is reserved for the sheep.'

'Sheep can't play football,' said Groucho. 'I just kicked the ball over to them, and they didn't even kick it back.'

'I'm sorry, sir,' said the bobby, 'but I just can't allow it.'

'Well, where can we play?' asked Groucho in a pathetic tone. 'We've been looking all over town for a place to kick the ball around.'

The bobby told us the name of a playground where we could go, apologized very effusively for breaking up our game, and then strolled off.

'What a wonderful place this England is,' said Groucho, as we were walking back to the hotel. 'If this had happened in Central Park, the cop would have said, "Get the hell off the grass before I turn you in." In England you can't play on the grass either, but they're so nice about telling you that it's a pleasure to get thrown off!'

Groucho was also very much impressed with all the pomp

and pageantry in London. His usual attitude is that when you've seen one parade you've seen them all, but in London he never got his fill – either of parades or of watching the Changing of the Guard ceremonies at Buckingham Palace.

One afternoon when he didn't have a matinée he took Mother, Miriam and me to the Tower of London. He thought it would be a good opportunity to teach me history first hand, to make up for the fact that I was missing so much school.

'This is where Henry the Eighth had all his wives' heads chopped off,' he explained when we were going through the grim-looking building with one of the guides.

'Why did he do that?' I asked.

'Because it was simpler than paying alimony,' he answered. 'Now – what else do you want to know about English history?'

Another morning, when we were walking by Buckingham Palace, I remembered that he had promised to introduce me to the Prince of Wales, and I reminded him of it.

'Good idea, since we're in the neighbourhood,' he said.

He walked up to the sentry box in which the guard was standing and knocked on the side of it.

'Anybody home?' he asked.

The guard ignored him.

'How do I get in this joint?' asked Groucho, indicating the Palace.

'What do you want?' asked the guard.

'I've come from across the sea,' said Groucho in a mock-serious tone, 'and I have business with Edward, Prince of Wales.'

'Who are you?' asked the guard.

'My name is Julius H. Marx,' replied Groucho, 'and the Prince told me to drop in on him when I came to London.'

The guard informed him that royalty didn't cater to drop-in business. Groucho, I'm sure, was well aware of this, but he pretended to be extremely indignant.

'All right for you,' he said, shaking a warning finger under the guard's nose, 'but the next time I see the Prince I'm going to tell him to get rid of you. Turning away good customers is no way to run a business.'

Later he tried to get in touch with the Prince through official channels, but he was told that the Royal Family was in mourning for a distant relative who had just died, and that they weren't seeing outsiders.

However, the Marx Brothers were invited to spend an afternoon and have dinner at the Duke of Manchester's estate (that Duke's dead now), and at the last minute Groucho wangled an invitation for me, too.

The Duke was a big, affable man and a charming host, with a reputation for being somewhat of a playboy. He lived in a huge stone mansion surrounded by acres of beautiful grounds. He had dozens of servants, and a stable that was larger than our whole house in Great Neck.

But it was a damp, miserable day in January when we went out to see him, and the house was freezing inside. There was an enormous fireplace in the living-room containing a very small, ineffectual fire, and unless you stood directly in front of it, you felt no warmth.

'Say, can't you turn the heat on?' Groucho finally asked the Duke. 'It's like the North Pole in here.'

'I can't afford to burn any more fuel,' said the Duke, with a sad smile. 'I'm flat broke.'

'In a place like this?'

'Because of it.'

'Can't you sell it and get a smaller place?'

He shook his head. 'We dukes have to keep up a front, you know. Why don't you wear a sweater? That's what my other guests do.'

The following Sunday we were invited back to the Duke's again. On the way out to the Duke's estate in a rented car, Groucho spotted a place by the side of the road that sold firewood. Ordering the driver to stop, he alighted and proceeded to buy as much firewood as he could get into the boot (and part of the back seat) of the automobile.

'I couldn't find a sweater,' Groucho explained when he presented the firewood to the Duke, who was delighted. 'So I brought some fuel for you instead.'

*

By his standards, Groucho was quite active socially when we were in London. He and Mother attended a number of formal dinner parties, and he got to meet some of his favourite authors – J. B. Priestley, Noël Coward, A. P. Herbert and Somerset Maugham.

But the thing that impressed him the most was how British men, even at the most informal dinners, thought nothing at all of wearing evening clothes. He grew so used to it that he actually reached the stage where he would put on his own tuxedo without protest, though he normally loathed 'dressing up'. Sensing that he was weakening, Mother gathered up her courage one day and suggested that he have a new tuxedo made.

'Since you're in London, you might as well,' she went on. 'They know how to make them properly here. And if you had a really good one that you could be comfortable in, you wouldn't mind wearing a tuxedo.'

He surprised her by not only having a new tuxedo made, but also a full dress outfit with tails, white tie and even a silk hat. 'I'll be the talk of the Cliveden Set,' he threatened.

It was the kind of progress Mother hadn't dared hope for. And they were on such good terms by the time we left for Paris that they were speaking to each other nearly all the way across the English Channel.

Groucho liked Paris well enough to stay there for two weeks, despite the fact that the rates at the George V Hotel were 'outrageous'.

In the first two days we were there, he methodically whipped us through all the main tourist attractions – Versailles, Notre Dame, Flea Market, the Louvre and the Eiffel Tower, where he got sick going up in the rickety, glass-enclosed elevator.

Then, while Mother spent the rest of her time in Paris shopping, he whiled away the days hunting for a restaurant with American cooking. The snails and the French sauces were getting him down. 'I just want a plain meal,' he kept complaining. 'Isn't there somewhere in Paris where I can get a meal that isn't cooked in wine?'

138

One day he took me to a Punch and Judy show in the park along the Champs Elysées. He left me in the audience while he went out and took a walk through the park. When the show was over and he hadn't returned, I went out to look for him. I found him on the boulevard rolling hoops with a group of French children, and apparently having the best time he'd had since we'd arrived in Paris.

Except for the night life, which he deplored, the main thing he didn't like about Paris was the language barrier. More than anyone I know, he is dependent upon the spoken language for his fun. If he can't get into ridiculous conversations with people, he feels that there's not much point in living.

He can speak German, but not French. And German got him nowhere in Paris.

One afternoon he and Chico decided to go to the horse-races, but they couldn't make the cab driver understand this. Desperate because he'd already missed two races, Chico finally got down on his hands and knees on the sidewalk, and motioned Groucho to climb on his back.

'Make like a jockey,' said Chico.

Groucho jumped on Chico's back, and started whipping him with a newspaper.

'Now do you know where we want to go?' Chico, still on his hands and knees, asked the driver.

'*Oui, oui,*' said the driver, motioning them into the cab.

As they drove away, Chico was rather pleased with his inventiveness. But his confidence in himself was shaken after the cab-driver dropped them off in front of a large building a little while later, and they found that they were not at a race-course at all. They were at a wrestling arena.

After that experience, Groucho decided he'd better learn the rudiments of the French language. But after spending two weeks in Paris, the only phrase he succeeded in mastering was '*Voulez-vous coucher avec moi?*' To Mother's embarrassment, he sprang this on every man and woman with whom he came in contact.

We sailed home from Le Havre on the German ship, the *Europa*.

The night before we docked, Mother and Groucho held a confab to discuss the strategy they would employ for getting through the Customs.

They hadn't made a great many expensive purchases while we were in Europe, but they had exceeded the limit, which at the time, I believe, was $400 per person. Groucho, as a matter of fact, had spent $500 on a single item – a combination lighter and watch – which he had bought at Dunhill's in London.

The duty on our excess, if it had all been declared, probably wouldn't have amounted to a great deal. But, as every American tourist knows, half the fun of going to Europe comes from the thrill of seeing what you can smuggle through the Customs on your return. And Groucho was in a gambling mood.

'I'll just put the lighter in my vest pocket,' he announced, 'and even if they should frisk me and find it, who'll be able to prove that I didn't buy it in the States before I left?'

'Just as a precaution,' said Mother, 'you'd better slip the Customs man a few bucks when we get on the dock, so he'll overlook some of the clothes in our trunk we're not declaring. Harpo and Chico are doing it, and they say that always helps.'

'Oh, no,' said Groucho, 'I won't resort to bribery.'

'But, Groucho – everybody does it,' protested Mother.

'Bribery is crooked,' he roared. 'I'll have no truck with it.'

'I suppose sneaking that lighter in isn't,' said Mother.

'That's different,' said Groucho. 'I'm simply matching wits with them. But it's not crooked, like bribery.'

He remained adamant. There would be no bribing the Customs men.

Nevertheless, everything probably would have gone smoothly – if there hadn't been a Declaration of Purchases Form to fill out. But, given a blank questionnaire, Groucho can't control his comic tendencies, and this was the result.

Name: Julius H. Marx.
Address: 21 Lincoln Road, Great Neck, L.I.
Born: Yes.
Hair: Not much.
Occupation: Smuggler.

List items purchased out of the United States, where bought, and the purchase price: Wouldn't you like to know?

When we finally arrived at the pier, the other passengers went through Customs without much delay, but we were detained for several hours while the Inspector carefully examined every inch of our baggage.

Mother, who hadn't seen the form after Groucho had filled it out, couldn't understand why the Customs Department was singling us out to make an example of. And with each new piece of undeclared clothing the Inspector discovered, she would whisper irately to Groucho, 'It's all your fault. I told you you should have slipped him something. And look how he's messing up my new dresses!'

'It's just routine,' Groucho assured her. 'Everyone goes through this.'

'This is the last ocean trip I take with you,' she said at one point.

'Never mind that,' said Groucho in a whisper just loud enough for the Inspector to hear it. 'What did you do with the opium? Do you still have it on you?'

That was all the Customs Inspector needed to hear. We were promptly taken to the Customs office on the pier, segregated by sex, and made to undress while they went through the clothes we were wearing.

Groucho hadn't counted on his practical joke getting so far out of hand, and he was nervous and pale for fear that they would discover the lighter. But somehow he managed to conceal it (he later confessed to me that at one point he had it in his mouth) and eventually we were released.

There's an interesting postscript to the story which ought to be a warning to all incipient smugglers.

About six months later, after we had moved to California and were living in a hilltop home in Hollywoodland, there came a knock on the door one afternoon, and Groucho opened it.

Standing there was a fellow in a grey suit and a fedora. He had that unmistakable look of a Government man about him. His manner was polite, but at the same time a trifle ominous.

He introduced himself, and said he was from 'Customs' – and quickly got to the point.

'We're interested in a little item you didn't declare when you returned from Europe last February,' he said.

'What kind of an item?' asked Groucho innocently.

'A lighter, Mr Marx.'

'That's absurd,' said Groucho.

Ignoring his protest, the Customs man went on resolutely reading from a notebook:

'A combination cigarette lighter and eighteen-jewel watch. According to our records, you bought it at Dunhill's London store on 16 January. Salesman: Y.Z., Third Floor. Purchase price: $528, American money.'

In the face of such incriminating evidence, Groucho had no choice but to confess, agree to pay the duty, and also an additional penalty charge.

But he was filled with admiration for the Customs Department.

'You boys certainly are thorough,' he said. 'How did you find out all that?'

'We have our ways,' smiled the Customs man.

'Well, it certainly teaches me a lesson,' said Groucho. 'That's the last time I buy anything at Dunhill's in London. The place is obviously full of stool pigeons!'

18

In Hollywood, the Marx Brothers continued as a team for nearly twenty years. They made eleven more pictures together, and Groucho appeared in three without his brothers. Two of them – *A Night at the Opera* and *A Day at the Races* – were, in the opinion of nearly every critic, outstanding.

Although they were box office favourites for many years, Groucho always felt that if they had fallen into the hands of Irving Thalberg earlier in their picture careers, and if he had lived longer and continued to guide them, as he did with *A Night at the Opera* and *A Day at the Races*, they would have had more films of that calibre to their credit. But their association with Thalberg lasted only a short time.

The Marx Brothers' early pictures in Hollywood — *Monkey Business*, *Horsefeathers*, and *Duck Soup* — may not have been great pictures, but they were successful in the eyes of the public. And they've held up surprisingly well over the years. Exhibitors apparently think so, too, for there always seems to be at least one of their old pictures playing around in the big cities, and audiences still enjoy watching them.

Groucho never enjoyed watching himself, however, even in his very best pictures. At previews, he'd sit slumped down in his seat, usually with his coat collar turned up, so that he wouldn't be recognized as one of the perpetrators, and afterwards he'd slink out into the lobby as if he were some criminal. His face would be a sort of off-white colour, and his comment would always be the same:

'Gee! I gave a bad performance. I'm certainly not the actor I used to be.'

This wasn't just false modesty, either. He believed it. He'd be depressed for several days, and he'd be convinced that he was 'washed up'. And during this period of depression, he'd pay particular attention to the advertisements in *Time* magazine telling how a man could retire on $200 a month and spend his 'sunset years' swordfishing off the coast of Florida.

But when we first arrived in Hollywood, shortly after our European excursion, Groucho was pretty enthusiastic about the moving picture business. The Marx Brothers already had two successful pictures to their credit, and he saw no reason why they couldn't continue to turn out more like *Cocoanuts* and *Animal Crackers*, especially if they made them at the leisurely pace of one a year, which they had insisted on in their contract with Paramount Studios.

Actually, it turned out to be quite a struggle for the Marx Brothers even to make one picture a year in Hollywood. And this came as quite a shock to Groucho.

He had quit Broadway mainly because he was looking for a more comfortable way of life, or 'a softer racket', as he phrased it. He was in good health, but as he used to remind us often, he wasn't getting any younger. He was in his early forties, his hair

143

was greying to the point where it needed to be touched up for public appearances, and he wanted to spend what he called his 'declining years' in front of a fireplace in the evenings instead of in front of footlights.

He accomplished this by moving to Hollywood, but in return for the comforts of a more normal home life, he discovered that there were certain disadvantages to being a picture actor that he hadn't anticipated.

Apart from the mechanical aspects, there had been no problems in connection with putting *Cocoanuts* and *Animal Crackers* on film. The important ingredients – the story, the jokes and the comedy routines – were all sure-fire. There had been few changes to make. In fact, they had practically photographed the shows exactly as they had been on the stage.

But in Hollywood they had to start from scratch, and this turned out to be exceedingly difficult.

True, they had to start from scratch when they were preparing a Broadway show, too, but there was one important difference. If they were not satisfied with a scene after an opening, they could tinker with it until they got it right. Lines that didn't get laughs would be thrown out, and they'd keep trying new ones until they found lines that did get laughs.

But in the movies, once a picture was on film they were stuck with it, good or bad. There was very little that anyone could do to improve it, beyond cutting, or perhaps shooting a scene over, if it was exceptionally bad.

At the time, Groucho and his brothers saw no way in which they could solve this problem satisfactorily. The only thing they could do was to try and see that their scripts were as funny as possible before they went before the cameras, and hope for the best.

And in those days it wasn't easy to get Marx Brothers scripts that even looked good on paper. Most of the writers around Hollywood were left over from the silent days, and the few who could write good dialogue weren't particularly suited for originating Marx Brothers material.

As I mentioned before, writing for them was a very special proposition. An author not only had to write a story conducive

144

to comedy, but he had to dream up one containing parts for comedians with three totally different styles, plus a love-interest role for Zeppo, the straight man. Probably the hardest one to write for was Groucho.

'A lot of authors thought because they wrote long speeches for me and had me talking fast and using a lot of non sequiturs and silly puns, that that was all there was to it,' explains Groucho. 'That's my style all right. The trouble is, a lot of writers forget to be funny along with it.'

Groucho's fast-talking style had its origin back in his *Fun in Hi Skule* days, when he was just blossoming into a comic. He had no confidence in himself as a comedian, and he was never sure whether his material was any good or not, so he decided that if he talked very rapidly there would be less chance of the audience getting bored.

His off-stage character also stems from the time when he didn't have much confidence in his ability to cope with people. Inherently shy, he discovered early in life that if you insult someone right off the bat or make a wisecrack, there is a good chance that the other person will be so taken aback that he won't make any remarks about you or notice your shortcomings.

When he became successful, he realized that fast talking by itself was not enough to keep an audience from being bored. But many of the men who wrote for him didn't realize this, and what they turned out was usually a very bad carbon copy of the Groucho Marx they had seen on the stage.

Groucho always contributed a good deal to the Marxes' picture scripts. He'd sit in on all the story conferences, work right along with the writers, if need be, and he'd occasionally take a script home and toil away on it by himself.

A good many of the basic premises for their stories were also his original ideas. I'm not sure which ones, but I have a hunch this was true of *Monkey Business*. We had just finished an ocean voyage, and most of the action in *Monkey Business* took place on a transatlantic liner. It couldn't have been simply a coincidence.

By the time the Marx Brothers finished *Monkey Business* and

145

Horsefeathers and were preparing *Duck Soup*, Groucho was beginning to realize that making movies wasn't the soft racket he had imagined it would be.

Not only was it becoming tougher and tougher to get good scripts, but he was beginning to dislike movie-making in general.

First of all, he had little respect for some of the producers and front office executives with whom he came in contact in those days. He was constantly fighting with them for script changes which they didn't feel were necessary. They were anxious to get the picture before the cameras, whether the script was good or not.

'It's like the story of the gas-house gang who went out to play football for the first time,' he used to tell me. 'They had never played in their lives, and didn't know the first thing about the game. They lined up for the kick-off, but they had neglected to bring the football. When some wise guy mentioned this to the Captain, the Captain said, "To hell with the ball. Let's get going!"'

He also didn't approve of the way many directors went about the business of shooting a picture. 'Their idea of directing me in a scene was to say, "Give 'em the eyebrows, Groucho", or, "When you come into the room, snap your fingers so the audience will know you just got an idea." That idea of snapping your fingers went out with the Keystone Kops.'

And he was rabid on the subject of directors who had to shoot simple scenes over and over again. 'If the actors know their lines, there's no reason for this sort of thing,' he'd say after a long day of shooting. 'The trouble is, this jerk we've got for a director doesn't know what the hell he wants. So he shoots everything twenty times, and hopes there'll be something good in it.'

He always had more dialogue, and longer, trickier speeches than anyone in the picture, but he was very conscientious about learning lines, and he rarely fluffed one, even on the first take. So naturally it infuriated him to have to do a scene more than a couple of times – either because the director was unsure

146

of himself or because some other actor hadn't bothered to look at the script the night before.

Another thing that rankled was the working hours during the shooting of a picture. A movie actor has to be on the set, ready to begin shooting, at nine in the morning. Groucho can barely be civil at nine in the morning, much less in the mood for cracking jokes.

'This is a hell of a time to have to be funny,' he'd complain bitterly every morning when he was leaving for the studio.

Ordinarily he rose at eight, so he didn't have to get up any earlier to be at the studio at nine. When he left the house he'd already have on his frock coat, striped pants and red tie. And he refused to bother with pancake make-up, claiming he looked just as grotesque with or without it, so when he arrived at the studio there was nothing left for him to do but slap on his painted black moustache.

But when he knows he has to be anywhere before noon he can't sleep the whole night before, so he'd be a wreck by the time he arrived on the set.

However, much as he hated getting to the studio early, he'd usually be the first actor on the set in the morning, and if anyone showed up late, he or she would have to answer to Groucho.

When Groucho was working with his brothers, Chico very often would be late arriving on the set. Harpo deplored this practice as much as Groucho, so one day the two of them put their heads together to try to think of a way to cure him of the habit.

They finally decided that they would impose a $50 fine on Chico every time he showed up late, and to make it fair the same rule would apply to themselves. Being a gambling man, Chico agreed to this, and Groucho was delighted with the whole arrangement.

The first morning that this new rule was going into effect, Groucho rose at his usual time, ate a leisurely breakfast, and then walked out to the garage to get his car.

We had a sliding overhead garage door that we had never had any trouble with before. But when Groucho went to slide it up, he found that he couldn't get it to move. Finally, he called me out to the garage, and the two of us went to work on it – but with the same result.

'We must do something,' said Groucho, looking at his watch frantically. 'I'm going to lose fifty bucks if I don't get to the studio by nine.'

The garage had a back entrance, and we entered through there and discovered that a four-by-four board was wedged into the complicated spring mechanism that worked the door. We tried to dislodge it, but it wouldn't budge.

'Why don't you take a taxi?' suggested Mother, who had come out to the garage to investigate the trouble.

'I don't want to waste money on a taxi, with two Cadillacs in the garage,' he said. 'Quick! Get me my saw!'

I brought him the saw, and after he had hacked away at the board for about forty-five minutes he managed to free the door. But he was late getting to the studio, for the first time in his life, and Chico was on the set, waiting for him with palm outstretched.

'My garage door jammed,' explained Groucho. 'You're not going to count that!'

'Never mind the excuses,' said Chico. 'Hand over the dough.'

'I don't have that much in cash on me,' said Groucho, annoyed. 'I'll write you a cheque later.'

'No cheques,' said Chico. 'I want cash – right now!'

'Me too,' said Harpo.

So Groucho had to go out and round up $100 in cash before they could begin shooting. But he saw to it that that was the last time they used the *fine* system on any of their pictures.

And although he never uncovered any evidence as to how the board got jammed inside the garage door, he has always suspected that there was foul play somewhere along the line, because his brothers were incorrigible practical jokers.

19

Groucho has been one of Hollywood's staunchest defenders ever since he first settled permanently in Southern California. He feels that it is the only place to live and work, and at the first word of criticism from an out-of-towner he'll rise to the community's defence more willingly than he'll come to the aid of a helpless lady.

He fell in love with Southern California's temperate climate and informal way of life the moment he was exposed to them. And he still can't get over the fact that he doesn't need galoshes in the winter, or that sport shirts are acceptable in most of the places he goes, summer and winter.

And yet, with all his loyalty, over the years he has consistently rebelled against many of the things that Hollywood stands for: the phoney glamour, the ostentatious living, the false adulation – in fact, the whole social scene as reported in the fan magazines.

For many years, for instance, he refused to have his own swimming pool. Apart from the initial installation cost and the upkeep, which he felt was an unnecessary extravagance, he believed that pools attracted too many uninvited guests. If there's anyone who's unwelcome at his house, it's an uninvited guest. But if you have a pool, it's practically impossible to keep friends from dropping in on you with their swimming suits and staying all day, no matter how frosty you are to them.

So when he bought his own home in Beverly Hills, he made sure that the backyard was bereft of any embellishments that would tend to make it a community playground.

Our new home was no slum. It had fourteen rooms, six baths and a three-car garage. And its grounds were spacious enough for a pool, and also a tennis court. But before Mother or Miriam or I could get any ideas, Groucho quickly filled up the backyard with citrus trees and a vegetable patch.

Without a swimming pool, we were definitely not part of the swimming pool set. Now that I think of it, I'm not sure what set Groucho was a part of. Certainly not the acting set.

Most of the people who used to come to our house were a desultory assortment of writers, producers, composers and relatives. Some were important people in town; some were still struggling, or perhaps out of work altogether. But all were his friends for the same reason – because he liked them and considered them entertaining people to have around. Not because they were big names, or could do him some good professionally.

Groucho is very loyal to his friends. He's not the type who gets a whole new set every six months. Once he's made up his mind that he likes you, nothing anyone can say about you will change his opinion of you or your talents.

Over the years, he has had occasion to know most of the important movie, radio and television stars. Some of them he only knows well enough to say 'Hello' to in a restaurant, or to kid around with when they get invited to the same parties. But there is a handful of them whom he sees fairly often, and whose company he really enjoys.

He eats lunch a couple of times a week at the Comedians' Round Table at Hillcrest Country Club, and though he rarely sees these comedians at any other time, he does enjoy having lunch with them. They discuss show business, world affairs, reminisce about the old Palace days, and try to top one another's jokes. Mostly the latter. No one in the crowd wants to be a straight man. No one even wants to listen to anyone else. If you want to get a word in, you have to speak fast and loud.

Big names that Father sees with any regularity are Humphrey Bogart, Lauren Bacall, and Fred Allen and Phil Silvers when they are in town.

He is also very fond of Bing Crosby, but they never see each other, except when they are thrown together professionally. Father likes Bing because he sings such good harmony, and what's more, enjoys doing it, even when he's not getting paid for it. The first thing they do, whenever circumstances throw them together, is organize a little quartet group.

One of Groucho's favourite stories about Bing concerns the time they were on a War Bond tour together. They were in Milwaukee, eating dinner one night at a German Hofbrau-type restaurant. Jerry Colonna was also at their table, but they needed an alto to complete the quartet.

'I'll find one,' volunteered Crosby, and, according to Groucho, he went to every table in the place, looking for someone who could sing alto. But everyone turned him down, and finally he returned to the table alone, and very disappointed.

'There's no big-punch finish to the story,' said Groucho, 'but

150

I don't think I'll ever forget that scene. There was probably the highest priced singer in the world — one of the most famous personalities of all time — going through some dumpy joint in Milwaukee, pleading with people to sing in harmony with us, and getting turned down. They didn't recognize him. They thought he was some screwball.'

When we first moved out to California, he used to see quite a bit of Charlie Chaplin, Will Rogers, and W. C. Fields. He was very fond of Fields and Rogers, and Rogers liked him because he played the guitar. They used to sit in one another's dressing-rooms and sing Western songs. And when Rogers thought it might be an asset for a cowboy actor to know how to play the guitar, Groucho taught him enough of the fundamentals to accompany himself.

I don't know where he first met W. C. Fields — in his vaudeville travels, I suppose. He considers Fields one of the all-time great comedians. He was one of the few people who's ever been able to make Groucho laugh out loud, and I'm sure they would have been closer friends than they were if Fields hadn't been such a serious drinker. But Fields was the top man in the drinking set. And when one drinks and the other doesn't, real companionship is pretty difficult, so Groucho only saw Fields sporadically, too.

Groucho also had a tremendous amount of admiration for Charlie Chaplin, considering him the greatest comedian of them all.

He first met Chaplin when they were playing the same vaudeville circuit in Canada, many years before his own first success in *I'll Say She Is*. 'Chaplin was just another baggy pants comedian at the time, recently immigrated from England, and he was making about $30 a week,' recalls Groucho. 'But he had audiences in the aisles, and I was among them.'

Their tours brought them together again in Los Angeles, on Groucho's first trip to California. They were on the same bill, and a movie producer spotted Chaplin and offered him $100 a week to work in pictures.

'I won't take it,' Chaplin said to Groucho.

'Why not?'

'Nobody can be worth that much money,' scoffed Chaplin.

Years later, when we moved to Hollywood, Chaplin was one of the most famous men in the world, and extremely wealthy. He had a palatial home, with liveried servants, and his own swimming pool, tennis court and projection room.

Groucho was a frequent guest there for a while. He liked being around his favourite comedian, and Chaplin enjoyed his company, too. Chaplin once told him, 'Groucho – you're the greatest comedian of them all.' It was a sort of mutual admiration society.

To my knowledge, Groucho, despite the bitter, caustic remarks he frequently makes and the insults he freely showers around, has never had a black eye; nor has he ever been involved in any kind of a fracas where he's had to resort to fisticuffs. However, he once was the cause of an incident that nearly succeeded in landing himself, Miriam and me in jail.

A few months after we had moved into our new home in Beverly Hills, Archie Mayo, a prominent Hollywood director, built a house with a swimming pool directly across the street from ours.

As frequently happens, the pool was completed and filled with water before the house was quite ready to be moved into. One hot day, while the house was still in the wall-papering and painting stage, Mayo happened to meet Groucho on the sidewalk in front of his place, and, being a very friendly fellow, issued him and the rest of the Marx clan a carte blanche invitation to use his pool.

Groucho didn't want to appear too anxious – after all, he was an important star, even if he didn't have his own swimming pool – so he waited until Mayo had driven off down the street before he told Miriam and me to get our bathing suits on, and that we were going for a swim.

Thirty minutes later the three of us were lolling beside Mayo's opulently tiled pool, thinking how fortunate we were to have such wealthy friends, when we heard the back door slam.

We saw, coming towards us, a rather nice-looking, matronly woman, who seemed quite incensed about something.

'Who are you?' she demanded. 'What are you doing here?'

I suppose this was a fair question, in view of the fact that in bathing trunks, and without his moustache, Groucho was completely unrecognizable, except to his family and his closest friends. And we had never seen this woman before. But Groucho was annoyed at her because he felt her manner was unnecessarily hostile.

'I'm swimming,' replied Groucho. 'What are you doing here?'

'It so happens I have a right to be here,' she answered, with indignation. 'I'm Mrs Dellar, and Mr Mayo, who owns this house, is my brother-in-law.'

'In that case, take off your clothes and come on in for a swim. Maybe I'll take mine off and we'll have a nude party.'

'Don't you know this is private property?' said Mrs Dellar, ignoring his invitation. 'Who gave you permission to swim here?'

Miriam and I were a little nervous by this time, and we hoped he would tell her the truth and vindicate all of us. But Groucho had no such intentions.

'No one gave us permission,' he said, looking Mrs Dellar straight in the eye.

'Then what are you doing here?'

'Swimming. I told you.'

'That's not what I mean. Who said you could swim here?'

'No one. The kids and I just happened to be loitering in the alley when we saw your pool, so we thought we'd go for a dip. After all, no one else is using it. It's silly to have it going to waste.'

Mrs Dellar was livid. 'Well, you can just pick up your things and get out of here before I call the police,' she threatened.

'We're not hurting anything,' said Groucho. 'Why should we?'

'That's not the point,' she snapped. 'This is private property, and we won't have just *anyone* off the street dropping in here.'

'That's the trouble with you rich,' said Groucho. 'You get a

153

little money and right away the people off the street aren't good enough for you. Well, we're not budging. This is a free country, and I insist on standing up for my rights.'

With that he removed his glasses, put down his cigar and nonchalantly swam three lengths of the pool, as Mrs Dellar watched, transfixed. Then he climbed out and started to dry.

'If I'm going to swim here,' he said in a complaining tone, 'I wish you'd see that the water is heated. It's a little too cold for my blood.'

Mrs Dellar bridled indignantly and stormed off in the direction of the house next door, announcing that she was going to phone the police.

'Do you think she will?' asked Miriam.

'Probably,' said Groucho, stretching out on a towel, unconcerned.

'I'm scared,' said Miriam, who was only six. 'I'm going home.'

'That's right,' said Groucho. 'Desert your father when he's about to be thrown in the jug.'

He finally persuaded the two of us to stick around, and then, when he saw Mrs Dellar return from making the call and go inside the Mayo house, apparently to wait for the police, he stood up and beckoned us to follow him.

He sauntered inside the house, and found Mrs Dellar admiring the freshly painted and papered living-room. It was really a beautiful room and the last word in luxury, despite the fact that it still contained no furniture.

Groucho cast an appraising eye around the empty room, then turned to Mrs Dellar and said, 'That's Hollywood for you! People can't even afford furniture, and they have to have a swimming pool.'

Mrs Dellar turned so white I thought she was going to have a heart attack, but two policemen arrived at that moment, and she managed to pull herself together.

'Here they are,' she said. 'I want you to arrest these people for vagrancy.'

I was sure Groucho would divulge his identity then, and tell them how we happened to be swimming there, but he double-crossed me by pulling the Julius H. Marx routine again, and stuck to it until they were actually herding us into the squad car. Then he glanced down at his bathing trunks and said:

'Would you mind terribly if I ran across the street and changed into something more formal?'

The officer looked at him as if he were out of his mind, and stiffly informed him that Groucho Marx lived in *that* house.

'I know,' said Groucho. 'Sometimes I go by that name, too.'

20

Duck Soup, which was about a mythical kingdom and was a satire on war pictures, was the last of the five films that the Marx Brothers made for Paramount.

While Paramount was trying to decide whether or not to re-sign them, Groucho and his brothers got wind of a possible deal in the offing with Irving Thalberg.

Thalberg, who was producing under the MGM banner, was supposed to be one of the true geniuses of the motion picture industry. And any performer who could get Thalberg for a producer was considered to be fortunate indeed.

Oddly enough, it was through Chico's bridge-playing that the Marx Brothers first got together with Thalberg. It seems that Chico's bridge-playing crowd consisted mostly of MGM executives, and Irving Thalberg was one of them.

One night, as their bridge game was breaking up, Thalberg said to Chico, 'What are you fellows doing now?'

'Loafing,' replied Chico. 'Between pictures.'

'Your contract's up at Paramount, isn't it?' asked Thalberg.

'Well, we haven't signed a new one — yet!' said Chico.

'Before you do anything,' said Thalberg, 'I'd like to get together with you boys and talk. I'm forming my own company at MGM. Of course, it won't be for a while yet, but as soon as I know something definite I'll call you and we'll have lunch together.'

That conversation was the only assurance that they might go to work for Thalberg, but since Paramount didn't seem over-anxious to re-sign them, they decided to leave and take their chances.

That was in the autumn of 1933. They still hadn't heard from Thalberg by the following January. Groucho was becoming a little panicky. That was the longest he'd been out of work in thirty years. He started looking around for another deal.

But the only deal he was able to come up with at that point was a job for him and Chico to do a coast-to-coast, half-hour radio show for the Esso Oil Company. This wouldn't have been so bad, except for the fact that it meant moving back to New York again. No national hook-up radio shows were being broadcast from the West Coast in those days. The facilities were too poor, and sponsors insisted on big shows emanating from New York.

Since they had nothing more promising to look forward to in Hollywood, Groucho and Chico went east and made their first plunge into radio in February 1934. The show was called *Flywheel, Shyster and Flywheel*, and was about a couple of shyster lawyers.

Groucho and Chico played essentially the same characters as they had been portraying on the screen, and, as I recall, the show was extremely funny. But I was only thirteen at the time, and apparently a very easy audience, for the sponsors dropped *Flywheel, Shyster and Flywheel* after the first twenty-six weeks.

While Groucho was alienating his first sponsor, we'd been living in an apartment on Park Avenue. After *Flywheel, Shyster and Flywheel* went off the air in June, Groucho decided he'd had enough of civilization for a while. He wanted to 'rough' it, so he packed up the family and we all moved to Skowhegan, Maine, for the summer.

There we roughed it in an eight-room cottage on lake Wesserunsett, with our own motor-boat and two servants. Groucho liked to be comfortable, even though he was unemployed.

Directly across the lake from our cottage was the Lakewood Playhouse, a summer stock repertory group that attracted many vacationing actors and playwrights.

Groucho hadn't intended to participate in any of the shows, but when the director of the company asked him to play the leading role in Ben Hecht and Charlie MacArthur's *Twentieth Century*, he decided he would.

He was curious to see how he'd do in a play that wasn't a slapstick comedy. He hadn't appeared in anything but a Marx Brothers vehicle since he had become a successful comic.

The show was a big hit, and he surprised many people, not only by being good in it, but by being able to stick to a straight part without playing it any broader than Hecht and MacArthur had intended it.

'What a racket this straight acting is!' he said, coming home after the first performance. 'Anyone can do it. It doesn't take any talent at all.'

This bore out a theory that he'd had for a long time – that being a slapstick comic was the toughest work of all.

'When you come out on the stage in funny clothes and funny make-up, the audience unconsciously sets up a resistance to you,' he claims. 'Right away their attitude is: so you're a comedian? Well, let's see how funny you can be. Go ahead. Make me laugh. I dare you to. But when you come out in street clothes and look like a normal human being, they don't expect to be in the aisles at the first word you say. When you do say something funny, they're pleasantly surprised and laugh all the harder.'

The ease with which he got big laughs in *Twentieth Century* started him thinking, and quite seriously, too, that possibly he ought to abandon his career as a Marx Brother and strike out on his own without a painted black moustache. Maybe Paramount was right. Maybe picture-goers really were tired of the Marx Brothers. Maybe their kind of comedy was getting old-fashioned.

At any rate, there didn't seem to be any great rush on the part of the studios to sign the Marx Brothers up again.

Before we had left Skowhegan, Groucho had told Chico, who was departing for the Coast, to be sure to let him know if anything was cooking for them in Hollywood. Chico had promised to keep his eyes and ears open, and assured Groucho that he would phone him long-distance at the first indication that there was interest in the Marx Brothers at any of the studios. They had long since given up on Thalberg. They were ready to settle for anything.

But now it was the middle of September. The leaves were turning brown and yellow. The other summer residents were beginning to move away from the lake. And the only time our very primitive six-party phone had jingled all summer had been when our landlady had called up to say that if our dachshund didn't stop eating her chickens she would let him have both barrels from her shotgun.

Then one night, just as Groucho was getting into his sleeping-coat and was preparing for bed, the phone rang eight and a half times. That was our ring, and he rushed to answer it.

'Hollywood calling,' said the long-distance operator. 'Just a minute, please.'

'This must be Chico,' he said gleefully to Mother and me. 'I guess he's heard something.'

After a pause, Chico got on the other end of the wire. 'Groucho?' he said.

'Yeah; this is Groucho,' he said, tense with expectation.

There was another pause, and then Chico said, 'What's new?'

After he got over the shock, Groucho replied, 'You're a hell of a businessman. You're in Hollywood, supposed to be arranging a deal. I've been in the woods for four months, with a six-party telephone and a bunch of farmers. And you have the nerve to call me up and ask *me* what's new!'

Chico hung up, very much chastened, and Groucho took two more sleeping pills and went to bed.

But things were not as dark as they seemed. When we arrived in Hollywood two weeks later, Chico did have news. Thalberg had phoned him, and was very anxious to have lunch with the Marx Brothers, presumably to discuss a deal.

They met him the following day.

Only three Marx Brothers — Harpo, Chico and Groucho — were at the table, and this was to become a permanent condition. After seventeen years of being a relatively unimportant member of the team, Zeppo had decided that he was a better businessman than actor, and had opened up a theatrical agency.

158

The break was completely unopposed by his brothers, who wished him good luck and agreed to become his first clients.

It turned out to be a very astute move for the whole Marx family. The Marxes functioned as a better comedy team without Zeppo, and he wound up making more money as an agent than he ever could have made as an actor. Moreover, after he'd been in business for about a year, he took in Gummo, who'd been in the dress business in New York, as a partner, and the two of them built the agency into one of the biggest in Hollywood.

But getting back to the Thalberg deal, it didn't appear too promising the way the lunch started off.

Groucho asked the producer what he thought of *Monkey Business* and *Horsefeathers*, and Thalberg replied:

'Not bad. Not good, either.'

This criticism just about coincided with what Groucho thought of those two pictures, but he resented it coming from a comparative stranger – even if he was a prospective employer.

'What was the matter with them?' he shot back indignantly. 'I thought they were pretty funny myself. And I think I'm as good a judge of comedy as you are.'

Harpo and Chico were writhing in their seats. This was no way to talk to a man who seemed to be the only one in Hollywood even remotely interested in hiring them.

'They were very funny pictures,' answered Thalberg. 'The trouble was they had no stories. It's better to be not so funny and have a story that the audience is interested in. I don't agree with the principle: anything for a laugh. For my money, comedy scenes have to further the plot. The comedians have to be helping someone who's a sympathetic character. With a sound story, your pictures would be twice as good and you'd gross three times as much.'

'What about *Duck Soup*?' asked Groucho. 'Didn't you like that?'

'It's just like the others,' replied Thalberg unenthusiastically.

'Well, I didn't come here to be insulted,' said Groucho. 'If you just want to knock our pictures, I'd rather have lunch by myself, somewhere else. If you want to talk a deal, that's something else again.'

Fortunately, Thalberg was more interested in signing them than he had let on. 'No offence,' he said to Groucho with an apologetic smile. 'I just thought it would be better for the four of us to understand each other before we actually started working together. If you're willing to go along with my theories, I think it can be very profitable for all of us.'

From that point on, there was never any question about whether or not Groucho was willing to go along with Thalberg's theories. Now that it had been pointed out to him, he could see for himself what had been wrong with *Monkey Business*, *Horsefeathers* and *Duck Soup*. The only thing that annoyed him was that he had been too stupid to realize it himself – it had had to be pointed out to him.

Groucho came home that day enthusiastic about making pictures for the first time in five years.

Soon after the Marx Brothers moved into their office on the Metro lot, the phone rang, and it was a secretary, asking them to be in Thalberg's bungalow for a story conference at three o'clock. Promptly at the appointed time, the three of them trooped into Thalberg's reception-room, only to be told by the secretary that the producer wouldn't be able to see them until he had finished reading the script of another picture he was making.

'But we had an appointment,' complained Chico.

'You'll just have to wait,' said the secretary.

When half an hour had gone by, and Thalberg still hadn't asked for them, Groucho and his brothers were fuming.

'How do you like that guy?' said Groucho. 'Who does he think he is – Irving Thalberg?'

'I could have had a bridge game this afternoon,' said Chico wistfully.

'We've got to do something,' said Harpo.

After a hurried conference, Groucho and his brothers took out big cigars, lit them and started blowing clouds of smoke under Thalberg's door. Pretty soon Thalberg noticed the smoke, and imagining that his reception-room was on fire, he rushed to the door to investigate. As Thalberg opened it and peered out, Groucho and his brothers stuck their feet in the door and wouldn't budge until the producer consented to let them in immediately.

Another time they had an appointment with Thalberg for three o'clock and were still waiting at five-thirty, when even the secretary was preparing to leave for home.

'Just be patient,' were her parting instructions as she left the bungalow. 'He'll see you any hour now.'

But their patience was exhausted. No one had a right to make them wait this long, no matter how bad *Duck Soup* was.

As soon as the secretary was out of sight, they shoved her desk in front of Thalberg's door, collected all the heavy steel filing cabinets in the room and piled them on top of the desk. Then they went home.

It took Thalberg an hour to escape, and after that he always took care to be punctual when he had an appointment with the Marx Brothers.

Once they settled down to work, however, there were no more pranks, and Groucho and his brothers were amazed at how methodical Thalberg was about making a picture, even a slapstick comedy.

The first thing he insisted on was that their new picture should have a dignified background. Upsetting dignity, he felt, was one of the basic tenets of good comedy.

'Hit a fellow in old clothes with a snowball, and it won't mean a thing,' explained Thalberg. 'But dress a man up in tails and a silk hat, and then knock his hat off with a snowball, and you'll get a laugh.'

After racking their brains, they decided on grand opera. There couldn't be a more dignified background than that – and where else could you find so many silk hats to knock off?

Secondly, their new picture had to have a believable love story. It didn't have to be as good as *Romeo and Juliet*, but it had to have some heart, nevertheless.

And last of all, to put all this together, they needed writers who not only knew comedy but who were good story constructers, too.

'Well, when you find a good place to get those,' said Groucho, 'let me know, I'd like to buy a half a dozen myself.'

'What's the matter?' asked Thalberg. 'You don't think there are any writers around who are any good for you boys?'

'I know two writers who are very good for us,' said Groucho. 'And their names are Kaufman and Ryskind.'

'So what's wrong with getting Kaufman and Ryskind?' asked Thalberg.

'We've tried,' said Groucho. 'But it's no dice. Kaufman says he won't go to any place where he can't be in Times Square in twenty minutes.'

'Let me try,' said Thalberg, and within an hour he was on the long-distance phone with George S. Kaufman, and had persuaded him to tackle the job in collaboration with his old partner, Morrie Ryskind.

In addition to Kaufman and Ryskind, they also were fortunate in securing the services of a gag man named Al Boasberg. It was Boasberg's job to punch up the script and to originate sight gags for Harpo and Chico.

Boasberg was no ordinary gag man. Many people, including Groucho, feel that he was probably the funniest man who ever lived. Whenever a group of comedians get together, as they do at the Hillcrest Round Table, they get stars in their eyes at the mere mention of Boasberg's name, and start regaling one another with Boasberg stories by the hour.

Boasberg had a rare gift. He wasn't much good at story construction, but no one could touch him when it came to dreaming up comedy routines or writing single jokes.

Like most big talents, Boasberg was what is known as a 'character'. He was a large, heavy-jowled man – well over six feet tall and weighing about 300 pounds – and he had an affinity for bath-tubs, and also bathrooms.

He did about eighty per cent of his writing in the bath-tub, immersed in hot water up to his neck. He kept a dictaphone by the tub, and another one, just a few feet away, next to the toilet. He also had a book-shelf filled with books in the glass-enclosed shower stall.

Groucho, Mother and I once spent a week with Boasberg at a dude ranch in Victorville. He spent the whole week in the bath-tub, and only came out for meals and to sleep.

162

Because the stable was close by, there were hundreds of flies swarming round the ranch house. Outside Boasberg's window was an electric fly-killer that knocked off a fly about every five seconds. It made a buzzing sound with each fly that bit the dust.

After our first night there, Groucho asked Boasberg how he had slept.

'Not so good,' replied Boasberg. 'Every time I was about to drop off, the Warden would lead another condemned fly up the thirteen steps, and I'd hear the fly saying, "You've got to believe me. I tell you I'm innocent. Don't send an innocent fly to the hot seat."'

He could not stand being rushed. As soon as a producer tried prodding him into turning in more pages a day, Boasberg would purposely slow down. If the producer kept it up, there was no telling what Boasberg would do.

Once, after Thalberg had been hounding him for a couple of weeks to hurry up and finish a certain scene for *A Night at the Opera*, Boasberg phoned the producer and said, 'Okay, Mr Thalberg. I've got that material you wanted. But if you want it, you'll have to come over to my office and get it. I'm going home and leaving it here.'

Groucho and his brothers were just as anxious to see the new material as Thalberg was, so the four of them walked over to Boasberg's office to pick it up.

But when they got there, they couldn't find the script anywhere. After considerable rummaging through desk drawers and filing cabinets, Groucho happened to glance up, and he saw some suspicious-looking objects overhead.

Further investigation disclosed that Boasberg had cut the script into tiny ribbon-like pieces – each just large enough for one line of dialogue – and had tacked them all to the ceiling.

'It took us about five hours to piece it together,' recalls Groucho. 'But it was worth it, for it turned out to be the nucleus of one of the most famous scenes we've ever done – the state-room scene!'

With all due respect to Kaufman, Ryskind and Boasberg, *A Night at the Opera* probably wouldn't have been a very good picture – much less a small classic – if Thalberg and the Marx

Brothers hadn't hit upon a very revolutionary way of making comedies.

It came about one afternoon during a story conference in Thalberg's bungalow. The final version of the script was completed, they had all read it, and now Thalberg was asking Groucho what he thought the chances were of their having a hit.

Groucho gave the question considerable thought, and then said, 'Frankly, Irving, I think the chances are pretty slim.'

'What makes you say that? I think the boys did a good job on the script.'

'I think so, too,' replied Groucho. 'But somehow I just don't have any confidence in any comedy that hasn't been broken in on the road first, in front of a live audience. You just can't sit in an office in Culver City and know what they're going to laugh at in St Louis. When we were on Broadway, we'd try a show out on the road for weeks before we'd bring it in to New York. Why do you think *Cocoanuts* and *Animal Crackers* were such good pictures? Because everything in them was sure-fire.'

'Why can't we do the same?' asked Thalberg.

'You're joking, aren't you? said Groucho. 'How can you try a picture out on the road?'

'You don't have to take the *picture* on the road,, said Thalberg. 'You simply take what you think will be your five big comedy scenes, and put them together into a sort of vaudeville show. And play them in a few cities for a few weeks.'

'How will the audience know what's going on?' asked Groucho. 'The comedy scenes are part of the story. They'll be meaningless unless the audience knows what the story's about.'

'Very simple,' said Thalberg. 'You just flash some narrative on a movie screen before each scene. In a few words, you can tell the audience which way the story is going at that point.'

Groucho doesn't know whether this was a stroke of genius or not. In retrospect, Thalberg's idea seems like a pretty obvious solution to their problems – one that anyone could have thought of. But anyone didn't think of it. It was Thalberg's idea, and for that Groucho will always be grateful to him.

After a month of rehearsing on an MGM sound stage, the Marx Brothers struck out for the north-west, to do six weeks of personal appearances in a cheaply produced vaudeville show called *Scenes from 'A Night at the Opera'*.

They opened in a movie house in Seattle, and laid one of the biggest eggs in the history of the Marx Brothers, if not all show business. In their most pessimistic dreams, they had never imagined that the five best comedy scenes from the picture, as originally written, could be so far off the track, that they themselves could be so unfunny.

'But it proved my point – that our stuff just had to be tried out,' claims Groucho. 'If we had shot *A Night at the Opera* with the material we opened with in Seattle, it would have been the end of all of us. Even the MGM lion wouldn't have been able to get a job.'

Practically everything that had been written at the studio except the basic story had to be thrown out.

Today many people consider the state-room scene from *A Night at the Opera* one of the funniest pieces of business ever shown on a screen. And it was one of the few scenes from the picture that Groucho had confidence in even before they worked it over on the road. Certainly it had all the basic elements of a good comedy situation – twenty people squeezed into a four-by-four cabin on an ocean liner, with Groucho trying to order dinner from room service, a plumber trying to repair some leaky pipes, and Harpo and Chico getting a manicure all at the same time. But at the Seattle opening it flopped along with the rest of the show.

Evidently it wasn't the kind of scene that could be written. Like most of their famous routines, it had to be worked out by the trial-and-error method, on the stage, in front of an audience. 'That was the trouble with being a Marx Brother,' says Groucho today. 'We weren't like other comedians. We had to try everything out first. Otherwise we didn't work well together.'

But gloomy as their prospects for getting a good picture out of *A Night at the Opera* seemed in Seattle, there was one comforting thought: they could still save the picture by working hard on the road.

For the next six weeks, they worked with beaver-like energy revising scenes and rehearsing. Morrie Ryskind and Al Boasberg made the trip with them, and they would sit in the audience with a secretary at every performance, making notes of the jokes and pieces of business that didn't get laughs, and trying, with considerable success, I might add, to think of new ones to take their place.

For a performer, this is the hardest work imaginable. There would be major changes in the dialogue to memorize and rehearse before every show, and they were doing five a day.

I wasn't along with Groucho on the *A Night at the Opera* junket, but I have accompanied him on subsequent tours for other pictures, and I've always been amazed at the facility with which he can learn a big chunk of new dialogue at such short notice. Except for Harpo, it was hectic for the other actors in the cast, too, but since Groucho always had the most lines the main burden of all this fell on him.

And he did plenty of griping about it. He was always saying during these tours, 'Well, this is the last time I let myself in for anything like this. I'm getting too old to lead this kind of a life. If you have to go through this routine to make a good Marx Brothers picture, then I'm getting into another racket.'

Despite his complaining, he worked hard, nevertheless, and he usually felt that the end-result was worth it.

Scenes from 'A Night at the Opera' wound up its tour at the Golden Gate Theater in San Francisco. On closing night the Marx Brothers were in a state of great anxiety, for Irving Thalberg was in the audience to give his verdict, and if he didn't approve of their offering — after he had let them have their way about breaking in the material on the road, at considerable expense to the studio — he was liable not to feel too kindly towards them.

Conceivably he could even find a loophole in their contract and wriggle out of his commitment with them.

There was no reason, however, for such dire pessimism. The show had improved steadily since their Seattle opening. The state-room scene was now getting bigger laughs than anything they had ever done on the stage previously. And during their first six days at the Golden Gate Theater they had broken every existing house record.

'Nevertheless, that was the most nervous I've ever been in my life,' recalls Groucho. 'Facing Thalberg was worse than going up against all the New York critics.'

Thalberg sat in the first row, and Groucho kept an eagle eye on him all through the performance, to see how he was reacting. He didn't crack a smile once – not even during the state-room scene, which got yells from the rest of the audience. Groucho was sure that this was his swan-song as a comedian. If not that, at least the Marx Brothers' finish with the Thalberg unit. For if Thalberg didn't like the state-room scene, then there was just no pleasing him.

But when Thalberg came back-stage after the show he was all smiles. 'You were right about playing the material on the road,' he said, shaking hands with all of them. 'What a dif-ference! Now we're going to have a great picture.'

'I don't get it,' said Groucho. 'I watched you tonight. You didn't laugh once.'

'Well, this isn't the first time I've seen it,' admitted Thalberg, with a grin. 'I've been out front watching you for the past four days. But I didn't want to tell you I was there, for fear I'd make you nervous.'

21

There isn't much more to the story of *A Night at the Opera*.

The picture, needless to say, was an immediate and huge success. It got raves from most of the critics, it broke many a house record, and it even contained a hit song, 'Alone'. It was the first time a hit song had ever emerged from a Marx Brothers vehicle, which I think is another tribute to Thalberg's producing talents. He had insisted that the picture have something in it for everybody.

Groucho had always felt that it was pointless to try to make a broad comedy that would appeal to women, too. From past experience, he had found out that it was mostly men who enjoyed the Marx Brothers. In fact, from time immemorial, it had been the men who enjoyed slapstick. Women preferred the kind of picture where they could take out their handkerchiefs and have a good cry. But Thalberg felt that by combining good singing, good songs and a believable love story with their comedy, women would go for their pictures, too.

The results speak for themselves. *A Night at the Opera and A Day at the Races* – the two pictures of theirs that Thalberg produced – not only grossed more than their other movies, but attracted a large female audience as well.

Two things happened while the Marxes were preparing *A Day at the Races* that made it extremely difficult for Groucho to be funny.

While they were on tour in the East, breaking in the new comedy scenes, their father, Sam, who was living in Hollywood, suddenly became very ill. The seriousness of his illness, however, had been underestimated by the doctors on the case, with the result that Groucho and his brothers felt that there was no necessity to leave a company of forty-five people stranded in Cleveland just to come out and sit by Sam's bedside. So when the end came, very suddenly, only the four wives and Zeppo were with my grandfather.

Groucho and his brothers were just getting over Sam's death, it seemed, when they received another blow. They were back in Hollywood by this time, shooting *A Day at the Races*, and everyone, including Thalberg, had high hopes that it would be another *A Night at the Opera*.

The script, by Bob Pirosh, George Seaton and Al Boasberg, concerned the efforts of a certain Dr Hackenbush (Groucho), who was really a horse doctor, and not a very good one at that, to save a ritzy sanatorium from going on the rocks. Horse-racing entered into it because the sanatorium was close to a famous race-course; and the hero, Allan Jones, owned the horse that won the big race at the finish (with Harpo in the saddle), thereby getting the money to pay off the mortgage.

The story was not quite the 'natural' that the opera background had been, but the road tour had been a great success, and the Marx Brothers had come back from it with comedy scenes that were every bit as hilarious – if not more so – than the ones that had resulted from the *Opera* junket. So everyone had good cause to feel elated when they finally went into production.

While they were making *A Day at the Races*, Louis B. Mayer bumped into Groucho on the studio street one day, and asked him, 'How's the picture coming, Groucho?'

'What business is it of yours?' quipped Groucho, who thought he was being funny. 'We're working for Thalberg.'

Three days later, Thalberg died suddenly of pneumonia, and the Marx Brothers were working for Mayer. The studio head, who didn't have much of a sense of humour, never forgot Groucho's remark and never missed an opportunity after that to harm the Marx Brothers' careers.

Thalberg was only thirty-seven years old at the time of his death, but he had always been a rather frail man, and he had worked much too hard for his own good. So when pneumonia struck he just didn't have the strength to fight it off.

Groucho was really broken up — more so than I've ever seen him — for he was extremely fond of Thalberg personally, as well as being a great admirer of his talents.

There were no jokes at the dinner table the night of the funeral. All Groucho had to say was, 'Why is it the great men always have to go early? The jerks live to be a hundred.'

Being human, Groucho was also upset about the loss for a very selfish reason. Thalberg had been the only one in Hollywood who seemed to understand the Marx Brothers. There was little likelihood that they would ever find another Irving Thalberg.

Actually, the production itself didn't suffer too much, for Thalberg had laid the important groundwork. The comedy scenes were solid from weeks of playing on the road. But the completed picture lacked a certain indefinable something, and that something was undoubtedly the gifted touch of Irving Thalberg.

When they were deciding on a name for Groucho's character in *A Day at the Races*, they felt they should give him the most ridiculous moniker a doctor could possibly have — and one that would also imply 'quack'. After much mulling, they hit upon Quackenbush. It was so outlandishly silly that it seemed as if there would be no danger of any real doctor having that name and taking offence.

But when it was time to shoot the picture, Metro's legal department informed them that there were dozens of real-life Dr Quackenbushes throughout the country, any one of whom would probably sue at the drop of a hat.

'That's their hard luck,' said Groucho. 'Let them change *their* names if they don't like it. I've already got Quackenbush painted on my shingle.'

His protests notwithstanding, the character's name had to be changed to Hackenbush. Since then Groucho has become so attached to the name that it's now replaced Jackson as his favourite pseudonym. He uses it all the time in everyday life, and has found that it comes in very handy when he's dealing with someone else's maid or secretary on the phone.

If he gets the usual 'Who's calling, please?' he's almost certain to reply:

'Who's calling? Why, Dr Hugo Z. Hackenbush, of course!'

'I find I get a lot more respect when I pose as a doctor,' he maintains. 'People who ordinarily wouldn't talk to me at all come to the phone right away.'

Something else that didn't get into the released version of *A Day at the Races* was a song called 'Dr Hackenbush', written by Harry Ruby and Bert Kalmar. It's a satirical song somewhat in the vein of 'Captain Spaulding', and one of the funniest pieces of special material that I've ever heard. It got yells during the vaudeville tour, but the shooting script was much too long, and something had to go. Since Groucho is essentially a lazy fellow, and was not particularly anxious to go through the agony of shooting a musical number, anyway, he saw to it that 'Dr Hackenbush' got the axe.

However, he performed the number several times on various radio shows, at Army camps during the Second World War and in the early fifties he made a recording of it for Decca. In fact, 'Dr Hackenbush' is one of his favourite songs, and it's the number most often requested of him at parties. He has even assumed the sobriquet of 'Dr Hackenbush', or maybe just plain 'Hack', when signing letters.

22

As Miriam and I grew older, it seems to me that life with Groucho got better. Or perhaps it wasn't really any better. Maybe I could just appreciate him more from a teenage vantage-point.

At any rate, the half a dozen years preceding the Second World War, when I was attending Beverly Hills High School, Miriam was going to Hawthorne Grammar School, Mother was reading *Gone with the Wind*, and Groucho was working at MGM and making occasional forays into the field of radio, were the ones I liked the best, because Groucho was at home so much.

After Irving Thalberg's death, Groucho took less and less of an interest in going to the studio. He didn't like MGM without Thalberg and apparently Louis B. Mayer felt the same way about the Marx Brothers, and Groucho in particular.

Groucho didn't like Mayer's attitude, which to him seemed to be: get the pictures made – it doesn't matter whether they're good or not. Just let the Marxes work out their contract and get them out of my hair.

The Marxes would suggest what they thought were important and necessary changes, pertaining either to the script or the production of it, and the front office would come back with, 'Why bother? We think it's okay the way it is.' Or, 'We've been in this business for years. We know what we're doing.'

Coming on the heels of their very rewarding relationship with Thalberg, this made Groucho and his brothers pretty discontented. And they were fighting mad when the script of *A Day at the Circus* was finished and the studio refused to let them try out the comedy scenes on the road.

'It's hopeless,' Groucho would mutter, coming home from an irritating day at the studio. 'They've seen what can be done when our pictures are made with some thought. And they've got the box office returns to prove it. And still they won't let us go on the road.'

Groucho, as a matter of fact, was not very happy with his

last three pictures at MGM, and he announced that when his contract was up he was going to quit.

'Why should I, at my age, let myself get upset over a movie — a movie that in three months will probably wind up on a double bill at the Oriental Theatre, with bingo and free dishes?' he said one night. 'It's not worth it. I'd rather retire than be constantly aggravated.'

During his last year under contract to Metro, he went to the studio as little as he had to, and spent most of his time around the house, supervising its management, writing an occasional magazine piece, and entertaining Miriam and me.

So what was bad for his career was good for us, for no adolescents ever had a better companion than Groucho.

There were some unhappy moments, too, for this was the period when the chasm between our parents was beginning to widen quite perceptibly. The divorce clouds were only forming during these years. They didn't actually burst until I was twenty and living away from home. In the meantime, I enjoyed a pretty average American adolescence, complete with the regulation amount of parents, a tomboy sister, dogs, report cards, braces on the teeth and no swimming pool.

Of course, it couldn't be completely average-American with a world-famous comedian as the head of the house. And Groucho realized this, too. In fact, he had long been aware of the pitfalls likely to be encountered by the children of celebrities, and he did his best to see that we had no more advantages or privileges than any of the other children in the neighbourhood. If anything, he leaned a little bit in the opposite direction.

In some ways, Groucho was almost mid-Victorian in his thinking. He was always very strict about the time I went to bed. On school nights he'd hustle me off to my room sharply at nine, even when I was a senior in high school. On Friday and Saturday nights he'd be a little more lenient. He'd let me stay out until ten or ten-thirty. But if I came in past then, he'd give me a long lecture the next morning on how a growing boy needed at least eleven hours' sleep, and threaten to take my car away the next time it happened.

If he caught me, that is. Many nights he was out late himself and wouldn't know whether or not I came in a few minutes past the curfew. But on the nights he was home it was very difficult to fool him, for his bedroom was right over the porte cochère, which you had to drive through in order to get to the garage, and Groucho, as you know, is a very light sleeper. He never failed to hear my car roaring under his bedroom.

Deciding that something had to be done about this, I tried an experiment one night. I turned my engine off at the corner of our block, and coasted down the hill, into our driveway, through the porte cochère and into the garage.

I was sure I had fooled him, but as I tiptoed towards the house he stuck his head out of the window, wiggled his eyebrows at me, and said, 'I still heard you.'

In other ways he could be extremely modern and liberal-minded.

When I was eighteen I took up smoking a corn-cob pipe, unbeknown to him. One afternoon, when I was in my bedroom, puffing away on the pipe behind closed doors, I heard the patter of Groucho's little feet approaching down the hallway.

I quickly stowed the pipe, still alight, in the drawer of my desk, and was sitting there with an innocent look on my face when he opened the door and walked in.

He detected the smell of tobacco immediately, and without saying a word turned round and walked back to his room. I was frightened, for I thought perhaps he had gone to get the snake-whip he kept in his closet (for what reason I never found out.) But when he returned he was carrying one of his good Dunhill pipes and a can of tobacco.

'Here,' he said, handing me the pipe first, 'I think you'll like smoking this better than that cheap corn-cob you've been using. And here's a can of good tobacco. Now you can stop stinking up the house with that cheap stuff.'

'Aren't you angry with me?' I asked.

'What for?' he said. 'Smoking won't hurt you as long as you do it in moderation. And that goes for everything else you do, too. I've been smoking since I was seventeen, and except for the fact that I usually feel awful, I'm fit as a fiddle.'

'Moderation' is one of the inviolate rules governing

Groucho's philosophy of life, and always has been. Many people think he is a heavy smoker because they see him with a cigar when he's performing. But actually he's one of the few people I know who has smoking completely under control. He never smokes before noon; he has one cigar after lunch and one after dinner; and after his evening cigar he'll generally puff on a pipe for a couple of hours. But that's the extent of his smoking.

He's just as moderate in his drinking and eating habits. A bourbon Old Fashioned before dinner and perhaps a glass of beer or wine with his meal will take care of him for a whole evening. If he drinks more, he'll get a hang-over. And he has never been a big eater. He can't be; he's too busy complaining.

In most respects, he treated Miriam and me more like close friends than children. He confided in us about his business and matrimonial problems, we had private jokes that nobody else understood, and he liked to take us with him wherever he went, provided we wouldn't be too much out of our element.

He revelled in the disrespect of his children. He'd pounce on any innocent remark or incident around the house and build it up into a routine. And, for my money, this was when he was at his funniest.

Basically he's more of a humorist and cracker-barrel philosopher than a straight comic, anyway.

After a long declamation on how his children chose to have dinner elsewhere because they had a 'better offer', he'd reverse himself and say: 'I don't know what the hell I'm talking about. When we lived in Great Neck, and I was working in Astoria, I used to drive past my mother's house in Little Neck every day. And I don't think I dropped in on her more than once every two weeks. It wouldn't have hurt me to see her for a few minutes every day. And yet I didn't, because it's only natural for children not to want to see their parents any more than they have to.'

Other children may have felt this way, but I know Miriam and I rarely did. If anything, being constantly around someone as amusing and stimulating as Groucho made it pretty difficult for us not to be bored with the company of children our own age.

23

A good deal of our family life in those days revolved around the game of tennis. Everyone was playing – even Groucho.

He had always been an ardent follower of the sport. He had watched Tilden and Johnson and Cochet and the rest of the greats of that era batting the ball around at Forest Hills, and he had also done some playing himself. Not at Forest Hills, but in Central Park.

Except as a spectator, he had given up the game during the years he was torturing himself on the golf-course. And had I not shown an interest in tennis when I was in grammar school, I'm sure he would have remained retired permanently.

But I was swinging a racket every day, and by the time I was thirteen Ellsworth Vines and Fred Perry, who owned the Beverly Hills Tennis Club, told Groucho that they thought I had a good chance of becoming a ranking player. This was all he had to hear. His old enthusiasm for the game returned immediately.

Not only did he take out a family membership at the Beverly Hills Tennis Club, but one day shortly afterwards he announced that he was coming out of retirement. (He had some free time on his daily calendar between lunch and his afternoon nap.)

Since amateur tennis was pretty much in the doldrums around that time – America hadn't won the Davis Cup in years – his announcement that he was going to start bludgeoning the ball again naturally created quite a stir in the racket-wielding world.

Groucho had the 'big game'. It wasn't good, but was big. His forehand, even though he frequently hit the fence with it, was probably his most formidable weapon, and it soon became known to the other club members as 'Iron Mike'. I'm not sure who first dubbed it this, but I think it was Groucho.

His other big *forte* was sitting on his racket between points, his legs astraddle, his racket propping him up, while waiting for his doubles partner to retrieve the balls or his opponent to get

175

into position. And sometimes, if he had a strong partner, he'd sit on his racket during the playing of a point. No other tennis player has ever mastered the science of racket-sitting to such a degree.

Because he played a scientific game, Groucho was extremely fussy about the kind of tennis racket he used.

One day, when he was picking out a new racket, the boy in the tennis shop handed him a Spalding–Bill Tilden model to try out. Groucho handed it right back.

'I can't play my best game with an American racket,' he said. 'They're too uncomfortable. Give me one of those Australian models, with the flat head. They're better for sitting.'

Sometimes, when she couldn't avoid it, Mother would be his partner in doubles. But they were not a very good team, because she took her tennis very seriously, and they were always fighting.

'For goodness' sake,' she'd say to him when he was about to receive service, 'will you please get off your racket and be ready for a change? We need this point.'

'Listen, Helen Wills. Don't worry about me,' Groucho would say, remaining calmly on his racket. 'I can handle my side of the court. They don't call me the Old Grey Fox for nothing, you know. Just take care of your side of the court, *Helen*, and we won't have a thing to worry about. I'll give 'em Iron Mike.'

He'd still be in the process of getting off his racket when the ball would fly past him for an ace.

'Some Fox!' Mother would exclaim with a derisive laugh. 'What happened to Iron Mike?'

'Never you mind, old girl,' he'd say, nonchalantly propping himself up with his racket again. 'Just remember, the race isn't always to the swift.'

Mother would grit her teeth, determined to show him up. If she happened to make an error, which was frequently the case, he would say, 'Well, who's got the last laaaaff now?'

According to Mother, it would always be Groucho's fault when they lost a doubles match. He'd take this for a couple of weeks, and then his fighting blood would come to the fore, and he'd challenge her to a singles match. He heartily disapproved of men in their middle forties playing singles, but in this case he was willing to make an exception.

Actually, Mother was the better player, but there wasn't enough difference in their games for her to be able to overcome the mental hazard, and she'd always wind up losing. He'd lob her to death, which she felt was terribly unsporting. And if this didn't work he could talk her into submission.

'Well,' he would say to Miriam and me in a gloating tone at the dinner table, the night of one of these victories, 'ask your mother how she came out against the Old Grey Fox today.'

'You're certainly not going to count today's match,' Mother would scoff. 'You know I couldn't play up to my usual game with a blister on my hand.'

'I don't know about that,' Groucho would say. 'All I know is that when the smoke cleared away I was the victor. Thoroughbred blood. It always tells in the final analysis.' Mother retorted, 'Thoroughbred blood – that's a laugh. You were extremely lucky.'

'Lucky?' he'd reply. 'I prefer to think it was Iron Mike that made the difference. No human being can stand up against Iron Mike when I want to turn it on. And you know that, old girl, as well as I,' he'd conclude, wiggling his eyebrows at her.

And after dinner perhaps he'd sit down at the piano and annoy Mother with ten or eleven choruses of a parody he had made up that was sung to the tune of 'Just Break the News to Mother.' I don't remember all of it, but the first two lines were:

> 'Just hit the ball to Mother,
> And you won't have to hit another.'

No man, not even his idol, Charlie Chaplin, could emerge from a match with him completely unscathed.

The occasion for their match was the grand opening of the Beverly Hills Tennis Club's new clubhouse. The feature court attraction of the day saw the best that America had to offer pitted against the best of Great Britain. America was represented by Groucho and Ellsworth Vines, and Great Britain by Charlie Chaplin and Fred Perry.

The match had been given a good deal of publicity, so in

addition to reporters and newsreel men, there was a large crowd of tennis fans on hand.

Chaplin played about the same brand of tennis as Groucho, but he took it more seriously and was very jittery before the match. He wanted to win, and was scared to death of playing before such a large crowd.

Groucho had never played in front of so many people before either, but he wasn't a bit scared, because, as he told Mother while she was giving him a rub-down before the match, 'I've got Iron Mike on my side.'

Not only Iron Mike, but when he finally walked out on the court with Vines, Chaplin and Perry, he was carrying twelve rackets and a large suitcase. To Chaplin's annoyance, he refused to divulge the nature of the suitcase's contents.

'Never mind what's in there,' he told Chaplin. 'Do I go around asking you what's in your suitcase?'

'I haven't got a suitcase,' replied Chaplin, failing to see the humour in the situation.

'Well, why the hell haven't you?' asked Groucho in a loud voice. 'What kind of a tennis-player are you, going around without a suitcase?'

Groucho played the first two games of the match quite seriously, with disastrous results. Chaplin and Perry won both games. Then, with Perry about to serve and Chaplin up at the net, Groucho, still sitting on his racket, held up his hand to stop play.

'What's the matter?' asked the annoyed Chaplin.

'I just want to warn you that I'm going to give you Iron Mike,' said Groucho, 'so you'd better get down behind the net. I don't want to be responsible for hurting you.'

The laughter of the crowd so unnerved Chaplin that he could hardly hit a ball in the court after that.

And just to make sure that there would be no more serious tennis play, Groucho got his suitcase from the referee's stand, brought it back to midcourt, opened it and started spreading a picnic lunch out on the blanket.

'Have a spot of tea?' he asked Chaplin.

'Let's play tennis,' demanded Chaplin. 'I didn't come here to be your straight man.'

'We're ready,' said Groucho, munching on a sandwich. 'Vines can do all my playing for me.'

Needless to say, the match broke up a couple of games later, with neither side emerging the victor.

During the days when the Old Grey Fox was still prowling the courts of the Beverly Hills Tennis Club, he and I had a favourite match we liked to play. He'd take either Ellsworth Vines or Fred Perry as his partner, and I'd play with Mickey Levee, another junior tournament player, and the four of us would go to it.

When we first started playing these matches, my partner and I were about fourteen, and we'd get drubbed. As time went on and our games improved, it became increasingly difficult for either Vines or Perry to overcome the handicap of carrying Groucho, for he was without doubt the worst man player at the club. We were still losing, but every match would be very close.

Then one day, when we were about sixteen, Mickey and I beat Groucho and Vines.

'Don't get cocky yet,' said Groucho. 'Tomorrow I'll play you boys with Perry, and that'll be a different story.'

So on the following day he played us with Fred Perry. Groucho was sure that he and Perry could turn the tables. After all, hadn't Perry wrested the world's professional title from Vines a few months ago?

But when he lost with Perry too, he realized that the whole thing was pretty hopeless, and decided that the time had come to hang up his racket for good.

'If I can't beat a couple of schoolboys with the two best players in the world as partners, then I think I'm definitely past my prime,' muttered the Old Grey Fox, making the announcement that officially ended his playing days. 'I want my fans to remember me as the great player I was – not the hollow shell of a man I am today. There's nothing more pathetic to see than the crumbling of a man.'

With golf and tennis out of the way, Groucho was now free to confine his sporting activities to brisk walks around the block, rooting for the Hollywood Stars baseball team, and watching me play tennis.

He was as serious about my tennis as he wasn't about his own.

When I was fourteen, I could beat most of the men at the Beverly Tennis Club. The only two I couldn't beat were Gilbert Roland, the silent film star and husband of Constance Bennett, and Norman Krasna, who took turns at being at the top of the tennis ladder. Groucho didn't mind my losing to anyone else, but he couldn't stand it when Krasna beat me, because Norman would gloat about it when he came to dinner.

So one day he asked Vines what would be the best thing I could do to improve my game, now that I was past the beginner's stage. Vines recommended tournament play, and since I was agreeable I devoted the next six years of my life to becoming a tennis bum.

I'd go straight to the tennis club from school. On Saturdays and Sundays I'd be at the club from nine in the morning until sundown. Our whole family ate, drank and talked tennis. And I played in all the tournaments.

From the first, this was quite a strain on Groucho, for even though I was starting out in the fifteen-and-under division, the competition was stiffer than any of us had bargained for. In addition to a number of other excellent boy players, Jack Kramer and Ted Schroeder were also in the fifteen-and-under division, and since they had already been playing competitively for a couple of years, their games were considerably better than mine.

This was never more evident than on the day Groucho and Mother drove me to Long Beach where I was to play a second round match in one of my first tournaments. Groucho was pretty elated that I had reached the second round, and since none of us recognized the name of the boy I was to play next – Kramer – it looked as if I had a chance to go pretty far in this tournament.

But before we knew it we were back in Beverly Hills, licking our wounds. I had lost 6 – 0, 6 – 0.

'Well, Flatfeet,' Groucho said after the match, 'it looks as if your game needs a little more work. You kept rushing the net and the ball kept flying past you. What kind of business is that

180

after I've raised and supported you all these years?'

Though he frequently joked about my losses, he felt worse about them than I did, but thinking I needed the comforting he'd always wind up by saying, 'Don't worry about it. It's only a game. It's not very important. Fifty years from now it won't make the slightest difference whether you lost to Kramer today or not.'

But despite this false bravado, he'd get so nervous when he was watching me play that he couldn't bear to sit next to my mother, and eventually he'd have to move to another section of the grandstand.

Mother would become more overwrought than Groucho, and on top of this she was always moaning about the bad calls she thought I was getting from the referee or linesmen.

'For the love of mike, shut up,' Groucho would say if they were sitting together. 'The bad calls even themselves up. Arthur is just playing like a *schlemiel*; that's all. Look how he's rushing the net. He gets caught half-way in every time.'

Although I was getting all kinds of professional instruction, there would be plenty of Monday-morning quarter-backing around our home after an important loss. After I'd been playing in junior tournaments for several years there wasn't anyone in our house, with the possible exception of Duke, our police dog, who didn't know more about how to play Kramer and Schroeder and the rest of the boys than I did.

But the only time Groucho would actually get angry at me for losing a match was when he thought it was because I had broken training. Then he'd really lay into me.

'Listen here, sonny boy,' he'd say in his grimmest tone, 'if you expect me to pay out good money for rackets and lessons and sending you around to all the tournaments, then you're going to have to take this thing more seriously. You can't stay out until twelve or one o'clock in the morning, necking in that little car of yours, and expect to play tournament tennis. I'll bet you Kramer and Schroeder are in bed every night at seven o'clock.'

My wife Irene, who was then my girl-friend, still shudders when she thinks of one which I lost, when she and Groucho were both watching from the same box. Every time I missed an important point Groucho would turn round and glare at her, as if to say, 'It's all your fault – keeping my son out so late.'

And when we all drove home together, he wasn't speaking to anyone.

After I had played in tournaments for several years, the gap between myself and the other junior players wasn't so wide. When I was seventeen, in fact, I was ahead of Ted Schroeder in the Southern California rankings, and had even beaten Kramer once.

By then the strain on Groucho was beginning to tell. His nerves couldn't take it any longer. He retired from watching me play, except on rare occasions.

That left it strictly up to Mother to bear the Marx standard in the grandstand. She carried on for another year, loyally going from tournament to tournament with me, cursing the linesmen under her breath, and always insinuating that they were deliberately plotting against me.

At the dinner table, after an unexpected setback, she would usually exclaim:

'Well, you should have seen that decision Arthur got in the second game of the third set. It was positively shameful. Van Horn hit the ball at least three feet into the alley, and the linesman didn't open his mouth. And it was probably the deciding point of the match. Up until then it was very even.'

'Unfortunately,' Groucho would point out, 'the only thing anyone is interested in is who won. When it goes down in the record book, they don't say, "Van Horn won the tournament, but Arthur Marx's mother claims he wouldn't have if her son hadn't got a bum call."'

Pretty soon Mother couldn't take the nerve-strain any longer either, and she, too, stopped going to tournaments. After that, the only time I ever saw either one of them on the sidelines was when I'd be fortunate enough to have reached the finals or else when I was playing one of the big name seniors against whom I wasn't expected to win.

Mainly because of me, all my uncles and their wives had

become tennis-minded, too, and they would also come to the finals if I was playing. They were desperately anxious to see me win, for no other Marx had ever succeeded in distinguishing himself in any sports but the ones where cards and pool-cues were the main weapons, and they wanted me to show the world that we were a family of athletes as well as comedians. But I don't think they ever saw me win a finals, though there was a period of about a year when I was runner-up in nine different tournaments.

24

Mother and Groucho were rapidly approaching the parting of the ways by 1941, and everyone in our household was perfectly aware of what was happening and expecting the worst. We didn't know just when the final explosion would come, but we knew it was inevitable.

How things reached this stage, or just when the situation really began to get serious, is difficult for a bystander – even one as close to the case as I naturally was – to know exactly. My own impression is that they never quite belonged together. They were completely opposite types, with different emotional needs and conflicting temperaments.

Mother probably never should have been married to a comedian and nonconformist. And Groucho never should have been married to anyone as shy and as sensitive as my mother.

Groucho had many admirable qualities that went into the making of a good husband. He had always liked his home, he loved his children, and most of his interests kept him pretty close to the family.

But at the same time I can see that he would be a very difficult man for the average woman to cope with around the house. Being something of an eccentric, and a male chauvinist to boot, Groucho was never easy to live with. But he and Mother managed to iron out, with a minimum of friction, most of the causes of their earlier disputes.

Groucho, for example, was no longer keeping such a firm hand on the purse strings. He hadn't completely conquered his insecurity syndrome. He'd still grumble mightily (as who doesn't) when the monthly expeditures were climbing higher than he thought they should be. But he had bestowed on Mother a generous monthly allowance to spend on herself as she pleased; he was supporting all her relatives (even the anti-Semitic ones); and he allowed her to buy anything she needed for the household, within reason, without having to ask permission.

They'd also reached an armistice on dining-room protocol that satisfied Mother's desire to conform to Emily Post while at the same time keeping Groucho from grumbling that he wasn't getting his meat and potatoes and vegetables at the same time. Whenever they had more than two extra to dinner, the food was served buffet-style.

Groucho had acquiesced on another key issue — dinner by candlelight, which he claimed was just another female ruse to keep men from getting a good look at their girl-friends or wives who no longer looked as young as they wished. He had eventually agreed to candelabras on the table provided Mother kept the electric crystal chandelier burning.

So for a number of my teenage years there was relative peace in the Groucho Marx family. If there were arguments, they were no more frequent or serious than those which go on between most supposedly happily married couples.

In retrospect, there was one indication that they were not quite so blissful as Romeo and Juliet — they were sleeping in separate bedrooms, each with the door locked. However, I was gullible enough to accept Groucho's explanation that they occupied separate rooms because he had insomnia and needed to turn on the lights and read if he couldn't fall asleep.

At any rate, I wanted to believe they were happy, because I liked both of them; they were fun to be around, when they weren't fighting; and I did not relish the prospect of ever having to decide which one of the two I preferred to have custody of me.

From time to time I'd been disturbed (as I'm sure my sister had, too) by vague but sinister feelings that someday I might have to make that decision. Times, for example, when we'd be on a trip or at a resort without Groucho, because he was working, and I'd see Mother sitting at the bar and becoming awfully friendly, I thought, with some handsome, single guy with whom we'd all played tennis during the day, and who was now buying the drinks. She might even be dancing with him to the piano music. But since Mother made no attempt to conceal these liaisons from Groucho when he came home, and Groucho, in turn, would simply kid her about her 'boy-friends', I assumed these relationships were precisely what they appeared to be – harmless resort friendships.

And since it didn't bother Groucho, I tried not to let it bother me. I figured that was the way life was supposed to be lived by a sophisticated couple. Noël Coward had nothing on them. So I'd dismiss my fears about divorce almost as quickly as they occurred to me.

But by my senior year in high school, the détente Mother and Groucho had managed to achieve – apparently for Miriam's and my sake – was beginning to show the strain of two personalities (with totally different ideas of what they wanted out of life) pulling against each other in a sort of marital tug of war.

A turning point in their worsening relations was, paradoxically, another ocean voyage – this time to Hawaii, in 1937.

Before leaving, they had their usual argument over whether or not to take Miriam and me. In this instance, Groucho lost out, and they sailed off on the *Lurline* without us.

They were barely speaking when they returned three weeks later.

According to Mother, Groucho had been in a miserable mood for the entire trip. He had suffered from one attack of seasickness after another, even though the Pacific was glassy calm. Furthermore, and even though they were given the royal treatment by Duke Kahanomoko himself, Groucho had hated everything about the Hawaiian Islands – the stench of gardenia leis that were always being thrown around his neck; luaus; fat women from Pasadena doing the hula; the native girls ('Their mouths are full of gold teeth!'), Hawaiian music; and even Waikiki Beach itself, which he claimed was too narrow and couldn't compare with the beach at Atlantic City.

185

At the time Groucho confided to Miriam and me that he could have taken the whole phoney milieu a little better if he'd had his children along to keep him company while Mother was getting loaded on Mai Tais and learning to do the hula.

'After all, it's basically a children's resort. What's there to do for a middle-aged Jew who wants to read *The New York Times*? I could do that in my comfortable house in Beverly Hills. At least you kids would have enjoyed the swimming. I could have kicked myself for not bringing you.'

But years later he admitted the real reason why he and Mother weren't speaking when they returned.

On the return voyage, Mother had followed her usual shipboard pattern of wanting to dance until the ship's musicians played 'Good Night Sweetheart' and started packing their saxophones and electric guitars back in their cases.

Groucho had followed his usual shipboard routine of announcing to Mother, every night around eleven, 'Well, you stay up if you want — I'm going to bed.' Following which he'd return to his cabin, leaving Mother in the company of whoever they had happened to meet that evening.

One of the group with whom they'd made friends was a personable man around Mother's age who ran the Arthur Murray Dance Studio on the *Lurline*. He liked to dance with Mother because she wasn't the usual klutzy housefrau he usually had to push around the floor, and she enjoyed being his partner because they performed so smoothly together that all the other dancers stopped and watched. Being in the spotlight obviously stirred up Mother's memories of her days as a professional dancer in vaudeville, and at the same time rekindled the dormant desire to be on the stage again.

Instead of resenting him, Groucho was pleased that the Arthur Murray instructor kept Mother entertained on the dance floor. It meant he could sit at the table and smoke his cigar.

The night before they were to dock, Groucho retired to his cabin at his usual witching hour, leaving Mother and the instructor on the dance floor. When Mother hadn't returned to their cabin by 3 am, he started to worry, threw on some clothes, and went up on deck to look for her.

He found Mother with the instructor out by the lifeboats, locked in a tight embrace, with their lips glued passionately together.

Groucho, refreshed from three straight hours of insomnia, gathered his strength, socked the instructor on the jaw, and dragged Mother back to their cabin.

Mother wasn't a promiscuous woman by nature, but she'd had more than she should to drink, which undoubtedly had had a liberating effect on her libido.

Drinking was beginning to become a serious problem with Mother, anyway, by then. And it was unquestionably compounded by another problem not uncommon in beautiful women approaching forty – she was afraid of growing old and losing her looks. And since she realized that she was still enormously attractive to men, she was determined to make the most of her life while she still had her youthful face and trim figure.

Groucho, on the other hand, was equally determined not to spend what he called his 'declining years' night-clubbing and consorting with the kinds of people who frequented the night spots – café society phonies, actors and actresses on the prowl for cheap publicity; big drinkers; and Arthur Murray dance instructors.

At the age of fifty, Groucho was a good thirty years away from being on the decline – either physically, mentally or professionally. He'd always lived a life of extreme moderation: one drink before dinner, none after; two cigars a day plus a few puffs on a pipe. He watched his weight, and kept regular hours. He couldn't sleep, but he spent a good deal of time supine.

Consequently, he was in excellent health, except for a mild case of low blood pressure, and a mysterious affliction that he referred to as 'a grippy feeling'. A grippy feeling was characterized by icy feet and a general lack of energy, which he felt was the precursor of the flu or a cold, neither of which ever actually came on. No doctor has ever been able to find the slightest shred of medical evidence to support the existence of his complaint. But despite its psychosomatic overtones, it was enough to incapacitate Groucho and confine him to his room a couple of times a week – usually when he had something unpleasant facing him, like having to escort Mother to Ciro's or the Mocambo, or attending one of those large Hollywood parties (generally given in a cold, damp tent in some celebrity's backyard), where the beef stroganoff wouldn't be served before eleven, and he'd have to dance whether he liked it or not — if only to keep warm.

If Groucho had a desire to stay home that was more compelling than the average husband's, it was understandable.

After years of appearing in vaudeville and on Broadway, when he had to be out every night, what greater luxury could a man have than the opportunity, which making films afforded him, of spending his evenings with friends or family in the comfort of a beautiful home. Everything he needed to keep him content was right there — his books, his guitar, his Capehart phonograph, a large collection of classical recordings and even a professional-sized pool table.

Groucho was an expert pool player, thanks to his many years in vaudeville when there'd be nothing better to do between shows than to hang out in the local billiard parlour. He wasn't as handy with a cue as Chico or Zeppo (who are close to being hustlers), but on a good night he could run the table a couple of times without missing.

Until I was a grown man he could spot me fifty points and still win. From the time I was twelve on, I spent most of my evenings trying to beat him, and rarely did.

When he wasn't entertaining his friends, Groucho liked to read or listen to classical music after he'd successfully fended off my nightly challenge at the pool table. In addition, he was turning into a Gilbert and Sullivan buff, having been introduced to the operettas by his good friends, Ira Gershwin and Newman Levy, the poet.

Groucho liked nothing better than to invite a few friends over for an entire evening of Gilbert and Sullivan. Everyone would have to sit around with the librettos on their laps, pay strict attention, and sing along with the D'Oyly Carte Company.

Mother liked nothing worse. She hated having to pay strict attention to anything, because it reminded her of school.

188

Besides, she liked the songs of Rodgers and Hart much better. 'At least you can dance to them,' she'd say.

When Groucho wasn't playing Gilbert and Sullivan, he was reading about them. He had enough biographies of the pair to fill an entire wall of our library. There were no intimate details of either of their lives with which he wasn't totally familiar, and he delighted in regaling both friends and relatives with his newly acquired Savoyard lore.

'Did you know,' he might say to Mother at the dinner table, 'that Gilbert hated Sullivan?'

'That's nothing,' Mother would retort. 'I hate the two of them.'

'If you'd just give it a chance,' Groucho would implore her, 'you might learn to like them. Now why don't you sit down with me this evening, and we'll listen to *Trial by Jury* together?'

But Mother would either go out to a movie by herself (or with me), or over to a friend's for a game of gin or backgammon. If she were really desperate, she'd retire to her own bedroom, and read. But never would she spend an evening listening to Gilbert and Sullivan.

Mother wasn't a baseball fan, either, and Groucho was – an avid one. During the summer he attended most of the Hollywood Stars night games, whether Mother accompanied him or not. Usually she'd find something else to do on those evenings. Her attitude about baseball used to annoy him, although he claimed the way she felt was typical of nearly the entire female race.

'There are few sensible girls who are real ball fans,' he used to say, 'but the average girl just pretends she likes baseball while she's trying to hook a fellow. Once the preacher says, "I now pronounce you man and wife," she'll never set foot in a ball park again.'

Things finally reached a stage where Mother was rebelling about spending an entire evening with Groucho and his friends, even if it didn't include Gilbert and Sullivan or baseball. Groucho rarely moved in the same circle as actors, finding them boring, uninformed and often a little bit on the phoney side. His friends were of the Hollywood intellectual establishment –

writers mostly, because he admired the men who put words down on paper, feeling that without them there could be no theatre or movie business. Norman Krasna, Harry Kurnitz, Nunnally Johnson, Arthur Sheekman, Dore Schary, Bob Riskin, Moss Hart, George Kaufman and Sid Perelman, and any other people who made a living punching a typewriter.

Bobby Sherwood, the guitarist, brought his niece, Judy Garland, when she was sixteen and not yet a star, to our house one evening for an informal musicale.

Andrés Segovia, the great classical guitarist, was a frequent visitor when he was in town; so was George Gershwin.

Harpo introduced Groucho to Gershwin first, bringing him along to a party one evening. Groucho was dying to have Gershwin play for his guests, but feeling the composer would think he was being imposed upon, he refrained from asking for a good part of the evening. Meanwhile, Gershwin fidgeted nervously in his chair, and occasionally scowled in the direction of the piano.

Finally Harpo came over to Groucho and whispered in his ear, 'Listen, Grouch, if you don't ask George to play pretty soon, he'll go home.'

'But I was afraid he'd be insulted if I asked.'

'He'll be insulted if you don't,' Harpo informed him.

Gershwin sat at the piano for five straight hours — until all the guests felt they were being brainwashed by his music.

As George Kaufman used to say, 'An evening with Gershwin is certainly an evening with Gershwin.'

Don't let me give you the impression that Mother disliked Groucho's friends. She admired them, and was fond of many of them. But they were cut out of the same bolt as Groucho. They'd rather sit around and crack jokes about the picture business, or discuss the horrible things that Hitler was doing to the Jews in Nazi Germany, than go dancing at the Trocadero.

Mother was swiftly acquiring her own coterie of friends: people she'd probably met at the tennis club or Lake Tahoe — people who liked to drink and dance, and whose idea of fun coincided with hers.

Groucho, quite understandably, couldn't stand her friends,

and would usually treat them coolly when she brought them home, if not insult them outright.

As a result, Mother and Groucho would usually argue about whom to invite to dinner. He'd want Morrie Ryskind; she'd want one of the instructors from the Arthur Murray Dance Studio in Beverly Hills, or perhaps the Murrays themselves.

They had become friendly with Arthur and Kathryn Murray through Ed Sullivan, who had brought them to dinner one night. Later, the Murrays sent one of their instructors round to our house, to give us all rumba and tango lessons, free of charge.

Mother was hoping that if Groucho could master the art of ballroom dancing, he might not object so much to taking her night-clubbing. But sensing what her scheme was, he retired after the first lesson, although he swore it was an arthritic hip that made him give up the rumba.

Because it was a form of advertising their business to be seen on as many dance floors around town as possible, the Murrays often went night-clubbing after dinner. They'd invite Groucho and Mother to accompany them. Groucho liked the Murrays, except for this mania they had for dancing. But usually he would elect to stay at home with Gilbert and Sullivan and me. And in this case, the Murrays would invite one of their instructors along to be Mother's date. This suited Mother fine, and in her eyes, made the Murrays the perfect dinner guests.

Occasionally Groucho would give in and take Mother out on the town on his own, but usually when Mother asked him, he'd have 'that grippy feeling'. She'd then accuse him of malingering, and they'd have another big fight – very often at the dinner table in front of Miriam and me – and she'd storm out of the house.

'I don't want to stay home here night after night and watch you read or listen to that damn phonograph,' Mother would scream.

'Your trouble is you have nothing to do all day,' he'd point out calmly. 'You need something to tire you out when I'm working, so you'll be willing to stay home when I'm too tired to go out.'

'I'd have something to do if you hadn't made me quit the act,' she'd reply. 'I could have been a great dancer – now it's too late.'

This would generally evoke a peal of derisive laughter from Groucho, who would tell her that she was damn lucky she didn't have to support herself with the little talent she had.

Following a crack like that she'd generally call him a son of a bitch, and run out of the house again.

As the front door slammed, Groucho would shake his head sadly, and say to Miriam and me, 'Your mother's a nice dame. Her trouble is she's bored. I've tried to get her to do charity work, or have another baby. Anything to keep her from running over to the damn club seven days a week. But she won't listen to me.'

She must have listened to him at least once, because I remember being called out of school one day, in the middle of a class, handed an address by the principal, and told to pick up my mother there.

The address turned out to be an abortion doctor's mill, in a run-down section of Los Angeles. But it wasn't until Mother – pale and troubled-looking, and clad only in bathrobe and slippers – got into the car, and we were on our way home, that she confessed what she had been doing in such a place.

I was shocked. An abortion, in those days, wasn't something you just ran over to your friendly neighbourhood doctor's and had done. It was a jail offence, and I couldn't see the reason why a respectable married woman, and a mother, would risk one.

'Like a fool I let your father talk me into getting pregnant,' she explained. 'But after I was two months gone, I knew I couldn't go through with it. I wasn't going to be stuck at home with a baby like a sweet little Ruthie, while your father's listening to Gilbert and Sullivan every night. I want to live and be gay – while I'm still young enough to enjoy it.'

It was one of those times when I realised that life with Father wasn't quite so much fun as his fans might imagine. Still, it wasn't Groucho's fault. He was doing his best to hold the family together. Frequently he took over the family responsibilities normally reserved for women, but which Mother refused to shoulder.

Like the time he went to the May Day Festival sponsored by the Hawthorne Grammar School PTA.

Miriam was dancing in the festival, and very much wanted Mother to come to watch her and her classmates perform. And in fact she exacted a promise from Mother that she would attend. But as much as Mother loved her children, she could not bear to waste an afternoon on anything so typically average-American as the Girl Scouts or the PTA when she could be at the tennis club having fun, and at the last minute she found an excuse not to go.

Being a very sensitive thirteen-year-old, Miriam burst into tears, so Groucho gave up a business appointment to go in Mother's place.

Mrs Pogson, the principal, was delighted to see someone as famous as Father standing among the parents and at one point in the entertainment she invited him to step up and say a few words.

Obliging, Groucho surveyed the young ladies gambolling around the May Pole, and said, 'It's hard to believe that in ten years most of you girls will be collecting alimony.' The line got a big laugh from everyone but Mrs Pogson.

Miriam, of course, was humiliated and angry. She refused to speak to Groucho until her allowance was due.

I'm pretty sure that, secretly, Groucho enjoyed playing the role of both parents, because that gave him the freedom to run the household the way he wanted, without female interference.

At the same time it angered him that Mother took so little interest in the house and family that she frequently remained at the tennis club, drinking and dancing, until 7pm — our usual dinner hour.

What started out to be a sociable cocktail after tennis would frequently wind up being two, or three and possibly even four. After a few drinks, Mother completely lost her sense of time. Very often she wouldn't arrive home until seven-fifteen or seven-thirty. When this became a habit with her, Groucho would tell the maid to start serving dinner without Mother, to teach her a lesson.

Mother's serious drinking actually started when we were living in Great Neck. Years later, she confessed to me that she had got into the habit of taking a nip or two whenever she had to face the prospect of mingling with Groucho's intellectual Broadway friends, around whom she felt terribly insecure and tongue-tied without the liquor to give her courage to speak up. Using liquor for a crutch was, of course, a bad habit to get into, because she soon started relying on it whenever she had to broach a sensitive subject with Groucho, which was nearly every day. With two or three drinks under her belt she was never afraid to ask him for more spending money on which to run the house or a larger personal clothing allowance. Unfortunately, her drinking accelerated to the point where it became her chief occupation.

Drinking always made Mother extremely argumentative. 'What's the matter?' she would ask when she finally arrived home. 'You couldn't wait five minutes for me? God knows, I've held dinner up plenty of times for you when you weren't home from the studio.'

'I happened to be working. I wasn't at the tennis club, boozing with a bunch of out-of-work actors.'

'Are you implying that there's anything—?'

'I'm not implying anything. I'm only saying it wouldn't hurt you to get home a few minutes early after you've been over there all day.'

'What am I supposed to do here – sit and twiddle my thumbs while you're taking a nap?'

'You could drop into the kitchen and see if everything's all right with dinner, or maybe take an interest in Miriam's homework.'

'Why should I? You won't let me run the house the way I want to, anyway.'

'Oh, for Christ's sake. You're too drunk to make any sense.'

Not wanting to face the truth, Mother would heap more verbal abuse on Father, and the battle would rage on.

It would usually culminate with Mother jumping up and

leaving the table, or else the four of us would have to sit there and finish our dinner in hostile silence.

'I don't know how much more of this I can take,' Groucho would complain to Miriam and me when we were finally alone with him. 'I could be a lot happier with nobody. The only reason I'm not doing anything about it is because of you kids.'

We really felt sorry for him. Mother was being impossible.

After a major battle, she might pull herself together for a few days, not drink quite so much at the club, and even pretend to take an interest in the house by arriving home prior to the dinner hour, as Groucho suggested. But her reformation would be short-lived, and things would soon revert to their former wretched state – only with a little more bitterness added, and a lot more booze.

The incident that made us all realise that Mother had finally developed into a true alcoholic occurred one Saturday night, when she and Groucho were having a few close friends in to dinner.

Groucho, being the instigator of most of their home entertaining, had issued his usual combination invitation and warning: 'If you want to drink, get here by seven. But we're eating at seven-thirty, regardless.' Knowing him, the guests were extremely punctual. But Mother still hadn't arrived home by eight o'clock. At Groucho's behest, I called her at the club to remind her of the time. She sounded a little giggly as she said she hadn't realized it was so late, and promised to leave immediately.

Ten minutes later I heard her car roar up to the front of the house, and screech of tyres as she attempted to turn without slowing down. I glanced out the window just as her car missed the entrance of our driveway and slammed into a palm tree.

The car was completely demolished. But Mother – more smashed from alcohol than the actual collision – merely broke a leg and sustained a few black and blue marks on her face.

While the doctor, who rushed right over, was setting Mother's leg in her bedroom, Groucho turned to me grimly and said, 'Well, there's one good thing about this evening – at least your mother won't want to go dancing.'

Following Mother's recovery and return to her life of total irresponsibility at the tennis club, no day passed without a major argument between her and Groucho – arguments of such grave proportions that they had to portend divorce.

Although we weren't looking forward to such an eventuality, Miriam and I were beginning to wish our parents would get divorced, if this was the best they could do. For selfish reasons alone, it was becoming just too damn uncomfortable to have to live in the same house with them, especially when one or other would expect us to take sides in their arguments.

More and more, I'd take Groucho's side, for he was generally right in criticizing her behaviour. And as the situation worsened, I even urged him to get a divorce and have some peace of mind, and to forget about staying together for the sake of his children.

But Groucho was a family man in that respect. He hated the thought of breaking up the family unit, with the custody battles that were sure to ensue. He preferred to ride out the storm, feeling that perhaps this was just a phase Mother was going through as she approached the change of life. I watched my parents drifting further apart until I entered the Coast Guard in 1942. I was away when they made the decision to get a divorce.

A few months later I received the following letter from Groucho.

'Your mother moved out today, and the whole thing was kind of sad. I was sorry to see her go, for I am still fond of her, but obviously this uncomfortable set-up couldn't continue.

'I said good-bye to her before she drove off in her car. It was one of those awkward, half-serious moments, and I didn't know quite what to say. Finally, I put my hand out and said, "Well, it was nice knowing you, and if you're ever in the neighbourhood again, drop in." Your mother seemed to think that was a funny line – so for once in my life I got a laugh when I wasn't trying for one.

'The house is pretty quiet now with just Miriam and me rattling around the fourteen rooms. Well, it's better than fourteen people rattling around in two rooms. I'll let things drift along – anyway, for the present.'

25

This was after Pearl Harbor, Corregidor and Guadalcanal.

With another world war in full swing, his family shrinking in size and petrol rationed, Groucho did not consider himself to be in an enviable position. In addition to everything else, he was out of work.

The Marx Brothers' last picture for MGM, *The Big Store*, had been released in 1941. Early in 1942 the Marx Brothers officially announced that, after more than thirty years as a team, they were disbanding for good.

Harpo wanted to retire, Chico had taken a band out on the road and was smashing all kinds of records. And Groucho, who'd never really enjoyed making pictures, except when he was working for Thalberg, was ready to get out of the movie business entirely.

But he'd had a taste of radio, and he liked that.

He considered radio a 'very soft racket', compared with making pictures or acting in a live show. In radio, there were no lines to memorize, no costumes or make-up to put on, and very few back-breaking rehearsals. Writers handed you a script, and you simply stood in front of a microphone, wearing your own comfortable clothes, and read off the jokes.

The trouble with radio was that you not only had to have a sponsor, but you had to keep a sponsor. You also had to have a formula that not only would fit your personality, but one that would appeal to a mass audience of people, a good percentage of whom had probably never seen you in pictures or in Broadway shows.

In 1941 and 1942 Groucho made a number of guest appearances on various radio programmes. He never had any trouble getting that kind of job. Writers liked to suggest him as a guest, because he was a big help when it came to punching up their scripts and having him on the programme therefore made their work easier.

But he was fed up with guest shots. He wanted a show of his own that would stay on the air indefinitely. Unfortunately, there weren't many sponsors around who were dying to have Groucho Marx star on a radio programme.

He felt certain he'd get some kind of offer eventually (he wasn't that washed up yet, he thought), and meanwhile he was content to bide his time during 1942, doing occasional guest shots, playing a great many Army and Navy camps and hospitals, and in general fighting the battle of Beverly Hills.

His biggest problem was transportation. He had an office in a Beverly Hills office building which he liked to go to every day. He also had to do the shopping, since he was now the woman of the house as well as the breadwinner. Being the woman of the house suited him fine, because there was nothing he enjoyed more than doing the shopping. But unfortunately his only means of transportation was a Cadillac that consumed more petrol a week than the Ration Board allowed him for a month. And Groucho wasn't the kind who'd trade on the black market, or try to get anything out of the Ration Board that he wasn't entitled to.

To get round this problem and still remain loyal to Uncle Sam, he bought himself a bicycle with a basket affixed to the handlebars. And henceforth he pedalled to and from Beverly Hills. He might have been thought a little old to take up this sort of thing, but as he said at the time, 'I regret that I only have one life to give for my country.' This had a familiar ring to it. I think he had read it somewhere.

He conformed to a rigid schedule during the war years. After an eight-thirty breakfast, he'd go direct to his study and read all the war news and latest magazines while he was shaving with an electric razor. He hadn't used an ordinary safety razor since the first electric shaver came out on the market, and he discovered that not only could he throw away his soap and old razor blades for good, but more important, he could also read while he was shaving. 'Of course, I get five o'clock shadow by around one in the afternoon,' says Groucho, 'but look how well informed it keeps me.'

Reading and shaving simultaneously is a feat very few men can pull off, but because he had always had so much reading to do he forced himself to master it. Otherwise he would never be able to devour the deluge of newspapers, books and magazines that arrives at his home through the mails every week.

After he had whittled down his beard, he would call up his secretary and dictate a few letters over the telephone. Then, dressed in shorts, sweat-shirt and a beret, he would get out his bicycle and pedal down to Beverly Hills, with Duke, his police dog, trotting beside him. They soon became a familiar sight along the streets of Beverly Hills. And if you've ever seen Groucho in a beret, you'll know what I mean by the word 'sight.'

His office was on the second floor of a building that had no elevator, and by the time he arrived there he'd frequently be so tired out from the bicycle trip that he wouldn't have the energy left to climb the stairs. When this was the case, he'd remain on the sidewalk and whistle up to Rachel Linden, his secretary, who would open the office window and lower any letters needing his signature down to him by means of a basket affixed to a long rope. He'd stand there for possibly twenty minutes, nonchalantly conducting his business affairs from the sidewalk, signing letters and perhaps even dictating a few more, which he'd have to shout up to Rachel. Then, his business for the day finished, he would go and haggle with the butcher and the grocer for a while, and after that with his bicycle basket full of groceries, he'd hop on his bike and ride back home.

Then, early in 1943, Groucho signed up with the Pabst Blue Ribbon Brewery for a half-hour, coast-to-coast, weekly variety radio show, in which he would star.

So he had two things to celebrate; not only was he among the employed, but he was getting rid of me. I was scheduled to get married to Irene Kahn on one of my leaves home, and there was a good chance that he would never have to give me a free room and board again.

Actually, when I first mentioned the subject, it came as quite a shock to him that a very low-salaried petty officer in the Coast Guard would dare to take on the responsibilities of marriage. 'What do you want to get married for now?' he said. 'You're already in the Service. It won't do you any good. You might as well stay single.'

But when I stood firm, he said, 'Okay. But just don't have

any babies for a while. I don't think the Pabst people would have hired me if they thought I was old enough to be a grandfather. And just remember, once you get married you're on your own. Don't come to me for any money.' Groucho spent the next year or so trying to make a success of the Pabst Show, entertaining Servicemen, and insulting everybody in general.

Because of the help shortage, he started doing his own gardening. One day he was out by the sidewalk, weeding a flower bed, when a dignified-looking lady in a Cadillac pulled in to the kerb. She was obviously in search of a gardener herself, and Groucho must have looked like a likely prospect.

'Oh, gardener – how much do you get a month?' she called.

'Oh, I don't get paid in dollars,' he said. 'The lady of the house just lets me sleep with her.'

As was the custom in those days, most of the important radio shows emanated from various Service camps around the country. The Pabst Show was no exception.

Groucho was willing to do anything to make the enlisted men happy, but he was a violent opponent of the officer caste system.

'I think I insulted more officers than any other living American,' he claims proudly.

He had nothing against any of the officers personally. It simply bored him to sit around with the brass and their wives, and whenever a general or an admiral requested him to do a special show just for the officers, Groucho would turn him down.

'Why should I just entertain you?' he said to one four-star general. 'You can go off the base and have a good time for yourself any time you want. Those poor enlisted men can never get off, unless you give them permission.'

When his option with the Pabst people came to an end, he was replaced by Danny Kaye; and, having failed to establish any new endurance record with one sponsor, and having no more prospective sponsors on the horizon, he devoted the remainder of the war to doing more camp shows and hospital appearances, and raising money for worthwhile causes.

In addition to putting on shows in the hospitals, he was exceptionally good at walking through the wards and cheering up despondent wounded GIs with conversation. When he wasn't in one of his grumpy moods, in which case he'd barely say 'Hello' to a person, he had a rare talent for drawing out people and making them talk about themselves. I had always been somewhat aware of this, but I didn't realise just how good he was at it until I went along with him once during the war on a tour of some of the GI hospitals around San Francisco.

He had no cast of entertainers with him. He didn't even bring his guitar. He simply walked through the wards, stopping at each bed to talk to its occupant.

'Where are you from?' he would ask.

'Racine, Wisconsin.'

'I played the Orpheum Theater there before you were born,' Groucho would say. 'Tell me – does Ed Hofheimer's restaurant near the theatre still have such wonderful potato pancakes?'

No matter what home town a GI might mention, Groucho could truthfully say that he'd been there in his vaudeville days, and he'd always be able to recall some landmark of the place that you'd think only a native would know about. Naturally, this approach struck a responsive note in the Servicemen he met, and soon each one would be chatting about his home, his mob, his girl-friend, or practically anything else except his immediate troubles.

Groucho would throw in a few funny anecdotes now and then, too, or maybe a couple of jokes; but I think what the men enjoyed most was the chance to reminisce.

In the course of his wartime travels – I think it was on a Victory Bond tour with a number of other stars – he wound up on the front steps of the White House, talking to Eleanor Roosevelt. This was a great treat, for he had been a liberal and staunch Democrat since the days of Woodrow Wilson, and he felt that Eleanor was one of the greatest women of all time.

In the midst of his conversation with her, the official US Marine Band started banging out a couple of very loud Sousa Marches on the White House Lawn. Groucho hates military band music, and after he had listened to a few bars he turned to

Mrs Roosevelt and said, 'Now I know why you travel so much.'

By the time Roosevelt had died, Groucho's personal life was about to undergo another change. Romance was in the air, and Miriam was on the verge of losing her position as head hostess of his house, which, incidentally, was no longer the same one I was brought up in.

He had sold his fourteen-roomed house in Beverly Hills shortly after I was shipped overseas. He figured he'd never need such a large home again. After all, he didn't need a room for me, since I was now married, and Miriam was about to embark on her college career in the East and would only be around in the summers for a while. Besides, his income wasn't what it had been when he was working, and what was the use of spending a lot of money to maintain a large establishment? Who could tell? He might never get another job again.

So he had bought a much smaller house in Westwood Village, and there he planned, once Miriam went off to college in 1945, to spend his 'declining years' as a lonely bachelor – all but forgotten by the brewery for whom he had toiled away for such a short time.

Groucho, if the truth be known, was rather looking forward to the life of an elderly recluse, and he certainly had no intentions of getting married again. He'd had a number of brief romances since he and my mother had split up, but he was a little wary of getting involved seriously for a second time, and he had always managed to sidestep nimbly away at just the right moment.

But as he firmly believed, man does not control his own destiny, and in fact it was not long before he was smitten by Kay Gorcey, the twenty-one-year-old former wife of Leo Gorcey, one of the Dead End Kids.

He kept saying, in the letters he was sending me in 1945, that he was 'not going to get hooked a second time', but I kind of suspected from his references to Kay that he would, and that it would only be a question of time.

The date they chose for the marriage ceremony was 21 July – my birthday. I'm not sure now – it's been so long – but I think this was supposed to be some sort of a tribute to a wandering son.

In 1946 Groucho became a father again, when Kay presented him with a daughter, Melinda. And in 1947 he became a grandfather, when my son, Steve, was born. Melinda and her nephew have been good friends ever since.

26

Groucho had always maintained that there is a great element of luck in show business, and he cites his success in *You Bet Your Life* as the prime example.

You Bet Your Life was broadcast for the first time in October 1947, and was on the air for fourteen years. But until the first show had been aired, and the reactions started pouring in, he was extremely sceptical that there would be an audience for it, or even that he could be good on that kind of show.

In fact, he had been pretty despondent about his entire career ever since he had been yanked off the Pabst Show so unceremoniously. It had seemed to him that the Pabst Show had been going along fine. Audiences liked it, and it was getting higher ratings by the week. He couldn't understand why the sponsors were dissatisfied with it and wanted to replace him with Danny Kaye.

By the time the war was over and he still hadn't landed another show, he had pretty well talked himself into believing that he might never become an important radio star, or even an unimportant one.

At any rate, it looked as if it might be months yet – maybe even years – before he'd get another chance to prove himself on radio. Sponsors were pretty wary of comedians who had flopped a number of times before. They'd rather take their chances with some of the young blood coming up, if they were going to gamble – and who could blame them?

In the meantime, mainly to keep himself from disappearing completely from the public eye, but also because Chico was running out of money, he consented to make one last Marx Brothers picture. So he and his brothers formed an independent producing company with David Loew, and Groucho took his trusty coat out of mothballs and started painting on the phoney black moustache once again.

The picture was called *A Night in Casablanca*, and it was allegedly a satire on Humphrey Bogart's *Casablanca*. Warner Brothers had made the latter, and when they heard of the Marx Brothers' plans to release a picture under a similar title they claimed that the name 'Casablanca' belonged to them.

Groucho immediately sat down and wrote the legal department of Warner Brothers Studio the following letter:

'Dear Sirs. — Apparently there is more than one way of conquering a city and holding it as your own. For example, up to the time that we contemplated making a picture, I had no idea that the city of Casablanca belonged to Warner Brothers.

'However, it was only a few days after our announcement appeared that we received a long, ominous legal document, warning us not to use the name "Casablanca".

'It seems that in 1471, Ferdinand Balboa Warner, the great-great-grandfather of Harry and Jack Warner, while looking for a short-cut to the city of Burbank, had stumbled on the shores of Africa and, raising his alpenstock, which he later turned in for a hundred shares of the common, he named it Casablanca.

'I just can't understand Warner Brothers' attitude. Even if they plan on re-releasing the picture, I am sure that the average movie fan could learn to distinguish between Ingrid Bergman and Harpo. I don't know whether I could, but I certainly would like to try.

'So they say that they own Casablanca and that no one else can use that name without their permission. What about Warner Brothers — do they own that too? They probably have the right to use the name Warner, but what about Brothers? Professionally, we were brothers long before they were. When Vitaphone was still a gleam in the inventor's eye, we were touring the sticks as the Marx Brothers, and even before us there had been other brothers — the Smith Brothers; the Brothers Karamazov; Dan Brothers, an outfielder with Detroit; and "Brother, can you spare a dime?"

'This all seems to add up to a pretty bitter tirade, but I don't mean it to. I love Warners — some of my best friends are Warner Brothers. It is even possible that I am doing them an injustice and that they themselves know nothing at all about this dog-in-the-manger attitude. As a matter of fact, I have a hunch that this attempt to prevent us from using the title is the scheme of some ferret-faced shyster serving an apprenticeship in your legal department. I know the type — hot out of law school, hungry for success and too ambitious to follow the natural laws of promotion.

'Well, he won't get away with it. We'll fight him to the highest court! No pasty-faced legal adventurer is going to cause bad blood between the Warners and the Marxes. We are all brothers under the skin and we'll remain friends till the last reel of *A Night in Casablanca* goes tumbling over the spool.'

In due time, thanks to Groucho's fine grasp of the law, Warner Brothers withdrew their legal action, and the picture was released under its original title. But after he saw the finished version, he was convinced that the Marx Brothers really had run their race, so they broke up as a team again.

In spite of *A Night in Casablanca*, Groucho got a picture offer soon afterwards to star in a picture without his brothers — this time from song-writer Sam Coslow, who had turned independent producer to make a musical called *Copacabana*.

This was Groucho's first solo attempt at picture-acting, and he considered it quite a challenge. It was what he had always wanted to do — play the part of a normal human being who spoke funny lines, but who didn't wear a grotesque, phoney moustache.

He did wear a moustache, however — a real one, which he had been grooming for some time. At first, no one in the family approved of his wearing a moustache in everyday life, but he said he would never shave it off, and he never did after that. His story was that he couldn't appear in a picture without some kind of an identifying mark, after having worn the phoney one for thirty years. Audiences would find it hard to get used to such a complete change. A real moustache would serve the same purpose as the phoney one, and yet it wouldn't give the illusion that he was a slapstick comic.

Copacabana, real moustache and all, did not do for Groucho what *It Happened One Night* did for Clark Gable. If he thought he was going to get away from the old Groucho character, which he hated, simply by shedding Harpo and Chico and the painted moustache, he was mistaken. *Copacabana* was a Marx Brothers picture without Harpo and Chico, and not anything Groucho was especially proud of. Soon after its release it, too, was playing second- and third-run provincial theatres, and before long he was again on the prowl for another sponsor or independent producer he could bankrupt with his sharp wit.

By the spring of 1947 it had been exactly ten years since he had appeared in anything remotely resembling the hits that *A Night at the Opera* and *A Day at the Races* were.

Financially, he wasn't too badly off. He had enough money salted away to last him the rest of his life, if he lived modestly. It was his ego that had been hit the hardest.

'I just don't understand it,' he used to tell me. 'I think I'm as good a comedian as Benny and Hope and the rest of those guys. As a matter of fact, I was once much bigger on the stage than they've ever been. And yet I lose every sponsor I get, and they go on year after year with the same sponsors. What's wrong with me that I can't click on radio?'

Then one day in April the phone rang, and it was Mannie Manheim, the radio and television producer, calling. 'Want to do a spot on the Walgreen Show?' he asked.

The Walgreen Show was an hour-long, star-studded radio extravaganza that the Walgreen Drug Store Company, one of the largest drug store chains in the United States, sponsored once a year for a single performance. The show was going to be recorded and broadcast at a later date, and Mannie Manheim and his collaborator, Charles Isaacs, had been assigned to write and produce it.

A steady job would have been better, but Groucho was in no frame of mind to turn anything down. He jumped at the opportunity.

There were a great many other stars on the show, including

Bob Hope and Art Linkletter. Hope's part ran all through the programme, but Groucho wasn't scheduled to make his first entrance, to do a 'two spot' with Hope, until about the half-way mark. Because there were so many other names in the line-up, and because, on the night of the actual performance, all the spots were running longer than they were supposed to, he had to wait about thirty minutes longer than he had expected, in order to get on. Meanwhile, Bob Hope had been in front of the mike most of the time, killing the audience.

The sketch that Groucho was to do concerned a radio station that Bob Hope was running in the middle of the Sahara Desert. And Groucho was playing a travelling salesman who was calling on Hope.

Hope's first line in the script was: 'Why, Groucho Marx! What are you doing way out here in the Sahara Desert?'

Groucho was supposed to announce that he was a travelling salesman, but he was so annoyed that he'd been cooling his heels in the wings for so long that he ignored the answer that had been written for him, and instead replied: 'Desert, hell! I've been standing in a draughty corridor for forty-five minutes.'

This succeeded in breaking up both Hope and the audience. Crazed with success, and in a reckless mood anyway, Groucho literally dropped his script from that moment on and started bombarding Hope with ad libs with the relentlessness of a panzer attack.

Hope, a pretty fair ad libber himself, quickly entered into the spirit of the thing, and before Mannie Manheim or Charlie Isaacs could figure out how to stop them, the two comics had made an absolute shambles of their carefully prepared show. The spot ran for twenty-five minutes overlength, and much of it would never have passed the censors.

Luckily for the sponsor, who had invested thousands of dollars in the programme, it was pre-recorded, and the censorable material could be cut out. 'But it was practically an impossibility to edit the spot and make it sound like anything,' Mannie Manheim confessed to me some weeks later.

He and Charles Isaacs still have nightmares when they think of what Groucho did to them that evening. But they'll also tell you that in twenty years of radio they had never before heard such a hilarious performance.

Here luck enters the picture because, if a man named John Guedel had not been in the studio that night to hear the best ad libbing performance of Groucho's career, *You Bet Your Life* might never have come into being. Nowadays Guedel is probably the most successful producer and packager of audience participation type shows in the business. But in 1947 his chief claims to fame were that he had originated *People are Funny* and *House Party*, and made a star out of Art Linkletter.

Groucho had never met or even heard of Guedel up until that night, and the chances are their paths never would have crossed if Linkletter hadn't been working with an unusual amount of props on the Walgreen Show, and needed an assistant to hand him the props during the broadcast. Guedel, being somewhat of a ham, anyway, volunteered for the job. But usually he wasn't in the habit of accompanying Linkletter to every show on which he was to make a guest appearance.

However, he *was* there, he saw and heard Groucho doing what he could do best, and he was so impressed that he sought out Groucho in his dressing-room after the performance, and said, 'Tell me something. How come you don't have a show of your own? Wouldn't you like one?'

'Very funny,' said Groucho. 'Who's writing your material these days?'

'I'm not being funny,' said Guedel soberly. 'I mean it.'

'Well, if you must know,' replied Groucho. 'I haven't got a sponsor. And when I get one, I can't keep one.'

'You want to know why?' volunteered Guedel. 'I can tell you.'

'Yeah – why?' said Groucho, slightly irritated that a young punk who wasn't even born when he was a headliner in vaudeville should be telling him what was wrong with his comedy.

'Very simple,' replied Guedel glibly. 'On all the shows I've ever heard you on, you were tied down to a script. In my opinion, you never quite came off on a script show. Lots of people can read lines better than you. But nobody can touch you when it comes to ad libbing. You should be doing shows without a script so you could utilize the thing you do best.'

'Well, if I had a good idea for one, and I could get a sponsor, I'd be glad to,' said Groucho, his interest definitely piqued.

'I'll go home and think of one,' said Guedel. 'Call you in a couple of days.'

Three days later Guedel dropped by with the original format for *You Bet Your Life* – a page and a half of hunt-and-peck typing, explaining how such a programme would operate.

Groucho wasn't too impressed with it. 'I can see where it might give me a chance to do some ad libbing,' he said, after reading it over hastily, 'but as far as I can see, it's still just another quiz show. There are hundreds of these audience participation shows on the air, all presided over by jolly MCs who double up with laughter at their own bad jokes, and who can't wait to give a contestant the right answer. Personally, I think they're pretty sickening, and I wouldn't be surprised if the radio audience doesn't tire of them pretty soon, too.'

'But this one is different,' said Guedel.

'What's different about it? It's a quiz show, isn't it?'

'Yes; but the quiz is only a gimmick so you can ad lib. If you'll look it over again, you'll notice that there are very few actual quiz questions anywhere on the programme. The rest is devoted to you interviewing them.'

'I'm still pretty sceptical,' said Groucho. 'I don't know whether or not the audience will accept me in one of these things. Whether I've been a success on the air or not, I'm still supposed to be a sophisticated comic. I don't know if I can do the gladhand bit, and be sincere. Give me a few days to think it over.'

He thought about it for a few days, showed Guedel's outline to all his friends to see what they thought about it, and eventually got round to letting me look at it when I came over to dinner one night.

I agreed with him. On paper, at least, it didn't seem like an unusual or strong enough idea to re-popularize a fading comic, or even to get him another sponsor. Except for the fact that the contestants came up before the quiz-master in pairs – like a spinster and a bachelor, or a lady driver and a motor-cycle cop—instead of singly, as they did on other interview shows, what was going to make this quiz programme better than the rest, or any different from them?

But Groucho had already decided to try it. 'What can I lose?' he asked me. 'No one else is beating any paths to my door with any better ideas. If we get a sponsor, okay; if we don't, the hell with it. All I'll be out is the couple of hours it took me to make an audition record. I've got nothing else to do, anyway. And who can tell? Maybe this guy Guedel knows what he's doing after all. He seems to have been pretty successful with Linkletter.' So he and Guedel formed a fifty-fifty partnership, and after a few conferences on the kind of contestants and interviews they should have on the programme, they set a date to make the audition record at NBC, rounded up a studio audience, and transcribed their first *You Bet Your Life*.

However, before he agreed to go through with it, Groucho had insisted on two conditions: (1) The quiz would have to be completely honest. He would not help, or even give hints to, any contestant who was stuck for the right answer. 'Either they know it, or they don't,' he said. 'If we're going to have a quiz show, let's make it a real quiz show.' And (2) the show would always have to be pre-recorded, even if a sponsor bought it.

He felt that it would be foolish – if not downright dangerous – to put an ad lib show on the air 'live'. Who could tell from looking at the contestants beforehand whether this was the type of person who would let an unsavoury remark slip out on the show and, as a result, shock 30,000,000 or 40,000,000 listeners and a jittery sponsor?

And for that matter, who could tell what Groucho might say? He was notorious for letting slip remarks that he afterwards regretted. His tongue was simply faster than his mind, and though he had often wished that it wasn't, there wasn't anything he could do about it.

Once, a friend of Groucho's who is a movie director invited him and me out to the studio, to watch him shoot his latest picture. The actor who was playing the lead is one of the biggest names in Hollywood, and, though Groucho had never met him previously, he had heard considerable talk to the effect that the man's masculinity was a little bit in doubt.

When the director introduced them they shook hands, and evidently the actor had a very powerful handshake. Pulling back his hand as though it were injured, Groucho said, 'Say — you don't shake hands like a pansy!'

Apparently the full import of the remark escaped the actor, for instead of being insulted, he threw back his head and laughed heartily. But Groucho was so embarrassed and ashamed of himself that if you had handed him a knife at that moment he would gladly have slit his throat.

Even he doesn't make many slips in such glaringly bad taste. In fact, I believe that is the very worst remark I've ever heard him make. But it would only take a couple of those to alienate a sponsor, and he didn't want to take that chance — especially considering the position he was in before *You Bet Your Life* became a hit.

And yet, if he made a conscious effort to curb his tongue, he'd probably tighten up so during the interview that he might never say anything funny. Not only that, he was supposed to be an ad lib expert, and very fast on the uptake. That was part of what they were selling. How would it look if, before each remark he made, he sat there for forty or fifty seconds, trying to decide whether or not it would be wise to say the thing that had just come into his mind?

But if they put the whole show on wax, and were able to edit out the questionable material later, he could feel as free and easy before the mike as he would if he were conducting the interviews in his own living-room.

I don't know how free and easy he actually felt the night he made the audition for *You Bet Your Life*. I wasn't there. But to judge by the jumpy way he always acted before a broadcast — and the insomnia he usually had the preceding night — I would imagine that he was pretty nervous when he faced his first pair of contestants. I remember, however, that he wasn't particularly elated about the results when I asked him how it went the next day.

'It went all right — if anyone's interested in listening to a washed-up comedian grilling a group of nonentities from the audience,' he said unenthusiastically. 'Personally, I have no faith in the whole thing. I don't see why any sponsor would ever buy it.'

However, there was one good reason why a sponsor might go for it, which he had apparently overlooked. *You Bet Your Life* was being offered at bargain rates. A sponsor could buy it for $5,000 per week, not including air time. This was about one-quarter of the budget for the average script show that had any kind of personality in it. The tremendous difference in cost was due to the fact that there were no major running expenses, except Groucho's salary, and he had agreed to take considerably less than the $2,500 a week he had received from Pabst. There was no one else in the cast, and they didn't need high-priced writers to write quiz questions.

Nevertheless, none of the big sponsors was interested. And it wasn't until about a month before the autumn radio season was about to start that Groucho and Guedel received word that there was definite interest in the show from a man named Allen Gellman, President of the Elgin-American Watch Case Company.

'Who the hell are they?' asked Groucho. 'I've never heard of them.'

'They make the cases for the Elgin Watch Company,' explained his agent. 'They have a new product called Elgin-American Compacts that they want to exploit. They've never been on the air before.'

'No; and if I know old Groucho, they won't be on for long, either,' he replied with his usual optimism.

When Groucho and Guedel started negotiating, they discovered, to their horror, that Gellman wanted the show for an even cheaper price than it had originally been offered. It wasn't a very good deal at all, but after thinking it over Groucho and Guedel decided that it was better than no show at all. So they accepted the deal on Gellman's terms, and neither they nor Gellman ever regretted it.

The show started to catch on almost immediately. First reactions were amazingly good the country over, from Vine

Street to Maine. And oddly enough, the show seemed to appeal to nearly every kind of person — not just quiz and audience-participation show fans, but the people who liked sophisticated comedy. All the radio critics but one raved about it.

Perhaps Groucho was a little out of his element in the beginning. I know he confessed to me that he felt slightly uncomfortable doing it — especially since he thought it wasn't the kind of show his friends and the people he respected would enjoy. But after a few months he became adjusted to the new format, and started to sound as if he had been doing quiz shows all his life. His adjustment to it was helped considerably by the fact that even his most intellectual friends thought the show was great.

He was astounded by the success of *You Bet Your Life*. 'I don't understand it,' he used to say to me. 'This certainly proves I know nothing about show business. We get a sponsor, not because he thinks the show is any good, or because he thinks I'm a great comedian, but because it's the cheapest show he can buy. And what happens? It sweeps the country and I turn out to be a bigger name than I ever was on Broadway.'

Not only was the show a success from the standpoint of the radio audience, but Elgin-American Compacts, which were given away to contestants on the programme, were selling so fast that the factory couldn't keep up with the orders. Elgin-American wasn't equipped to handle such a sudden rush of business, and by the time early spring came the product was completely sold out. As a result, Gellman took the show off the air four weeks before the regular season was supposed to end.

He said it was foolish to spend any more money on advertising that fiscal year, since he had nothing left to sell. However, it wasn't much of a blow to Groucho, because Gellman had already bought the show for the following season. Gellman, in fact, was so grateful that he sent Groucho a solid gold watch. And Groucho was so grateful that he wrote Gellman the following letter:

'Dear Mr. G., — You could knocked me over with a compact when one of your hirelings arrived here last week with a solid gold watch in his hands. My previous sponsors sold gasoline, corn-flakes and beer. These, needless to say, have their value, but how would a man look walking around with a bottle of beer tied to his wrist?

'The watch is a thing of beauty and will be a joy forever, and I would have thanked you sooner, but I purposely waited a week, for I wanted to be sure that the lousy thing would run.

'Sincerely,

'Groucho Marx.'

27

In 1958 a panel of English critics was discussing on the BBC what constituted a 'great comedian'. One of them said that a comedian could never be considered great, no matter how funny he was, if his comedy didn't have an ingredient called 'heart'.

'With one exception,' piped up another member of the panel. 'I think Groucho Marx is a great comedian, and he has no heart at all.'

This story was told to me by Victor Saville, the English movie producer, who had just lately returned to Hollywood from a visit to his homeland. 'Isn't it amazing,' Saville went on, 'that so many people got that impression of Groucho before he started doing *You Bet Your Life*? People recognized the fact that he was terribly funny, but at the same time they thought he was a little bit cold and heartless. Anyone who knows him personally knows this isn't true, and the masses who see *You Bet Your Life* every week realize it today. But *You Bet Your Life* hasn't been seen in England yet, so they still have the other impression over there.'

Corny as it may seem, the lack of heart or warmth or whatever you want to call it in Groucho's comedy was probably one of the main reasons why he was never able to recapture a mass radio audience before he started doing *You Bet Your Life*. And it was John Guedel who was responsible for changing his radio character into one towards whom audiences felt sympathetic. It has always been Guedel's theory that, if it came down to a choice, it was far better to be not so funny and be a person the audience liked than to be the funniest man who ever lived and have the audience not give a damn about you as a person.

With this in mind, Guedel took Groucho aside about ten minutes before they were to do their first show for Elgin-American, and said, 'Now, Groucho, when you go out on stage to do your warm-up, the first thing I want you to do is tell the studio audience some kind of cute little story about your small girl, Melinda. It doesn't have to be full of big laughs. The main purpose is to show the people in the studio that you have a little girl, that you love her very much, and that underneath that cold-blooded exterior of yours is a very devoted father and warm person. That'll make them like you, they'll want to laugh all the more when you say something funny during the show. And that feeling will carry right over the air waves too.'

As he finished his words of advice, Guedel suddenly realized that it was pretty nervy of him to be telling a man who'd been in show business forty-five years how to get an audience to like him. It would probably be taken as an insult.

'I'm sorry,' he quickly added. 'Don't pay any attention to what I said. Just go out there and do what you feel like doing. I have no right to be telling you how to get an audience to like you. You were bigger in show business once than I'll ever be.'

'Don't apologize,' snapped Groucho, 'I'm going to take your advice. I've lost every sponsor I've ever had. All your shows have been successful.'

He went out and told several stories about Melinda during the warm-up, and he found it to be such a successful formula that he never stopped doing it. He has even had Melinda appear in person on the programme itself several times, and they have sung duets together, quite successfully.

Fifteen years ago he would have cringed at this sort of thing and even now he can't stand seeing other people's children perform. But in Melinda's case he's willing to make an exception, since the public seems to like it, and he thinks Melinda is very talented.

Of course, there are other reasons, too, why he has become such a likeable personality on the air. I think one of the things that have a lot to do with his popularity on air is the fact that he's now dealing with average people. His jokes are motivated by situations in real people's lives — not phoney characters dreamed up by gag-men. He can be funny on the air in the same way as he's funny at home — commenting on life itself. His humour around the house was always as sympathetic and warm as it was amusing — especially when he was playing the down-trodden father.

Furthermore, if a contestant is good, he is willing to let him or her do most of the talking. The audience gets a big kick, for example, out of watching him try to get a word in edgeways with a housewife who won't stop talking. They also love it when Groucho, with his reputation for fast talk and cutting remarks, gets squelched himself by someone who is not supposed to be a comedian. That makes him sympathetic in the eyes and ears of the audience.

Naturally, it took more than audience sympathy alone to make him a success on radio. The show itself had to be basically sound. And for this John Guedel deserved most of the credit.

What was even luckier than the way the two of them first met was that *You Bet Your Life* turned out to be such a natural for television, which was in its infancy at the time the show came into being. In those days, television was something that most comedians who were a success on radio didn't want to contemplate, for in the majority of cases, radio shows didn't translate to the new medium. You couldn't, for example, just set up television cameras in a radio studio and shoot the Jack Benny or Bob Hope shows as they were.

But *You Bet Your Life* didn't have to undergo any but the most trivial changes — like getting an attractive back-drop. Groucho could keep right on doing what he had always done — sitting on a high stool at a desk, with the quiz and interview questions typed out in a notebook in front of him, and talking and joking with the contestants.

Nobody expected a quiz-master to commit questions and answers to memory, and since the contestants didn't have any lines to learn either, and no scenery was necessary, it would be comparatively easy to set up movie cameras in the studio and simply film the radio show exactly as it was. In that way, *You*

Bet Your Life could be on both media, without Groucho having to do any work, and the audience had a choice of hearing the show on radio or seeing it on television.

In the autumn of 1950, when the programme started being broadcast both on television and on radio, it was an immediate success. Groucho, needless to say, was sublimely happy, for not only had he succeeded in an area where previously he had failed – even winning the 1949 Peabody Award for the best radio comedy show – but he was also a hit on television, getting his picture on the cover of *Time* magazine for the second time in his life.

Ironically, some of *You Bet Your Life*'s most hilarious moments were never heard by anybody outside the studio. Most of the off-colour remarks that wound up on the cutting-room floor were not made intentionally. But when you are doing an ad lib show such as that, it was inevitable that either a contestant or Groucho would occasionally let something slip.

One evening, for example, Groucho asked a contestant, a travelling salesman, to relate his most embarrassing experience. The salesman promptly launched into a detailed account of a harrowing escape he had once been forced to make from a hotel fire.

The blaze had started while he was asleep, and was out of control by the time he awoke and heard the alarm. All exits were blocked, and the firemen were raising the hook and ladder to his window. Being a nude sleeper, the salesman looked around for some clothing, but all he could find was a pair of trousers belonging to his three-hundred-pound room-mate, who was still out on the town. He stepped into them and headed for the ladder outside his window. Once on the ladder, he found he had to hold on for dear life with his left hand and on to the oversized trousers with his right hand. Suddenly he felt he was losing his balance and had to let go of the trousers to grab the ladder. 'It was highly embarrassing,' the salesman concluded. 'The pants fell down to my ankles, and the crowd below could see my whole predicament.'

This brought down the house, but was cut from the broadcast programme.

Another time, Groucho was questioning a bride of two days, and made the mistake of asking her how she spent her wedding night. She told him *exactly* how she spent it.

Occasionally, it would be Groucho who couldn't resist making a censorable remark.

'How many children do you have?' he asked a housewife on his show one night.

'Why, twelve, Groucho,' she replied demurely.

'Twelve kids? That's quite a habit your husband has.'

'Well, everybody has habits, Groucho,' said the housewife. 'You have that silly cigar of yours.'

'Yes,' he replied, 'but at least I take it out once in a while.'

I didn't attend the broadcast that night, but I understand from people who were in the audience that Groucho's cigar line got the longest, loudest laugh in the history of NBC. Needless to say the remark had to be cut.

In the spring of 1950 NBC had succeeded in purchasing the Groucho-Guedel radio and television package for the tidy sum of $3,200,000, payable in weekly instalments over the next ten years. Under this arrangement, which was one of the biggest deals of that sort ever negotiated, NBC owned the show outright, and Groucho would get paid for his services whether he had a sponsor or not. It was up to the network to see that the show had a sponsor, which wasn't much of a problem.

Many sponsors, including Elgin-American Compacts, wanted the show, but unfortunately it had become such an expensive property that Elgin-American could no longer afford it. So when *You Bet Your Life* went off the air for the summer its first sponsor had to let it go, and the De Soto-Plymouth Dealers of America picked up the tab immediately.

After Groucho had been on the air a few months for De Soto-Plymouth, he got the notion that he'd like to own one of those small sporty cars that were becoming all the rage in Hollywood. He intended to keep his Cadillac too, but he wanted a lighter, easier-to-handle car for driving in city traffic.

At the time he didn't have a De Soto or Plymouth to his name. Not that he didn't think his sponsor made fine cars, but because he had been driving Cadillacs for a good many years, and he saw no reason why he should make a change simply because he was working for a rival company. And besides, De Soto-Plymouth hadn't offered to give him a car for nothing, so he figured they couldn't care much about what kind of an automobile he did drive.

He was more naïve in the ways of sponsors than he should have been. He started looking around for a lightweight car to buy, and soon came upon a dealer who offered to knock $1,000 off the purchase price of a Sunbeam-Talbot, provided he would pose for a few publicity stills standing beside the car.

Thinking nothing of it, Groucho agreed to the man's terms, posed for the pictures, and started riding around town in a very sporty convertible Sunbeam-Talbot. He liked the car quite well for a little car, and he even boasted to his brother Gummo about the good buy he had made.

'Are you crazy?' exclaimed Gummo. 'You can't work for De Soto-Plymouth and advertise another car. That's a violation of your contract. It's bad enough you don't even own one of their products.'

'I'll own one when they give me one,' Groucho said.

Nevertheless, he had to give the Sunbeam-Talbot back. He didn't like it well enough to pay the full retail price for it, which the distributor insisted on if he didn't promote it. But he still wanted another light car, so he bought a convertible Ford.

De Soto-Plymouth couldn't complain about this. It was perfectly ethical for him to drive any kind of car he wanted, just as long as he didn't accept money for exploiting it.

He drove the Ford for about three months, all the while stoutly maintaining to his friends that he was a free man in a free country, that he was technically employed by NBC, and was therefore under no obligation to drive either a De Soto or a Plymouth. But underneath this bold front he was beginning to feel more and more ashamed of himself for being such an ingrate to the people who were actually paying his salary. Eventually when he was out in his Ford or Cadillac he couldn't bring himself to look strangers in the eye.

Then one day, at the height of the noon rush-hour, he stalled his Ford right in the centre of the intersection of Beverly Drive and Wilshire Boulevard. What was worse, he couldn't get the motor started again, no matter how hard he tried. But what was even worse than *that*, he had the top down, and everyone who drove by recognized him and shouted, 'Why don't you get a De Soto – like you tell everyone else to do?'

Within twenty-four hours, he had traded his Ford and Cadillac in on two De Sotos.

28

When he married Kay, Groucho was living in a small bungalow in West Los Angeles, which he had purchased during the war. This was suitable for a bachelor, but not a man trying to raise a family. So when Kay became pregnant in 1945, Groucho bought a larger house on a hillside overlooking the Sunset Strip in West Hollywood. This was adequate for him and Kay when Melinda was still an infant, but when she reached the toddler stage, living on a hillside was no longer practical for there was no place for a little girl to play except in the street in front of the house.

In view of those developments, Groucho sold the house on Sunset Plaza and bought one on a palm-tree-lined street in Beverly Hills, not far from Hawthorne Grammar School, where I had matriculated when I was a kid. The new house was a traditional two-storey Mediterranean-style villa, with sixteen rooms, including a billiard room, and an acre of ground featuring a citrus fruit orchard. It was more house and grounds than Groucho actually needed, and the price was more than he had intended to spend, but he just couldn't resist a place that had an orchard and a regulation-size pool table that the owners had offered to throw in, along with the carpets and curtains.

For about three years, Groucho seemed reasonably contented and happy living in his new abode with his beautiful, young, vivacious wife and precocious daughter.

Even though there was a vast difference in their ages, I felt that he and Kay were reasonably well matched. Both enjoyed parenthood; both enjoyed staying home in the evening, listening to music or entertaining friends; and both abhorred the Hollywood night-club scene.

I was aware that they had an argument every now and then, but I must admit I never thought their differences were serious enough to lead to a divorce. If they fought, it was over minor matters: he didn't like mayonnaise on his sandwiches or flowers on the dinner table. She was a night person and liked to sleep until noon. He, on the other hand, enjoyed going to bed at a reasonable hour and rising early enough the next morning to read all the newspapers from front to back, dictate a few letters and practise the guitar before going off to Hillcrest Country Club to have lunch with his fellow comedians and perhaps follow that up with a round of golf.

When he complained to me occasionally that Kay never liked to go out anywhere with him – to a ball game or a movie, for example – and that all she wanted to do was 'stay home and wash her hair', I thought he was kidding. But one day, early in April 1950, when I was in my office at Columbia Studios, he phoned me and said, 'Guess what? Kay and I are going to get divorced. I'm too old to spend the rest of my life arguing. She wants it too. I'm going out in a few minutes to buy her a house in Westwood.'

It was as sudden and unexpected as that.

The break-up was a friendly one, however. He made a fair settlement with her. He gave her a hundred thousand dollars and custody of Melinda. And he got to keep the house and all the furniture. They still saw each other occasionally and spoke over the phone when there were matters of Melinda's upbringing to discuss.

But they simply couldn't get along under the same roof.

After the divorce became final, Groucho decided that his house was too big for him, and he began talking of selling it and buying a bungalow in which he could live without having to negotiate any stairs. He had hated walking up and down stairs even when he was young. Now that he was getting on in years, he'd frequently spend the whole day in his study on the second floor, even though he preferred to be outside in the garden, rather than walk down the stairs and then up again later.

So he and a real estate agent started combing every inch of Beverly Hills, in search of a bungalow that would meet all his specifications. But he couldn't find one to his liking.

Finally, when I was over at his house one day, I noticed that the 'For Sale' sign was down, and I asked him if he had sold it.

'No; and I'm not going to,' he said. 'I don't want any of those cracker-boxes I've been looking at. I'm going to stay right here where I can be comfortable.'

'But what about the stairs?' I asked.

'I've taken care of that,' he said. 'I've bought an Inclinator.'

And he led me to the back staircase, and proudly showed me the strange-looking chair device that was affixed to the wall on a track and ran up to the second floor. 'Greatest thing I've ever owned,' he went on enthusiastically. 'All you have to do is sit down on this seat, press this button, and before you know it you're upstairs. No home should be without one – not even a bungalow.'

With the stair-climbing problem out of the way, he had no more qualms about living by himself in such a tremendous house. His foremost concern was that the Inclinator didn't break down. But this was wishful thinking for anyone who had an eight-year-old daughter and two grandchildren who seemed to think that an Inclinator was a wonderful plaything.

'Hey, you kids, get away from the Inclinator,' he'd roar out as soon as he saw any of them heading for it. 'That's no toy for your enjoyment. Now go on outside and play.'

He'd then turn to whoever he happened to be with and exclaim, 'Only people under thirty have the vitality to enjoy the company of small children.'

Actually he loved having Melinda and her playmates around, and he devoted a good deal of time to keeping them entertained.

After two marriages, Groucho seemed determined to remain a bachelor, and for a time he apparently enjoyed being single. But there was one aspect of bachelorhood he didn't like – all the rigmarole of making dates, picking up girls, and taking them home. This resulted in some unique romantic experiences.

A couple of years ago, he had occasion to escort Deborah Kerr to a large party. This was the first time he had ever taken the actress out, and he didn't have any idea where she lived, because he hadn't picked her up at home. She had come down to his broadcast in a cab, watched the show, and they had proceeded to the party from NBC.

Around midnight the party, which was in Beverly Hills, began to break up, and he asked Deborah Kerr where she lived.

'Pacific Palisades,' she answered.

'Pacific Palisades?' Groucho was shocked. Pacific Palisades was a good fifteen-minute jaunt from Beverly Hills, a thirty-minute round trip, and he'd be damned if he'd go that far for anyone – even Deborah Kerr.

Climbing up on to a chair, he commanded the attention of the other guests, and yelled, 'Anyone for Pacific Palisades?'

Considering everything, Groucho has changed remarkably little during his lifetime – or at least since I've known him.

He's still the devoted father he was when he used to tell me a joked-up version of Little Red Riding Hood when I was barely old enough to understand the story as told conventionally. Of course, he doesn't tell it to me any more. But Melinda is privileged to hear one of his bedtime stories every night that she spends at his house. And she appreciates his story-telling talent too. One night, when he was about to go out to dinner, Melinda rushed up to him in tears. 'What's the matter?' he asked.

'You promised me Little Red Riding Hood,' she cried.

'Well, I haven't got time tonight,' he said. 'Get Sarah to tell it to you.'

'I don't like the way she tells it,' complained Melinda. 'You tell it better.'

'Ridiculous,' said Groucho. 'It's the same story no matter who tells it. Why is mine any better?'

'Because you put more food in Red Riding Hood's basket,' said Melinda.

He still expects his children to play straight man for him. Melinda got hardened to this sort of thing quickly.

'Daddy, will you tie my shoe?' she asked him one day. 'It's too loose.'

'Too loose? He was a painter,' said Groucho. 'Too Loose Lautrec.'

'Will you tie my shoe, please?' persisted Melinda. 'It's too loose.'

'Too loose?' exclaimed Groucho. 'Didn't John Huston just make a picture about him?'

'Daddy,' said Melinda with Job-like patience, 'I know you want to be funny, but will you please tie my shoe first, so that I can go out and play with the kids?'

Groucho is still insecure about money, and during the daytime he'll occasionally wear a beret, because he can fold it up and put it in his pocket instead of handing it over to a hat-check girl.

But he's not insecure to the degree he once was when he was still worrying about what he would live on when he was completely washed up. Last year, in fact, he finally put a swimming pool in his backyard – even though he never cared much for swimming and likes it even less today. How he came to spend $7,500 for this luxury still amuses me.

My wife and I and our family live in the Pacific Palisades, and Groucho is always complaining that he doesn't see enough of his grandchildren, Steve and Andy, because we live so far out. But if he wouldn't drive out there with Deborah Kerr in the car, you can be sure he wouldn't make the trip very often just to see his grandchildren, especially since he has a small child of his own in his house a good deal of the time.

One hot day, a couple of summers ago, my family and I were invited to go swimming at Sol Siegel's house in Beverly Hills. Siegel, who is a movie producer, lives directly behind Groucho's house, and Melinda was welcome to use his pool whenever she felt like a swim.

This arrangement suited Groucho, until the day Irene and I took our children swimming at the Siegels'. On that afternoon, just before we arrived at the Siegels' house, Groucho, who was out cruising around in his De Soto, spotted our car, and yelled out, 'Where are you going?'

I told him we were going swimming at the Siegels'. 'A fine thing,' he said indignantly. 'You bring Steve and Andy all the way into town to go to a stranger's house, and you never bring them to my house during the day.'

'We wouldn't have brought them in if we weren't going swimming,' I explained to him. 'We can't go swimming on the grass in your backyard.'

Two days later, while I was dropping a book off at his house, I noticed that there was a steam-shovel in the backyard. Seeing that I had noticed it, Groucho said in a disgruntled tone, 'I'm putting in a pool, so that when you take the kids into town next summer you can bring them to my house instead of the Siegels'. It's a hell of a note when I have to pay $7,500 for a swimming pool in order to see my own grandchildren.'

Groucho uses the pool, too, but only if the temperature rises above 100. On most days he's still content to get his recreation by taking a brisk walk round the block, or inspecting his orchard. Or if he's in an exceptionally good mood he might take Melinda to the Griffith Park Zoo or the Beverly Playland Amusement Park, where he'll sit on a bench reading a magazine while his daughter goes on all the rides.

He never lets himself be caught without a magazine. He keeps one on the front seat of his automobile at all times, so that if he ever gets stuck with some time to kill – even if it's just a prolonged traffic jam – he can put the time to good advantage.

He is still reading and shaving simultaneously, too. And he still indulges in what has always been one of his favourite pastimes – proselytizing. When he reads something he considers particularly worthwhile, he'll first give you a verbal summary of it, and then he'll hound you for days until you read it for yourself. He's very dogmatic in his views, and heaven help you if you don't agree with him about the merits of a book, a movie, a certain restaurant, a joke or even a particular line of thinking. Unless you're one of the few people whose intellect he really respects, he'll take it as a personal affront if you disagree with him about anything, and he's liable to get quite angry and upset about it.

He's still doing all the shopping for his household, and he's still insisting that no bogus pumpernickel or rye bread be smuggled in. He still eats lunch at the Hillcrest Comedians' Round

Table a couple of times a week, and he still reverts back to the 'World Telegram golf swing' on the rare occasions when he can be lured on to the course.

In the late thirties, when our whole family was very much into tennis, Groucho decided to drop out of the Hillcrest Country Club, because he didn't want to have to pay dues to two clubs, the other one being the Beverly Hills Tennis Club. But he found he just couldn't phone the Board of Directors and tell them he was quitting. They insisted he write an official letter of resignation. This request resulted in one of his most oft-quoted lines:

> Dear Board,
>   I don't want to belong to any club that would have me as a member.
>
>   Sincerely yours,
>   Groucho Marx.'

After the war, he decided to rejoin Hillcrest, so that he could eat lunch at the renowned Comedians' Round Table in the corner of the Men's Grill. Since he had sold his membership after his resignation letter for $750, and it cost him $7,500 to rejoin, he suffered quite a financial loss in order to be able to crack a few jokes at lunch-time with his fellow comedians while chewing a corned beef on rye.

When he wants to have lunch with his friends who don't belong to Hillcrest – Harry Ruby, Nunnally Johnson and Arthur Sheekman – he'll take them to Nate 'n Al's Delicatessen in Beverly Hills. 'Take' may not be the exact word. They usually toss a coin to see who pays.

His relationship with his brothers is the same as it's always been. He sees Gummo perhaps the most frequently, because the latter handles his business affairs and they share the same office in Beverly Hills. He sees Harpo almost as often. They live within a few blocks of each other, and generally exchange dinner invitations a couple of times a week. They also meet at Hillcrest for lunch, or when Groucho brings Melinda over to Harpo's house to play with his children.

But Chico is still as elusive as ever, and it would take the combined forces of the Pinkerton Agency to keep track of his activities, and a roulette wheel, or at the very least a gin game, to attract him over to dinner.

Zeppo dissolved his theatrical agency in 1949, and he can be found managing his plant in Inglewood, which manufactures aeroplane parts under Government contract. And Chico is usually on the road, playing night-club engagements, either solo or teamed with Harpo. Together they are a very successful and much-sought-after team in the night-clubs, but Harpo is like Groucho in many ways, and he's not crazy about travelling around the country just to make money.

The word 'moderation' still governs Groucho's every move, and it's one of the reasons, I'm sure, why he always enjoyed such excellent health. Until he reached sixty he'd been in a hospital twice – once for an appendectomy in 1930, and more recently to undergo a prostate operation at the Cedars of Lebanon Hospital in Los Angeles.

Upon showing Groucho to his room the day he was admitted, the floor nurse, a rather prim, middle-aged woman, handed him a white sleeping-gown and told him to get into it. She then bustled out of the room, and when she returned a few minutes later, she found him standing in the middle of the room with the sleeping-gown on over his suit.

'You're supposed to take your clothes off first,' she said.

'I won't take mine off unless you take yours off,' said Groucho firmly.

It's possible that the nurse might have been offended, but in the years he was doing *You Bet Your Life*, Groucho discovered that most people enjoyed being insulted by him. Which was probably the secret of the show's success.

One day, while he was having lunch at Nate 'n Al's, an elderly couple approached his table. 'Mr Marx,' said the husband, introducing himself. 'Would you do me a favour? My wife is just dying to be insulted by you.'

Groucho looked at the wife, who was short, fat and ugly, and said, 'I'm surprised at you, sir. With a wife who looks like that you ought to be able to think of your own insults!'

PART TWO

29

Four days after I mailed off *Life With Groucho*, my agent wired me her reaction:

GREAT. AM SENDING IT RIGHT OVER TO SIMON & SCHUSTER.
NAOMI BURTON

Two weeks later, Edith Haggard, my magazine agent, rang to inform me that Ben Hibbs, the editor of *The Saturday Evening Post*, loved *Life With Groucho*, wished to run it in eight instalments, and had offered to buy the serial rights for $45,000. Was the offer acceptable to me?

Was it acceptable? I'd seen the last of the two thousand advance from Simon & Schuster months before; I hadn't been able to get an assignment from *Collier's* since July; and I'd just spent most of the afternoon waiting in line at the Californian State Employment Bureau for my unemployment compensation – which came to a grand total of $27 in those days.

I gleefully shouted into the phone to take the money before Ben Hibbs changed his mind, then Edith went on excitedly, 'The funny thing, Arthur ... Ben didn't even want to read the book when I offered it to him. He didn't think your father was a warm enough personality for *The Post*. But after he read your manuscript, he said you convinced him what a warm, wonderful family man Groucho really is.'

The sale, Edith added, hinged on only two conditions: could I assure Hibbs that Groucho would co-operate in plugging the book and the magazine on his TV programme once it started to run in serial form in *The Saturday Evening Post*? And could I possibly persuade him to write a few more footnotes?

Since I'd written all the footnotes myself, the latter was no problem – I could dash off as many as they wanted in no time. And I was positive Groucho wouldn't mind plugging his own life story on his television show in return for all that loot his son would be getting – the first really big money of my life.

In fact, I could hardly wait for Edith to hang up so I could phone him. I knew he'd be bowled over by my success, and very proud.

When I reached him, I said, 'Hey, Padre' – my sister Miriam and I had always called him that rather than 'Father' – 'You know that book I've been writing about a certain TV star? The one you said wouldn't make me any money?'

'What about it?'

'Well, I just sold it to *The Saturday Evening Post* for forty-five thousand dollars!'

'The government will get most of it,' he responded sourly.

One evening, after my deal with *The Post* was made official by the arrival of a very large cheque in the morning mail, I dropped a copy of *Life With Groucho* off at Father's house, fully expecting him to get back to me the following day (if not that same night) and tell me how pleased he was with it.

But when several days had passed without my hearing anything, I grew nervous and phoned him.

'You'd better get over here right away,' Groucho commanded, in a tone that boded no good. 'I want to talk to you about your book.'

My pulse rate must have tripled with anxiety as Irene and I travelled the seven miles between Pacific Palisades and Groucho's house.

He met us at the front door in his cashmere bathrobe and slippers. He looked at my wife as though she were some kind of an intruder, then ordered her to wait in the living-room. 'I want to talk to Art alone.' Whereupon he quickly escorted me to his upstairs study, closed the door and sat down at his desk. On top of it was my manuscript, dog-eared and looking as if it had been maltreated by the KGB.

'You certainly don't intend to publish this?' Groucho said, shooting a disdainful glance down at what represented nearly a year's work.

'What are you talking about?' I said. 'I just sold it to *The Saturday Evening Post* for $45,000.'

'It's scurrilous,' he said. 'You've made me out to be some kind of an ogre – and a cheap one, at that.'

'Where is it scurrilous?' I asked, feeling I could assuage him by rewriting a passage or two.

'Not one place. Just the whole tone of it.'

Treading carefully so as not to upset him further, I said I felt he was being overly sensitive and that he had to be mistaken, because I really hadn't depicted him any differently in my book than I had in the *Collier's* article, which he had liked – I had just expanded the material. And besides, how could he possibly think I'd made him look like an ogre when the editor of *The Post* had brought the book solely because Groucho came over as a warm family man?

'I don't care what the editor thinks – he's not printing a word of my life until I'm satisfied with it. I'm one of the biggest names in show business, and you're not going to make a horse's ass out of me for a few thousand dollars.'

'But I just told you what Ben Hibbs thinks –'

'Editors will print anything to sell copies. Now sit down at that typewriter and I'll start dictating to you from the beginning. And the first thing we're going to do is eliminate the footnotes – it's an old fashioned device.'

'The editor particularly likes the footnotes,' I said, beginning to tremble with anger – and fear.

'What does he know? Now listen to me if you know what's good for you.' And he pushed the typewriter, on its rollered stand, in the direction of my chair.

'Be reasonable, Padre,' I said, trying to appeal to his common sense since it was obvious I could no longer rely on his fatherly feelings. 'We can't rewrite the book now after I've accepted a cheque for $45,000. The most they'll stand for are a few changes – but certainly nothing structural. They bought this book, not the one you want to write. Do you want me to have to give back $45,000?'

'I make that much in a month,' said Groucho.

'Well, it's a lot of money to me.'

'Look here,' he said threateningly. 'Either you rewrite this book starting from page one, or I'll call my lawyer!'

Lawyer! My own father! I couldn't believe it.

However unbelievable, I realized I either had to take a firm stand, or be ground into the carpet under his heel. My whole reputation in the magazine business hinged on the outcome – not to mention my bank account, which had been severely depleted by devoting most of 1953 to working only on the book.

'Call anyone you want,' I said, in an emotion-filled voice. 'I'm not rewriting my book, and you can't stop its publication.'

And with that daring announcement, I picked up my manuscript and walked out of his house. For all I knew it might be our final parting.

I was quivering slightly, but at last I was my own man.

30

Feeling in my heart that I'd depicted Groucho affectionately — and not scurrilously — helped me get through a rather sleepless night. And having, through my association with *Collier's*, a layman's knowledge of libel laws and invasion of privacy statues regarding 'public figures', I didn't really believe that he had a leg to stand on in court.

Awareness of my legal rights, however, didn't alleviate the emotional pain I was experiencing from my father's unreasonable reaction to *Life With Groucho*. Nor would this knowledge get me off the hook with the editor of *The Saturday Evening Post*, who expected Groucho's full co-operation in plugging the series on his highly-rated television show.

I suspected that Groucho was much too sensitive about his public image ever to sue his son, but I also knew that if I didn't bow to his demands, he wouldn't publicize *The Saturday Evening Post* on the air, as I'd promised Ben Hibbs he would.

What bothered me even more was — how could he do this to me, his own son? Me, Big Feet (as he sometimes called me)? The son he had proudly shown to audiences in the opening scene of *Animal Crackers*? The boy who used to sit on his knee and listen, somewhat bewilderedly, to his joked-up versions of *Little Red Riding Hood* and *Jack and the Beanstalk*? The son who'd put the Marx family on the sports page with a victory over Jack Kramer in a major tennis tournament?

What was going on?

Did Groucho really believe I'd written something damaging? Or had I simply hurt his feelings by not letting him read the manuscript before I'd sold it to *The Saturday Evening Post*? Or, like many a superstar, was he merely being difficult to call my attention to himself?

Knowing my father, I couldn't believe it was a simple case of egomania. He wasn't a typical ham actor (although he was showing signs of turning into one since the enormous success of *You Bet Your Life*). On the other hand, I was certain I hadn't defamed him in my book, either.

Which led me to yet another theory.

I was no psychiatrist, but I'd learnt enough psychology in college to realize that Groucho's reaction to my manuscript had all the ingredients of the classic father-son rivalry. Could it be possible that my father had a subconscious desire to keep me in a subordinate position, so that he could remain top dog in the family and thereby hang on to his youth a little longer?

There wasn't much danger that he would ever be known as the father of Arthur Marx. And it was hard to believe he could be fearful of such a possibility rather than proud of it. Still, it made the most sense, since his behaviour was consistent with his negative reaction to almost everything else I'd written without his help. And when I checked it with a psychiatrist I sometimes played tennis with, he admitted my theory could very well be correct.

Whatever the reason for Groucho's behaviour, I finally decided I had two possible courses of action open to me.

I could either go straight to Martin Gang, the Kahn family lawyer, and ask him to take action to prevent my father from doing something that would endanger *The Post* sale – a move that might well push Groucho so deep into a corner that he couldn't extricate himself and still save face. Or I could wait out the situation for a few days, and see if he was really serious about stopping the book. Perhaps if I gave him the silent treatment, his more normal paternal instincts would finally show themselves.

I didn't have to wait long. The phone rang that evening, and it was Groucho calling.

'Big Feet?' he began in a penitent tone. 'Why don't we be sensible and talk this thing over?'

'Okay ... what do you want to talk over?' I said, trying not to sound too jubilant. He was obviously beginning to feel guilty.

'You don't have to rewrite the whole book. I just want you to take out the parts I don't like.'

'From what you told me,' I said, 'that's the whole book.'

'Well, it does need a lot of work still – don't you think?'

'No,' I said uncompromisingly. 'If *The Post* likes it, Simon & Schuster like it, and my agents like it, I'll go by their opinions.'

A long pause, and then he resumed in a more ominous tone, 'I don't know if you're aware of it or not, but I'm a very rich man. I'm going to leave a lot of money when I die someday – which I hope won't be soon.'

'I hope so, too,' I quickly interjected.

'So why don't you be sensible and listen to me? In the long run there'll be a lot more money in it for you than a lousy $45,000.'

The old will bit! I never thought I'd see the day when a man with Groucho's sense of humour would employ a corny gambit like that – and seriously.

'Why don't you be sensible, and stop badgering me?' I said. 'You come over in the book as a great guy – everybody who's read it thinks so.'

'I guess I'll just have to call up Beilenson' – Beilenson was his attorney – 'and ask him to get out an injunction. He says he can do it.'

On that note, he hung up.

Whether it was pure gamesmanship or the truth that he had already obtained a legal opinion from his lawyer, I'd probably not find out until I was in jail.

I still didn't actually believe he'd sue, but it was enough of a worry to keep me from thinking about anything else for a couple of weeks. I couldn't even concentrate on the new book I'd promised Simon & Schuster.

My wife was pretty upset too, for she was counting on using the money from the magazine to redecorate the living-room and buy some much needed furniture for the children's rooms. But we were afraid to touch any of the $45,000 for fear *The Post* would make us return it if they got wind of possible trouble.

A few more suspenseful days passed, with no further developments, leading me to believe that Groucho was just bluffing. Nevertheless, every time the phone rang I jumped. I finally reached the point where I wouldn't answer it at all. I just didn't want to hear any bad news.

One day, however, while I was standing out by our mailbox, collecting our daily allotment of bills, a man jumped out of a car and shoved a subpoena into my hand.

I figured it was finally happening. But when I opened the document, I discovered it was only a small claims action from a repairman I was refusing to pay because he'd done such a bad job of fixing our washing machine. Even that seemed a relief.

A call from Gummo, Groucho's brother and business manager, came that evening.

'Your father's very upset,' he told me in a cajoling tone. 'Why don't you be nice to him?'

'Why doesn't he be nice to me?'

'I think your wife is turning you against your father,' said Gummo.

'I think my father is turning me against my father,' I retorted. 'He's impossible.'

The next day I got the call I'd been dreading – from Larry Beilenson, Groucho's lawyer.

'You know we can stop publication,' he said threateningly.

'I don't think you can,' I replied confidently. 'I know my rights.'

'Okay,' said Beilenson. 'Your father just wanted me to warn you that we're sending off a letter to *The Saturday Evening Post* today, informing them that Groucho's biography is completely unauthorized, and that we're going to get out an injunction if they don't withhold publication voluntarily until Groucho is satisfied with the material.'

I swallowed hard and said, 'Go ahead and mail it.'

As I hung up, I was sure they were bluffing, otherwise they wouldn't be talking so much about what they were going to do – they'd just do it.

On the other hand, if they did send that letter, who could tell what *The Post*'s reaction would be? I had never guaranteed them that the book was 'authorized,' but since Groucho's apparently signed footnotes ran throughout the entire text, and the editors had requested that I ask him to write more of them, and I had assured them he would, they evidently assumed he had co-operated with me in the writing of the book. If they now found out otherwise, they might very well claim I'd put one over on them, and wish to renege on the whole deal.

That panicked me into bringing my own lawyer, Martin Gang, into the case.

After reassuring me that I wasn't in any kind of trouble, Gang said he felt that Groucho's lawyers were mishandling the whole affair: that since the trouble was between father and son it should be handled on an informal basis, with the two sides sitting down together and talking it over, unemotionally.

'We'll ask them to pinpoint the parts of the book they don't like, and then if their demands aren't too unreasonable, so you'll make a few changes. *The Post*'s got to accept that if they expect your father to plug the book.'

Because I felt that compromise often led to complete surrender, it was against my better judgement to give in on any points. However, in the interest of getting the case settled so that I could think about other things, I told Gang I wouldn't mind a few changes, provided they didn't take the guts out of the book.

'Let's worry about that when the time comes,' said Gang. 'Meanwhile, the important thing is to settle this in such a way that the book is published without destroying the relationship between you and your Dad.'

I was in favour of that, and Gang contacted the Beilenson office, settling on a meeting date for the following Thursday.

Groucho was so pleased at the news that he invited us to a dinner party at his house on the Saturday, and we were so relieved that we accepted.

There was no talk about the book at the party – Groucho was all sweetness and light. That was one nice thing about my father – he could be suing you, and still not carry his animosity to the dinner table.

On Thursday afternoon, Gang and I met with Beilenson in Gang's office. Groucho, being somewhat cowardly, especially when he knew he was in the wrong, had wisely decided to stay at home.

On the conference table in front of him, Beilenson had an open copy of my manuscript, with a number of suggested revisions pencilled in the margins in Groucho's hand. Many of these were minor and I agreed to them. But there were two important things I wouldn't change: a chapter showing how eccentric Groucho was in his spending habits, and the letter he had written to me on the day Mother moved out of their house, which included the line, 'If you're ever in the neighbourhood again, drop in.'

Groucho felt the one made him look like a miser, which it did not, and that the other made him seem cruel, which was also not true. It was warm and sentimental – even Beilenson had to admit as much.

'But he still wants it out,' insisted Beilenson.

We reached an impasse on that point, and the meeting broke up, with Beilenson threatening to sue again, and my own lawyer telling me not to worry – just to go home and make the changes I had agreed upon.

Shortly after dinner that night, Groucho phoned the house and said he understood I wouldn't make any of the changes he wanted. I said that wasn't true – I just wouldn't make all of them. 'Well, I guess I just have to turn it over to Beilenson and let him handle this in court,' he said with finality as he hung up on me.

Relations in the Marx family see-sawed back and forth for several weeks, always following the same pattern: first threats, sometimes combined with a little cajoling from Groucho, Beilenson, or Gummo, then peace overtures, and short-lived détentes, when Groucho would invite us to dinner.

To make the situation even more suspenseful, two men from *The Saturday Evening Post*'s public relations department phoned me from Philadephia, and asked me whom they should contact regarding the TV plugs Groucho had promised to film in advance. They had already written the copy, and now wanted to come to Los Angeles, and get his approval. 'Maybe he'll throw in a few wisecracks of his own,' one of them suggested.

They also wanted me to take them down to one of the filming sessions of *You Bet Your Life* – 'So we can meet the old gent, and tell him how much we loved your book on him. You really made him a whopping good character.'

That was just what I needed – to put them together with Groucho, who'd spill the whole pot of beans, and I'd be back in the queue for unemployment compensation.

On the other hand, I couldn't let on that anything was wrong, so I played it as cool as I could, and put them in touch with John Guedel, Groucho's producer and partner in the *You Bet Your Life* venture.

Having no idea that there was trouble between Groucho and me about the book, John Guedel was naturally delighted to co-operate with *The Post*'s PR men. As soon as he heard from them, he started making arrangements for the filming of the TV plugs, and the recording of radio blurbs. A good showman, Guedel was well aware that an eight-part serial of his star's life in a magazine with a circulation the size of *The Post*'s was certainly not going to hurt *You Bet Your Life*'s ratings. Only two other celebrities' lives – Bob Hope's and Bing Crosby's – had ever rated eight parts in *The Post*.

I just hoped Guedel could handle my father, if and when he started balking at doing the plugs.

I also hoped that *The Saturday Evening Post* PR men weren't planning to come out too soon. If I could just buy some time, I might be all right. I didn't want the whole thing to blow up in my face before I could work out my problem with Groucho.

While I was worrying about the PR men, I received a phone call from Gene Lester, the Hollywood photographer who did most of of the picture coverage for *The Saturday Evening Post*'s personality pieces.

'I've been assigned to do the picture layout on your book for *The Post*,' he began. 'When's your old man available? I'd like to start with some shots of him around the pool with some broads. It never hurts to have a lot of tits in a layout.'

Knowing how Groucho hated being photographed under ordinary circumstances, I shuddered at what his reaction would be to this.

'Why don't we put it off for a few weeks?' I suggested casually. 'It's only the spring. The series isn't scheduled until the fall.'

'Are you kidding? I've got my work cut out for me if I start right now. You need a bundle of pictures for an eight-parter.'

'He's kind of busy,' I said nervously. 'And he's not too fond of posing for pictures.'

'I know. He's a bitch when it comes to that,' said Lester. 'I've had to deal with him before. But I can handle him. Just tell me when.'

'You're sure you don't want to wait a few weeks? He'll be in a better mood.'

'Listen, kid, if you're afraid to ask him, give me his number and I'll set it up. I've got to get going on this now while I've got the time.'

I couldn't let on that anything was wrong, for fear it would get back to The Post, so I told him I'd try to arrange a session – preferably for the coming weekend – and I'd be in touch with him after I had.

I had no idea how I was going to manage it. Not only that, I was beginning to wonder if the $45,000 was worth all this agony and apprehension.

What with Lester's insistence that he get started right away on the picture layout, continued harassment from Groucho's legal beagles, and the likelihood of The Post's PR men arriving in Los Angeles any day now and a possible confrontation between them and my father, I was beginning to show signs of cracking up.

I wasn't sleeping very well. When I finally did drop off, I had nightmares about having to return the $45,000 to The Post. I had also acquired what had to be a psychosomatic cough, because my doctor couldn't find any physical reason for my hacking now that I'd stopped smoking. And I couldn't concentrate on anything. I couldn't even knock out a 2,000 word article on Jack Benny that the editor of The New York Times Magazine had assigned me to write.

In short, I was a real mess, and I knew if I didn't do something soon to break this stalemate myself – the lawyers seemed to be getting nowhere – I'd wind up spending the $45,000 on psychiatric bills.

So I devised a plan. It was inspired by a letter I received from *The Saturday Evening Post*, informing me that they were sending galleys of the eight instalments of *Life With Groucho* under separate cover, and that I should make my corrections – 'if possible, a few more footnotes from Groucho, please' – and return them to Philadelphia as quickly as possible.

I immediately wired Hibbs to send me two sets of galleys. 'I always like to keep one set for my records,' I explained.

When Hibbs replied that he'd be delighted, I phoned Groucho, and said that Gene Lester wanted to start photographing him at the weekend.

'You still refuse to cut that letter about your mother?' he asked.

'It's too late to take it out of the manuscript,' I said. 'They're already setting it up in print. But as soon as I get the galleys, I'll let you see them, and you can delete everything you object to then.'

'Now you're talking,' exclaimed Groucho. 'I'll tell Beilenson not to send the letter.'

He sounded more relieved than I.

'Now, what about posing for the pictures?' I asked.

'I suppose I can't get out of it,' he replied. 'Okay, tell Lester to be here with his Brownie at eleven o'clock Sunday, I'll give him fifteen minutes. And, oh, yes bring Steve and Andy. I might as well get some free pictures of my grandchildren while I'm at it.'

Groucho behaved remarkably well with Lester, and the photographer managed to squeeze in several very fruitful photo sessions with his subject before the galleys arrived.

I quickly went over my set of proofs, and dashed off a few more funny 'Groucho' footnotes to please the editors.

On the second set, I deleted all the material Groucho had objected to which amounted to half the book. Then I took the galleys over to his house and sat there while he examined them.

He made a few more corrections, and handed them back to

me with the comment, 'I hope this is the end of it. I'm getting pretty sick of my life.'

Needless to say, so was I.

I dropped the second set of galleys in a trash can on the way to the Post Office, and mailed my set off to *The Saturday Evening Post*.

By double-crossing my father, I'd bought myself a little temporary peace of mind. It was a dirty trick to play on him, but after what he'd put me through, I didn't feel guilty. Besides, what he didn't know wouldn't hurt him – and he wouldn't know until the magazines were already on the stand.

Between the reading of the galleys and the publication date, however, he was to give me quite a few more sleepless nights.

31

As mid-summer of 1954 approached, and time for the serialization of *Life With Groucho* grew nearer, rumours were suddenly rife around Hollywood that Groucho was planning to marry a twenty-one-year old brunette and former model named Eden Hartford, whose real name was Edna Higgins.

An aspiring actress with no films to her credit, Eden was the sister of Dee Hawks, the skeleton-thin *Vogue* cover girl who was married to movie director Howard Hawks. Eden came from Mormon stock, and except for a few years in New York where she tried to follow in her sister's footsteps, she had spent most of her life in the tiny community of Bell, California.

She had been married previously, to a man from Bell, and not unhappily, she had once confessed to me. But when her sister had suggested that life could be more rewarding in the big city, she simply packed up, walked out on her first husband, and got a divorce.

She had met Groucho on the set of *A Girl in Every Port*, where her sister had brought her to meet its producer, Irwin Allen. Allen introduced her to Groucho, and the two had been having an on-off romance ever since. Eden had everything that appealed to Groucho. She was young, pretty, gentile and quiet.

Irene and I had double-dated with Groucho and Eden on a

number of occasions, and they obviously liked each other, judging by the seriousness of their necking in the back seat when I was doing the driving. Occasionally, the Groucho of yore would predominate, and I'd hear a line or two from one of his early shows. 'Edna, your eyes shine like the pants of my blue serge suit,' he might exclaim, or 'Your scent maddens me!' But for the most part he'd be as dedicated to the pursuit of sex as a horny kid.

Dedicated or not, his conversations with me in private were full of steadfast avowals that he would never marry again.

I knew that he was unpredictable, and that one could never rely on anything he said – especially regarding his relationships with the fair sex. 'The trouble is, I'm a sucker for a pretty face,' he once told me. Still, I believed him when he said he wouldn't get married again, until the rumours became so persistent that I figured they had to be more than malicious gossip.

That worried me – not because I didn't like Eden, or think my father was old enough to know what he was doing – but if he was intending to marry, I had to know about it long before the magazine hit the stands and the book went to press, so that I'd have time to rewrite the chapter about his bachelorhood.

I finally put the question to him bluntly. 'Do you intend to get married before the book comes out?'

'We're just good friends,' he answered shiftily.

'Why do all the gossip columns say you're going to get married?' I persisted.

'Listen,' he said, 'don't be so nosey. Do I ask you if you're going to get married?'

'I have to know,' I pleaded, 'because I don't want the book to be out of date by the time it's published.'

But I couldn't pin him down. 'Listen, Big Feet, I didn't consult you when I married your mother – and I'm not going to start now.'

'But you also promised me I could come to your third wedding,' I reminded him.

'There's not going to be a third wedding,' he insisted.

In late July he, Eden and Melinda took a trip to Sun Valley, and from there he sent me the following telegram:

IF YOU'VE HEARD ABOUT THIS, PLEASE
FUND THE PRICE OF THE TELEGRAM
LOVE FROM US BOTH.

GROUCHO

I can't say that I was surprised, but I was pretty disgusted that he had to play this game of oneupmanship with me so late in the proceedings.

It was back to the typewriter again, for a complete rewrite of the last chapters of the book. Luckily, it wasn't more than that, for the first few instalments had already gone to press by the time I'd finished a new draft.

In the final scoring, I guess I finished one-up on Groucho, for he never suspected that I'd double-crossed him with two sets of galleys, or noticed, when his life started running in the 28 September 1954 issue of *The Post*, that the text was considerably different from the one he had approved. I know he read it, because he had all eight issues of *The Post* on the nightstand next to his bed. As a matter of fact, when he was writing his own memoirs several years later, I walked into his study unannounced one day and caught him copying from the hardcover edition of *Life With Groucho*, which was open on the desk in front of him.

Life With Groucho sold well in hardcover, probably as a result of a spate of better reviews than I had ever hoped for. *The New York Times Sunday Book Review* called it 'great.' *The New Yorker* said it was 'an excellent piece of work'. And *The Herald Tribune* wrote, 'Many sons of distinguished men have written biographies of their fathers, but none has done so with a greater combination of affection and irreverence than the scion of Julius H. Marx.'

This latter convinced me that my analysis of Groucho's behaviour had been correct – it wasn't *what* I'd written, but *who* had written it.

And if I needed further proof, it was supplied me by

245

Confidential Magazine — a scandal-mongering publication that was popular during the fifties — when it published a real muck-raking article about America's 'favourite quizmaster'.

Their story on Groucho was incredibly vicious. Among other things, it accused him of being an old roué, with an insatiable appetite for young girls; it also said that his quiz show was fixed, and that he was meaner to his writing staff than Simon Legree, and more miserly than Silas Marner and Jack Benny combined.

'That's what I call scurrilous,' I chided Groucho when he showed me the piece. 'Why don't you get your lawyers after those bums?'

He shrugged, and said, with complete unconcern, 'What'd they say that's so bad? Just that my quiz show's crooked and that I like young girls! Well, I do like young girls — a hell of a lot better than old girls.'

From his pleased tone, you'd have thought the piece was a tribute to his virility.

He never consulted his lawyers, of course. The most he felt compelled to do was to dash off one of his inimitable letters to the editor of *Confidential Magazine*.

DEAR SIR:
IF YOU PERSIST IN PUBLISHING LIBELLOUS ARTICLES ABOUT ME, I WILL HAVE TO CANCEL MY SUBSCRIPTION.

VERY TRULY YOURS,
GROUCHO MARX

Any man that unpredictable was bound to keep a young bride in a constant state of turmoil and bewilderment. I figured he'd be lucky if his marriage to Eden lasted six months.

But Eden was cast in a different mould from his other wives. Extremely phlegmatic in nature, Eden was not easily upset by Groucho's dogmatic home rule, or his idiosyncrasies. She may have been young, but she didn't have the sensitivity usually attributed to youth. Frequently she wasn't even aware that he was criticizing her. Or perhaps she just wasn't listening.

Intellectually, of course, she was no match for him in an

argument. But she made up for this in bulldoggish persistence — until she finally wore Groucho down, and she got her way.

Either that or Groucho was finally mellowing — having learned from the bitter experience of paying alimony to two wives that it was really a lot cheaper in the long run, and less taxing physically, to give in on certain issues rather than fight them.

Another thing in Eden's favour was that she was a good mother to Melinda, who now lived with her and Groucho most of the time. Melinda's mother, Kay, gave up custody of her daughter when she was ten years old because Groucho insisted that, because of her heavy drinking, she was not a responsible person. Besides, she was away from home a lot trying to pursue an acting career. As a result, Melinda preferred living with her father, and Eden provided the mother figure and emotional support that she couldn't always get from her real mother.

In money matters, Groucho was more generous with Eden than he'd been with his other wives, probably because his income was larger than it had ever been. His NBC contract assured him of a practically life-long annuity. He had a very healthy bank account. And the time he had left for spending it all was growing shorter, if you could trust the actuary tables.

In addition to financial security, he was enjoying more fame because of *You Bet Your Life*'s success than he'd ever had in his life. There was nowhere he could travel without being instantly recognized — even the Vatican City in Rome.

The summer after his marriage he took Eden and Melinda on an extended honeymoon through Europe, first visiting his mother's birth place in Dornum, Germany, then Paris, and ending the vacation in Rome. There, on a rainy day, he decided to visit the Vatican. But on his way up the steps in a crowd of sightseers, someone jostled him from behind causing him to drop the three-dollar cigar he was smoking in a puddle. 'Jesus Christ!' he exclaimed, bending down to retrieve the soggy stogey from the water. As he straightened up he found himself face to face with a solemn-faced priest, who happened to have been the one who had bumped into him. Pulling a cigar from his own pocket, the priest handed it to Groucho and said,

'Congratulations, Mr Marx, you just said the Secret Word.'

When they returned from Europe, Eden persuaded Groucho to sell his Mediterranean-style house in the flats of Beverly Hills, and build a plush, contemporary dwelling of stone and glass on a fifty thousand dollar Trousdale lot. The new layout wound up costing somewhere in the neighbourhood of $300,000, all cash, of course. He still didn't believe in mortgages.

When I asked Groucho why he was going to all the expense when his present home was more than adequate, he answered, 'Because Eden's a young girl. She's entitled to have a house that an ex-wife didn't live in. Besides, she wants a sunken bathtub and a round bedroom.'

'Why a round bedroom?'

'I guess she figures it's harder for me to corner her in it.'

Eden not only got her sunken bathtub and round bedroom, complete with circular bed, but after they were in their new palatial home for a while, she also talked Groucho into buying a second house in Palm Springs, for weekends.

A second house, purely for recreational purposes, was an extravagance Groucho had studiously avoided all his life. I remember Charlie Farrell, who was promoting Palm Springs when it was little more than an Indian reservation, trying to persuade him to buy a house near the Racquet Club, because it could be picked up for $7500, and would be a good investment. Groucho was tempted, because he liked the sun, and riding, but in the end he put the money into securities instead.

Groucho's spending didn't go completely berserk as a result of Eden's influence. He was still a little apprehensive of that proverbial rainy day. Which is the reason why the insides of his homes were never as attractive as their outsides (if you're going to spend three hundred thousand dollars you have to cut corners somewhere), and why there wasn't always enough white meat for a second helping, and sometimes even a first.

But the net result was that he loosened up considerably.

He was more tractable in other ways, too. Realizing that Eden was so much younger than himself, with the need for a more active social life, he would frequently let her stay on at a party and continue having a good time long after he had gone to bed.

If it was not a party night and Eden felt a need to go out, Groucho was happy to accept her explanation that she was attending an acting class.

'Look, let her have a good time,' he'd tell me. 'She's a young girl. If she wants to have an affair with someone else, let her. As long as I don't know about it, I don't care.'

It was sad to think that at his age, and with so much else going for him, he had to make such a compromise in his personal life. But at least he was wise enough to realize that material things alone couldn't keep a young girl completely contented.

Years later, Groucho admitted to me, 'I never had an ideal marriage. I guess I always looked for the wrong things in a wife.'

For fourteen years, however, he believed that he and Eden were happily married.

He also thought my wife and I were happily married, which we were, more or less, until 1951 when she had a nervous breakdown that completely changed her personality. Oh, we'd had problems before that, despite outward appearances that we were very compatibly matched.

None of our friends suspected anything because at parties, Irene, who was wanting in self-assurance, used to grab my hand for security.

Groucho used to say, 'Beware of couples who hold hands.' And then he'd quote an old vaudeville joke: 'They hold hands because they're afraid if they let go they'll kill each other.'

Groucho was closer to the truth than he thought – although I didn't wish Irene any harm. Platonically, I was still fond of her. She just wasn't the person I cared to spend the rest of my life with.

Lois Kahn, my sister-in-law, who was married to Irene's brother Donald, was that person, and she felt the same way about me. But did we dare break away from our respective spouses in order to be together?

This wouldn't be just an ordinary case of divorce and remarriage. This was all in one family. My kids were Lois's nephews –

they called her 'Auntie Loie'. And Lois's Linda was my niece. And she called me 'Uncle Artie Boots'. And Lois and I had the same white-haired matriarchal mother-in-law, who was given to boasting to all her friends about the wonderful marriages her Donald and Irene had effected with her daughter-in-law the model and her son-in-law the son of Groucho.

As you must suspect by now, my father was no prude when it came to divorce and remarriage or relationships between men and women in general. He certainly didn't believe that couples should remain unhappily married 'till death do them part,' at least where it concerned himself. He liked Lois: she was his kind of woman. She was pretty. She had style. She could sing. She was a good cook and homemaker. And she had a great sense of humour and loved to laugh. Comedians liked to have her in the audience, because her own laughter would generally spark a hitherto unresponsive audience into joining in with her. Once, before comedian Don Adams had made a name for himself in TV, he was playing the Mocambo nightclub on the Sunset Strip. We were there for his early performance, and a couple of jokes he told literally had Lois in the aisle.

After the first show, when we were about to leave, Adams came over to her and begged her to stay for the second show. 'I need you,' he said in a plaintive tone.

Groucho liked a good audience, too. But there was another consideration that prevented him from giving us his whole-hearted blessing – his long-term friendship, dating back to his vaudeville days, with our mutual mother-in-law, Grace Kahn. He felt that my leaving Grace's daughter to marry her son's wife would harm that relationship, so he openly opposed my marriage to Lois, and sided with Irene when she tried to prevent me from divorcing her. He even went so far as to phone Lois one night and accuse her of wanting to marry me for *his* money.

If he was trying to break us up, it didn't work. All he succeeded in doing was losing me as a loyal son and friend for the year it took Lois and me to get our divorces. As a matter of fact, I don't believe I ever quite trusted him again.

We didn't speak for a year.

However, I was able to keep track of him and his career

through the trade papers. From what I read, his career wasn't going particularly well. *You Bet Your Life* was still popular in 1959 and 1960. But *The Untouchables*, starring Robert Stack as Elliott Ness, on CBS at the same hour, was cutting badly into its ratings, and had in fact knocked Groucho's programme out of the top ten for the first time in nearly twelve years, and there was talk of the show being dropped by NBC the following season.

Aside from the precipitous drop in ratings, NBC had another reason for wanting to dump Groucho's quiz show. They had twelve years' worth of shows on film, which they wanted to start running in syndication before the public tired of the programme. But if they aired the re-runs on local TV stations in the same season as *You Bet Your Life* was on prime time, the show would be competing against itself. The network could save money by dropping the prime time programming and just show the re-runs.

With the writing on the wall, Groucho started accepting other offers.

In the spring of 1959, he appeared with Harpo and Chico in a half-hour comedy on television for the General Electric Theater. The show was called *The Incredible Jewel Robbery* and was a dismal exercise in comedy. It contained hardly a laugh. Apart from a bad script, Harpo, in his early seventies, was beginning to look too old to play the blonde-chasing mute with the angelic face. He just seemed like a lecherous old man. By the same token, Chico's face, which was terribly thin with sunken eyes with black circles under them, had the look of impending death about it, due to an angina condition.

The critics panned *The Incredible Jewel Robbery*, and the ratings were nowhere. It was the end of the Marx Brothers as a comedy team.

Groucho was still a good name, however. Early in 1960 he was engaged by the Bell Telephone Company to portray Ko Ko in *The Mikado*. A Gilbert & Sullivan fan for most of his adult life, he was delighted to have the opportunity to interpret *The Mikado* before a mass audience.

As outspoken as he was about nepotism in Hollywood,

Groucho made certain that Melinda, an aspiring fifteen-year-old actress, was given the role of one of the 'Three Little Maids From School'. He also found a bit part in the show for Eden.

The Mikado was broadcast on 29 April 1960. It was directed by Martyn Green, who though insisting that Groucho's Ko Ko remain faithful to the spirit of the masters, nevertheless allowed his mannerisms to show through enough for the public to know who the funny man was beneath the bald pate and layers of makeup.

The reviews were okay, and the Bell Telephone Company was pleased enough with Groucho's Ko Ko to offer him another role in *The Pirates of Penzance* the following season. For some reason, he turned that offer down. Since we weren't speaking, I never found out why, though I suspect he felt that having to memorize those rapid-fire tongue-twisting Gilbert lyrics was a little too arduous for a man of seventy.

By then a year had passed, and Irene had agreed to give me a divorce, because she, too, had found someone she wanted to marry.

As a result, my father sent up the white flag of truce.

He never openly apologized either to Lois or me. His way was to phone up out of the blue one morning and invite us to dinner that night, just as if there had been no rift in our relationship.

During dinner, there was no mention of the bad blood between us. The conversation remained general, the atmosphere was relaxed, and after dinner Groucho took me into his study and handed me a cheque for five thousand dollars as a wedding gift.

My father may have been strong-willed, stubborn, and a martinet when it came to ruling over his family, but there was one facet of his character that remained constant throughout his life — he never held a grudge.

32

A few months after Lois joined the Marx family, my Uncle Chico left it.

Chico, the eldest of the Marx Brothers, was seventy-four when his big heart finally stopped beating one night when he was asleep in his bedroom in the unpretentious bungalow that he and his second wife, Mary, had been renting in a modestly priced neighbourhood of Beverly Hills.

Groucho had always predicted that Chico's life would come to an end in bed – but as a result of shotgun wounds, not angina pectoris; and not in his own bed, but in some other husband's.

Chico had had a chronic heart ailment for several years, and had grown progressively weaker, thinner, and more hunched over, until, when I last saw him alive – at a gathering of the Marx clan at Groucho's house – I could hardly believe this wizened old man was the same Chico Marx who could never pass a good-looking girl without reaching out to pat her rear, or be in your home for more than half an hour without succumbing to the urge to start dealing out the cards.

Chico had many faults – chief among them, a total disregard of responsibility – but his friends will always remember him for his sweet nature and a certain joie de vivre that only serious illness could subdue. When, during his last few weeks, he had to take to his bed I don't believe he really cared about living any longer. What good was life if you were too weak to shuffle a deck or lay the manicurist?

As Groucho had also predicted, Chico, who'd earned millions, died broke, having gambled or foolishly thrown away every cent he had ever earned. Whenever I think of Chico's happy-go-lucky attitude towards money, I'm always reminded of *The New Yorker* cartoon which shows a lawyer reading the will to the family: 'Being of sound mind, I spent every penny while I was alive.'

During Chico's waning years, when he'd been too ill to work, he was forced to live off the generosity of his brothers. If they resented, just a little, having to shell out money to support a man who ought to have been as well-heeled as they, they didn't complain. They perhaps realized that there might not have been as much to shell out if it hadn't been for Chico's contribution to the Marx Brothers' act. Maybe he wasn't Paderewsky, but nobody, including Paderewsky, has ever been able to duplicate his piano tricks, or to mesmerize an audience with quite the élan of the audacious Chico Marx.

The legacy he left to everyone who knew him or saw him perform, is the memory of him at the piano, in his little green hat, playing 'On the Beach at Bali Bali', while fending off Groucho's wisecracks in his atrocious but inimitable Italian accent.

GROUCHO: (*to Chico at the piano*) How much do you get an hour to play?
CHICO: Six-a-dollars.
GROUCHO: How much would you take not to play?
CHICO: Oh, you-a couldn't afford it.

Audiences lapped it up – even complained bitterly when a Marx Brothers film didn't contain at least one Chico Marx number. Groucho never forgot that, much as perhaps he would have liked to.

The morning of the funeral – 14 October 1961 – the immediate family was asked to assemble at the bereaved widow's house, there to be picked up in Cadillac limousines and driven to the service at Forest Lawn's Wee Kirk of the Heather chapel.

Lois and I arrived at the house a few minutes before ten, to be greeted solemnly by Mary, Chico's widow; my cousin Maxine, Chico's forty-four year-old daughter, who had flown out from New York; my sister Miriam; and my Uncle Gummo, who was looking after the funeral arrangements; and his wife, Helen.

Groucho and Eden arrived shortly afterwards. Groucho, looking properly solemn but making no sartorial concessions to the grim reaper, was dressed in a light grey business suit and tie, and might have been going to the Brown Derby to have lunch. His wife, however, was clad in black from the tip of her shoes to the crown of her cloche hat. This outfit combined with her dead-white complexion, shoulder-length black hair, and tall, willowy figure, gave her somewhat the appearance of the ghoulish lady in the Charles Addams cartoons.

As the two of them stepped into the living-room, where the

rest of us were sitting around trying to make cheerful small-talk with Chico's widow, Groucho seemed to notice Eden's sepulchral mien for the first time.

Indicating her with a jerk of his thumb, he remarked loudly to the rest of us, 'The way my wife's dressed you'd think I was the corpse!'

A few minutes later, Harpo and Zeppo arrived with their wives. After paying his respects to Mary, Harpo turned to Groucho and asked him how he felt.

'Better than Chico,' he answered.

Harpo grinned impishly, and said, 'Wanna make a bet on which one of us goes next? I'll give you three to one, and take either corner. Zep'll hold the money.'

'Oh, no,' shot back Groucho. 'I wouldn't trust him with my money any more than I would Chico.'

Lois and I rode to Forest Lawn in the same limousine as Harpo and Susan and Groucho and Eden.

During the slow drive, Groucho kept our minds off the grimness of the occasion by telling a few of his favourite 'death' jokes (including the one about the husband on his deathbed sniffing the aroma of freshly-baked coffee cake and requesting a piece. 'Don't be silly, Sam — that's for after the funeral!'); improving on Shakespeare and Longfellow ('Life is short, and the goal is but the grave.') And spouting a few comforting clichés ('It's nothing to feel sad about. Chico had more fun out of life than the rest of us combined.')

At Forest Lawn, a tremendous crowd of fans, mourners and the merely curious swarmed the walks and grassy areas around the chapel as our limousine pulled to a stop. As we approached the chapel, I heard my name called, and turning, was surprised to see my mother standing among the uninvited throng lining the walk.

Although she and I talked on the phone occasionally, and maybe even had dinner once a year around Christmas time, she and I were practically strangers now — just as she was to the rest of the Marx family.

'Hello, Grouch,' she whispered as he walked by.

He acknowledged her presence with a grim smile, then quickly ducked inside the chapel.

I believe it was the last time they ever saw each other. She died in 1972.

Inside the chapel, which pulsated with soft organ music and reeked of that cloyingly-sweet miasma of too many flowers under one roof, there wasn't an empty seat.

Chico's silver casket rested in the appropriate place before the altar, and as we filed past it in order to reach the cloistered section of seats reserved for 'family', I was shocked to see that the lid was open. Father averted his eyes as he walked past the waxen-looking Chico.

We were the first to sit down in the family space, except for a complete stranger who had taken one of the better seats for himself.

I nudged my father and asked him if he knew the fellow. Groucho studied him for a moment, then shook his head. 'He must be left over from the last funeral,' he said.

The rabbi who delivered the eulogy had never met Chico. He gave a long, dull, cliché-ridden speech that would have fitted just about anybody except the man we were there to remember.

Eventually the torturous service came to an end with a short prayer, and we rose to leave. At that moment, I heard a commotion in the rear of the chapel and saw three precocious children — about eight years old and all wearing Harpo-type wigs — and a man, who was evidently their manager, rush down the aisle towards the open casket.

The three midget-sized Harpos struck a theatrical pose in front of the casket, while the man aimed a camera and flash gun at them and took three quick pictures.

'I'm surprised he didn't ask Chico to say cheese,' muttered Groucho as he looked with contempt at the publicity seekers.

To my relief, Groucho and Harpo chose to skip the grave-side ceremonies, and the six of us piled into the limousine for the long drive back to Beverly Hills from Burbank.

The mood in the car wasn't exactly light-hearted, but there was a feeling of relief that it was all over, and the exhilaration that springs from being still alive, and not the unfortunate one in the casket.

As Groucho leaned back and made himself more comfortable, he suddenly exclaimed, 'For Christ's sake, Harpo. Why in hell did Mary have to hire a rabbi who didn't even know Chico? Have you ever heard such a goddamn pack of lies?'

'Nobody could know Chico unless he was a card hustler,' Harpo reminded him.

'Or a madam in a whorehouse,' added Groucho.

'I guess Mary didn't know who to get,' commented Susan.

'She should have got me,' said Groucho, a little testily. 'I should have done the eulogy. I could have told the congregation plenty about Chico that they didn't know.'

'You certainly could have,' said Harpo. 'I could have too.'

'Imagine that schmuck getting up there in front of all those people and saying Chico was so generous he'd give you the shirt off his back,' exclaimed Groucho. 'Sure, he'd give you the shirt off his back. It would be the one he borrowed from you the day before.'

'The rabbi also said he was charitable,' interjected Harpo.

'He was charitable all right,' said Groucho. 'I'd like to tell them about the time he stole the bass drum from a Salvation Army band so he could hock it to pay off a debt. I don't think that he gave a penny to charity in his life.'

'But he was kind to his family and good to his kids,' said Harpo.

'Sure – he was cheating on Betty from the first day he married her.'

'And the only time he ever saw Maxine was at dinner-time between golf and his bridge game,' added Harpo.

'He wouldn't even take her to Europe when I took my kids,' said Groucho. 'I'll never forget Maxine standing on the dock crying as all of us sailed for France on the *Paris*.'

'He was especially charitable to his family,' said the normally mild Harpo. 'Mary tells me he didn't have a dime of life insurance. That's what I call being kind to your family. If you had Chico for a husband, you didn't need an enemy.'

'I suppose he was so good to us,' said Groucho, really warming to his subject. 'Will you ever forget that time we were playing Scranton when we nearly got lynched by a mob of angry coal miners because one of them found Chico in the hay with his daughter?'

'Or the time in Chicago,' chimed in Harpo, 'when we had to do the show without him for a week because the son of a bitch had given a bum cheque to Al Capone and was hiding out across the Canadian border.'

'Yeah,' said Groucho. 'I'll never forget what the manager of the theatre told us when we went to collect our salary after the last show Saturday night; "Not one red cent. I hired four Marx Brothers, not three!" Yes, you couldn't help loving Chico after all the charitable things he did for everybody. I still can feel the thrashing I got from Pop when he blamed me for losing Stuckfish's trousers, when actually Chico had hocked them.'

'You just got a licking,' said Harpo. 'But what about poor Mom and Pop? They couldn't come up with the rent because Stuckfish refused to pay them, and we all got evicted from the flat on 92nd Street.'

'If you couldn't love him for that, then you just don't know a charitable fellow when you see one,' concluded Groucho with a shake of his head. 'Well, it's the old story – the people who are really nice and charitable, like you and me, never get the credit for it.'

They panned Chico irreverently all the way back to the house. Then, just as the limousine was pulling in to the kerb, Harpo said, as though he'd just thought of it, 'Yeah, Grouch – you should have done the eulogy.'

'At least I wouldn't have been hypocritical,' said Groucho, getting out of the car. 'They'd have known what Chic was really like when I got through with him.'

That evening, Groucho took Lois and me to dinner at Chasen's.

For the first time, I saw him completely abandon his guiding principle of 'moderation'. In rapid succession he had four straight whiskies, and got so loaded we practically had to carry him to the car after dinner.

I guess he felt worse about losing Chico than he let on.

33

As well as losing his eldest brother, which reminded him of his own mortality, 1961 was not a good year for Groucho professionally, either.

After a fourteen-year run, NBC had officially cancelled *You Bet Your Life* that spring. He filmed the last programme of the series on the night of Wednesday 17 May, and according to a letter he wrote to his friend Norman Krasna, who was living in Switzerland, he wasn't shedding any tears about it. The show had brought him wealth and security and made his name more well known than it had ever been as a member of the Marx Brothers team.

In June he was saddened by the death of the man he most admired in the world, playwright George Kaufman, who with Morrie Ryskind had written the book of two of the Marx Brothers' biggest Broadway hits, *Cocoanuts* and *Animal Crackers*, and the script for their most successful film, *A Night at the Opera*.

Surprisingly Groucho wasn't overwhelmed with offers after *You Bet Your Life* went off the air. George Axelrod had offered him the lead in his new play, but Groucho turned him down because he didn't wish to undergo the rigours of trying out a play on the road. But over the next couple of years he appeared in TV roles in the General Electric Theater, and the Kraft Comedy Hour. In 1962 he hosted the *Tonight* show before Johnny Carson took over. And in 1963 he played the leading role in *Time for Elizabeth*, the play he had written in collaboration with Norman Krasna (and which had flopped on Broadway) in the Bob Hope Chrysler Theater. He also toured *Time for Elizabeth* in stock the next two summers to sell-out crowds from Phoenix to Cape Cod. This was something of a moral victory for him, since he had always claimed that if he had played the lead on Broadway instead of Otto Kreuger, the play would have been a hit.

But none of his television appearances was received with any enthusiasm from either critics or viewers.

By 1965 he was in semi-retirement. He spent his mornings

reading, writing funny letters to his friends around the globe, practising the guitar and dabbling in literature. His autobiography, *Groucho and Me*, had been published in 1960 and sold well enough to be included in the *New York Times* best-seller list for several weeks. This inspired his publisher, Bernard Geis, to get out a collection of Groucho's funny magazine pieces, under the title *Memoirs of a Mangy Lover*, in 1964. Its title was probably the funniest thing about the book, which, though it contained a few humorous observations about life, was not up to his usual high standards.

He spent his lunches either at Nate 'n' Al's Delicatessen in Beverly Hills with a few of his cronies such as Harry Ruby or Nunnally Johnson, or sitting around the Comedians' Round Table at Hillcrest Country Club exchanging wisecracks with Jack Benny, George Burns, Danny Kaye, Danny Thomas and George Jessel.

Although he had been friends with George Burns since their vaudeville days, my father, now that he was out of work, became extremely resentful of Burns's success. And for some reason, he was especially vulnerable to Burns's mischievous brand of kidding. Once, Burns and Groucho got into an argument over who was the funniest man ever.

'I think Charlie Chaplin was,' ventured Burns.

'I disagree,' said Groucho. 'I think I am.'

'Well, if you think you are,' retorted Burns, 'then I must be because I know I'm funnier than you.'

The other comedians roared with laughter, upsetting my father so that he didn't speak to Burns for weeks.

Next to ribbing my father, Burns's favourite Round Table feature was the chef's broiled sea bass, and he would order it without fail whenever it appeared on the menu. And every time Burns told the waiter, 'I'll have the sea bass,' Groucho would sing a parody of the old Sophie Tucker song: 'If you can't see mama every night, you can't see mama at all.' When Burns ordered sea bass, that was my father's cue to start singing, 'If you can't see bass every night, you can't see bass at all.'

The first time Groucho burst into song, Burns thought the

play on words mildly amusing. But after a year and a half, it began to wear a little thin.

Finally Burns believed he had a solution. The next time the waiter took his order, Burns pulled his head down and whispered into his ear very softly. 'I'll have the sea bass.' Without a moment's hesitation, the waiter sang back at him, 'If you can't see bass every night, you can't see bass at all.' Burns switched to whitefish.

In the evenings, Groucho either went to the movies or stayed home and watched television with Eden and any friends he might have invited over to dinner.

In the winter, he spent some of his weekends in the small cottage he had bought in Palm Springs, out by Tamarask Country Club, a section of the desert to which Harpo, Gummo and Zeppo had already retired and where they lived full time.

At the Springs, he whiled away his time riding his bicycle or hacking his way around the golf course with his brothers. His game hadn't improved any in the twenty-odd years since he had thrown his clubs over the cliff in Monterey and renounced golf for good. But in Palm Springs, there was little else to do.

Being a desert rat wasn't a bad life. He particularly enjoyed Harpo's company. But when Harpo died, following open heart surgery in September 1964, Groucho, who was more broken up than I'd ever seen him, lost his taste for the desert. Without Harpo's clowning to make him laugh, he felt he had no more reason to go to Palm Springs. It contained too many memories that saddened him. Zeppo and Gummo were still there and alive, of course, but he didn't enjoy their company as much. There was something special about his relationship with Harpo.

With his two favourite brothers gone, together with many of his contemporaries, such as George Kaufman, and his best friend Norman Krasna residing permanently in Switzerland, Groucho had to turn more and more to his family for company.

Unfortunately, his marriage to Eden was going the way of his other two marriages. Eden, as I have said, was no match for my father intellectually. She couldn't stand up to him under the barrage of insults that he bombarded her with in the name of humour.

From what I could observe, Eden wanted to be a credit to Groucho. She embarked on a curriculum of study in an effort to develop her own intellect, but he invariably had a devastating comment to make. When she took up French, he told her that she didn't speak it as well as de Gaulle. When she began studying the piano, he complained that her teacher was trying to seduce her. 'He keeps feeling your leg when you're on the piano stool with him,' he commented, sometimes right in front of the teacher.

Eden gave up the piano when the music teacher died, and started to take acting lessons from Jeff Cory, one of Hollywood's leading coaches. After appearing in her first production, in a small non-equity house in Hollywood, Eden invited the members of the cast (plus Cory) home for a nightcap. Groucho was furious that these actors, only a step above amateurs, had come into his house while he was asleep and drunk his liquor, and he told Eden that she'd have to choose either to be a housewife or an actress. She couldn't be both. (Actually, he was jealous of Cory, a younger man than himself, believing that Eden had a crush on him.)

As a result, Eden retired from the theatre and returned to painting. My father encouraged this pastime, because she could do it at home and not leave him alone in the evenings. He even offered to pay for an exhibition of her paintings at the Hammer Galleries in New York City. But Eden didn't believe she was ready for this yet, and turned the offer down.

As my father chipped away at Eden's self-confidence, she turned to alcohol for an escape. But even had they been intellectual equals, and even had she been able to hold her own in those witty conversations that took place at my father's dinner parties, there still would have been problems caused by the huge discrepancy in their ages.

Like Ruth and Kay before her, Eden liked to go out on the town at night rather than stay home and watch television and go to bed at ten. Although Groucho frequently confided in me that he didn't mind if she went out by herself occasionally, I don't think he really meant it, judging by his reaction to *The Cannibals*, a *roman à clef* written by actor Keith Brasselle and published in 1968. In this trashy story, two of its main characters — an elderly comedian with a young wife — bear a startling resemblance to Groucho and Eden. The book's protagonist, a young entertainer, revenges himself on the ageing comedian by seducing his young wife.

Groucho's own confidence was shattered when he read the book, even though Eden denied that anything like that had ever happened. I'm not sure whether he believed her or not, but his reaction was to throw the offending book into the living-room fireplace and never mention the episode again. The episode certainly belied what he had told me about not caring whether Eden had outside affairs.

From that point on, their marriage went rapidly down hill, although they managed to stay together until the following January.

Melinda, now twenty-two, was also beginning to give Groucho sleepless nights. Failing to recognize that she was no major acting talent, he'd been encouraging her Thespian career ever since she was five years old, when they had sung an Irving Berlin number together on *You Bet Your Life*.

In addition to putting her on his own programme a number of times over the fourteen years he'd been on the air, he'd also insisted, whenever he made a TV or movie deal, that Melinda be given some kind of a bit part in it. In addition to giving her prime-time exposure, it was also a way of saving tax dollars. He'd take less than his usual asking price and give the difference to Melinda as her salary.

Her appearance on the tube actually led to Melinda receiving a call from an independent movie producer named Mack Gilbert, whose father owned a large shoe store in Columbus, Ohio, Gilbert cast Melinda as the romantic lead in a cheap budget film called *No Deposit, No Return*. Before the film was half completed, Melinda accepted Gilbert's proposal of marriage. Groucho was delighted. Not only did his prospective son-in-law come from a family with money, but he also was a Gilbert & Sullivan addict.

As the father of the bride, Groucho threw a $10,000 wedding and reception on 8 December 1968, at his Trousdale house, inviting all his and the groom's friends and relatives. It was the glitziest wedding ever to take place in the Marx family, and half of Hollywood was there when the proud father solemnly (for him) walked his daughter to the altar.

Two weeks after the wedding, Melinda left Gilbert and ran off with her long-haired leading man in the film, Sanh Berti. 'The marriage was so short,' quipped George Jessel, 'that the bride got custody of the wedding cake.'

Groucho was understandably upset, but he was enough of a realist to know that 'these things happen' – especially in the Marx family.

By then he had recovered from the trauma of my divorce and remarriage to my erstwhile sister-in-law. Despite his lingering friendship with Grace Kahn, he openly admitted that he had misjudged Lois, and that his son could have searched the world over and not found a more caring, loyal and attractive wife.

In addition, he had seen me enjoy the biggest success of my career up to that point.

With Lois's daughter, Linda, as my inspiration, I wrote, with my collaborator, Robert Fisher, a comedy about her called *The Impossible Years*, which opened on Broadway in 1965 and ran until the end of 1967. MGM had also made it into a successful film starring the late David Niven.

A success on Broadway was just the kind of thing to impress Groucho. He didn't come to the opening in October, claiming, 'It'll be too hard on my nerves.' Which I could understand, because it certainly was hard on mine. At the same time I wondered if his reluctance to be there on opening night might have been motivated by a little professional jealousy. Even before our New York opening *The Impossible Years* had been heralded as a hit, for it had broken box office records in Philadelphia, New Haven and Boston. By the time we opened in New York, we had a nine-month advance sale and had already sold it to MGM for $300,000.

So even though there was no guarantee that the New York critics would like it, the play was assured of being a financial success — which was more than could be said for Groucho's only attempt at playwriting, *Time for Elizabeth*.

Still, having a hit on Broadway was a hollow victory if I couldn't get my own father to see the show. But Groucho finally came through, like the loyal father I'd always hoped to have.

Shortly after the beginning of the new year, my father couldn't contain his curiosity any longer. He fabricated a reason for going to New York on business, and told me he expected 'good seats, and for nothing' to *The Impossible Years*.

I immediately phoned the box office to make sure they gave him my house seats and charged them to me.

A week later, Groucho flew back into town.

'How'd you like the show?' I asked.

'It's a hell of a funny evening in the theatre,' he replied, without a moment's hesitation. 'The most laughs I've had in a long time.'

I couldn't believe it. There wasn't even a qualifying statement.

'There's just one trouble,' he suddenly added, after I thought I was home and dry. 'The management tried to charge me for the tickets.'

'Well, I told them not to let you pay,' I explained, feeling embarrassed. 'The dumb girl at the box office must have slipped up.'

'That's all right,' he said. 'I finally got in for nothing.'

'How?'

'I demanded to see the manager. And when he came out in the lobby. I yelled at him in front of all those people milling around, "I'm not paying money to see this turkey. You know who I am? I'm Arthur Marx's father!"'

My status in the Marx family did get a boost with the success of *The Impossible Years*. To my uncles, I was no longer just their nephew the tennis player who was always losing in the finals of a tennis tournament when they were sitting in the grandstand — I was the author of a Broadway hit, to which everybody expected free tickets.

And Groucho paid me the supreme compliment.

He invited me out to lunch, and insisted that I pick up the bill.

34

Groucho's fortunes continued to slide. By January 1969, he was in no demand at all, making his retirement more or less mandatory. Not that he was bothered by that any longer. On the following 2 October he'd be seventy-nine years old. That was old enough to retire without having to make explanations to his peers at The Round Table. And financially he was set for the rest of his life, even if he lived to a hundred. His income from NBC had been spread out over thirty years, so that even though he was no longer doing *You Bet Your Life* money from it kept rolling in.

Two things were preventing him from enjoying his sunset years: he had a chronic bladder problem, resulting from a flawed prostate operation when he was in his sixties. A second operation a few years later only compounded the problem, and a third operation was required. His regular doctor believed that he was too old to undergo any further surgery. He never complained about this condition, except to me, so most of his friends – and also the public – believed he was in excellent health for a man of his age.

As if his physical condition wasn't debilitating enough, his emotions took a severe blow when Eden surprised no one (except Groucho) by packing her bags and walking out on 7 January, and serving him with divorce papers the next day. In her divorce complaint she asked for half of the four million dollars she claimed he had accumulated during their fourteen-year marriage.

Despite his outward cynicism about women and their predatory motives, Groucho, deep down, was a romantic. He truly believed that Eden still loved him, and was deeply hurt and surprised by her decision to walk out on him.

At the time that it happened – early evening – he was in bed with a bad cold, and I was at General Service Studios in

Hollywood, working with Desi Arnez on the filming of a part of the *Mothers In Law* TV show that my partner and I had written. Suddenly I was called away from the set by Desi's assistant, who said, 'Your father's on the phone, and he wants to speak to you. He says it's an emergency.'

As I picked up the receiver, I heard Groucho say, 'Hello, Art?' He sounded on the verge of tears. 'I have to talk to you. Eden just walked out on me.' He was so forlorn that I felt like shedding a few tears myself. The only other time in my life that I'd ever seen him cry was when he received news of Harpo's death.

I was not surprised by Eden's departure, even though at a party a year before, she had told Lois and me, in a very frank confession induced by several martinis, 'I've waited this long. I might as well stick it out all the way.'

'Can you come up to the house?' asked Groucho. 'I need company. Badly.'

'I can't right now,' I told him. 'We're shooting our show and Desi wants us here. We won't be finished until after midnight.'

'Well, come when you can,' he said, putting down the receiver.

I phoned Lois, and she went over to Groucho's house and kept him company until he fell asleep.

'He's a wreck,' Lois told me when I got home at two in the morning. 'I really feel sorry for him.'

He was even more of a wreck after Eden's high-priced attorney, Marvin Mitchelson, filed papers in court, charging Groucho with an uncontrollable temper and alleging that he had threatened to kill her on one occasion.

I doubted that charge, for I'd never seen him lose his temper. I'd seen him angry, but as far as I knew, the only person he'd ever threatened to kill was himself, after he lost all his money in the 1929 stock market crash.

Along with her allegations of physical violence, Eden asked for a division of their community property, which she said was in excess of three million dollars, and $5500 monthly alimony, plus possession of the Trousdale house, valued at $350,000.

After the initial shock, Groucho claimed not to be worried

about Eden's financial demands. His ace-in-the-hole, he figured, was an agreement he had persuaded her to sign before he married her. According to that, she'd take none of his assets, and only enough alimony to provide her with food and shelter.

Mitchelson, however, claimed that a pre-nuptial agreement would never hold up in court if a couple had been married as long as Groucho and Eden had. But Groucho believed he had even more ammunition. In addition to the pre-nuptial agreement, he had fairly good evidence that Eden had been having an affair with her acting coach. Provided he had actual proof, that charge might have helped his cause before 1 January 1970. On that date the 'no fault' divorce law was to go into effect in California, making it irrelevant whether or not either partner was having outside sexual relations.

Since there was no possibility of a contested divorce hearing being held before the law was changed, Groucho took his attorney's advice and capitulated to most of Eden's demands. He wound up giving her close to a million dollars, but not the house with the round bathtub.

As I mentioned earlier, Groucho's never been one to hold grudges. He's always remained on friendly terms with his ex-wives, no matter what they accused him of in court, or how many pounds of flesh their attorneys tried to exact. He continued to pay my own mother alimony, even after she had remarried and legally was entitled to no more.

He invited Kay, Melinda's mother, to stay with him and Eden and Melinda in a house he had rented on the Rhode Island seashore while he was appearing there in *Time for Elizabeth* in stock, so she could be with her daughter. He paid all her medical and dental expenses, and he financed her stay in a sanatorium to kick the drinking habit, which she eventually did.

Consequently, it was no surprise to me to find out a few months after his divorce from Eden, that he was dating her occasionally.

'How can you keep taking her out, after what's she's done

to you?' film producer Irwin Allen asked Groucho one evening. 'What have you two got to talk about?'

'There's a wealth of material,' explained Groucho blithely. 'We talk over our old fights.'

All through 1968 and the early part of 1969, I'd heard vague talk from my father about a Broadway musical Arthur Whitelaw, producer of *You're a Good Man, Charlie Brown*, was planning to do on the lives of the Marx Brothers.

'Neil Simon's going to write the book,' Groucho told me.

'That's nice,' I replied. 'It should be a big hit.'

A few weeks later, while Lois and I were having dinner with him at his house, he handed me a script in a spring-back binder and said, 'This is *Minnie's Boys*. Tell me what you think of it. Take it home and read it.'

I opened it up to the title page and was surprised to see it hadn't been written by Neil Simon at all, but by comedian David Steinberg.

'What happened to Neil Simon?' I asked.

'He turned it down,' said Groucho, somewhat embarrassed. 'So we decided to give Steinberg a crack at it. He's a pretty funny writer and he likes the Marx Brothers.'

'Why David Steinberg? What's he written?'

'Nothing. But he's a very funny comedian.'

I was slightly annoyed that my father had gone from Neil Simon to Steinberg without even considering my partner and me for the job. After all, we'd had a hit that lasted on Broadway for three seasons. 'Why didn't you ask us?'

'Tell me what you think of it,' he said, avoiding my question.

After taking it home and reading it, I phoned him the next morning and said I didn't like it.

'That's what I think,' he said. 'Amateur night.'

I let the matter drop. But a few days later I received a phone call from Arthur Whitelaw, asking me if my partner and I would consider doing a new book for the musical.

When I asked him why he hadn't come to us in the first place, he explained that he had wanted to, having enjoyed our first play. But that my father wouldn't permit it. 'He said he didn't believe in nepotism,' explained Whitelaw.

'That never stopped him from putting Melinda on his show,' I said. 'What's changed him?'

Whitelaw smiled and said, 'Frankly, we can't get anybody else to do it. At least nobody as qualified and who knows the Marx Brothers as well as you two.'

At the time I was flattered. Also pleased. So my collaborator and I embarked on the project with great enthusiasm. But a year later, when we opened at New York's Imperial Theater on 45th Street, in the midst of a raging snow storm, with a star who didn't belong in the show at all, and hostile critics everywhere the eye could see, I realized how wise Neil Simon was to have turned down the project.

Although I hadn't foreseen it at the time, the whole notion of doing a musical about the Marx Brothers was fraught with peril, if not madness. Who but the Marx Brothers themselves were funny enough and talented enough musically to play the Marx Brothers?

I should have paid attention to a comment Larry Gelbart – author of *On the Way to the Forum* and the hit TV series *M.A.S.H.* – once made about musicals. When someone asked him what should be done to Hitler if they ever captured him alive, he said, 'Send him on the road with a musical.'

Bob and I had no trouble knocking out an acceptable first draft. We did that in about six weeks. Arthur Whitelaw was pleased. So were the song writers, Larry Grossman and Hal Hackaday.

In late spring the three of them came to my house in Bel Air, where we did the finishing touches on the libretto. The problems started there. Although Arthur Whitelaw liked what we had written, he didn't think the second act should be as 'realistic' as the first act. He insisted on its being done in some kind of free-form nonsense that the choreographer and director would work out when we were in rehearsal. Bob and I figured he knew what he was doing. After all, he had been responsible for producing other hits, so we let him have his way.

Another mistake he made was giving Groucho the title of

'production consultant'. My father, by the summer of 1969, was in no shape to be consulted about anything. In addition to his bladder problem, he'd been slowed down by several minor strokes, which had brought him to the brink of senility. He was frail and painfully thin. In his seventy-ninth year, he was forgetful, repeated himself constantly, and had to wear a hearing aid, which was concealed in the ear piece of his spectacles.

Aware of all this, Whitelaw was smart enough to keep Groucho away from our script conferences (he didn't even let him read the finished libretto), but he was more or less bound by his contract to give him some sort of say in the casting of his mother Minnie, which was the starring role.

Arthur Whitelaw had his heart set on the late comedienne, Totie Fields, playing Minnie. She was not only funny, but she could sing and dance.

But my father became enraged when he got wind of Whitelaw's casting idea. 'I won't have that Jew broad playing my mother,' he yelled at me over the phone when I called him from Reno, where I had flown with Whitelaw to see Totie in her night-club act, and had got her verbal acceptance to play the part.

'What are you talking about?' I said. 'Aren't the Marx Brothers Jewish?'

'Yes,' he replied, 'but the world thinks we're Italian.' And he wasn't trying to be funny.

He wasn't anti-Semitic. He donated money to Jewish charities, paid lip service to all the Jewish causes, was outraged by what Hitler and Mussolini had done to the Jews. He was all for the Jews having a homeland in Israel. And he loved a good corned beef sandwich on rye with a kosher pickle washed down with Dr Brown's celery tonic.

But he wasn't proud to be a Jew. He never sent any of his children to Temple, claiming that all 'organized religion is hogwash'. He never married a Jewish woman or got married by a rabbi. Perhaps his denial of being Jewish stemmed from the fact that when he was a kid growing up in a tough upper East Side New York neighbourhood, the Irish were the dominant race on his block and were always beating up on the Jewish kids.

But whatever his real feelings about the Jews, my father remained adamant about not casting Totie and eventually Whitelaw, who was afraid to jeopardize his relationship with Groucho, gave in.

Later in the summer, Whitelaw hired Shelley Winters, who physically fitted my father's image of his blonde, Germanic-looking mother, to play Minnie. My father was delighted to have the two-time Oscar winner in the show. But ironically, Winters ended up looking and sounding more Jewish in the role than ever Totie Fields would have done.

During most of the rehearsal period, Arthur Whitelaw, recognizing the shape my father was in, kept him on the West coast by telling him that everything was going smoothly and that we didn't need him for consultation. But somehow my father got wind of the fact in early January that *Minnie's Boys* was in trouble (which it was), and the next thing we knew he had flown East, checked into the Regency Hotel and started attending every rehearsal. His contribution, unfortunately, turned out to be more destructive than helpful. All he wanted to do was sit on stage and reminisce about the Marx Brothers' early days in show business. His anecdotes were often amusing, but they only served to slow down our progress and confuse the cast. Desperate to keep Groucho away from rehearsals without offending him, Whitelaw finally had to pay one of his attractive female secretaries to take him on long walks around the block or through Times Square whenever we didn't want his interference.

One of the show's problems was our book, for which Bob and I take only part of the blame. The first act, written in old-fashioned vaudeville style in keeping with the material – the rags-to-riches ascendancy of the Marx Brothers – seemed to work, as far as we could tell from the way Shelley Winters was handling her lines. She never delivered a line the same way twice, making it impossible to know if a joke was any good or not.

But even before our first preview, we realized the second act, written in a completely different style as per Arthur Whitelaw's instructions, didn't work, and would have to be rewritten. Whitelaw agreed with us, but our director didn't. So he was fired, and Whitelaw hired Stanley Prager. The new director put Bob and me immediately to work writing an outline for a new second act. If he approved it, we were prepared to go ahead and start writing the dialogue. Quite by accident, I discovered that Whitelaw and Prager, behind our backs, were paying Joe Stein, author of *Fiddler on the Roof*, to rewrite the second act from *our* outline.

Bob and I confronted Whitelaw about his unethical behaviour. His excuse was that the morale of the cast was so low that the only way to lift their spirits was to hire a 'big name' playwright like Joe Stein to work with them. The logic was that if Stein thought the show had enough of a future for him to work on it, then it still had a chance of success and everybody could stop panicking.

Reluctantly, we went along with this.

By now the show was in a shambles, in our opinion. Anything was worth a try. Unfortunately Joe Stein wasn't a miracle worker. The new jokes he wrote couldn't change Shelley Winters' uncertain performance. When she couldn't remember a line, she'd stutter a lot, until she could come up with the proper words. When told that was not the way to do jokes, she claimed it was her 'method acting' approach, which gave her performance realism. Method acting might have worked in a Tennessee Williams play, but not in what was supposed to be a slam bang old-fashioned Marx Brothers musical.

In February, when we started previewing in front of paid audiences, Winters still didn't know her lines and actually came on stage with the book in hand to read from.

At that point, Arthur Whitelaw had had enough. He decided to fire her and hire Totie Fields, who was still keen to play the role of Minnie. He was desperate enough about his investment not to give a damn any more about what Groucho thought.

Shelley Winters blamed her poor performance on a case of the flu, which she couldn't shake off. In any case, it turned out she couldn't be fired because, contractually, Whitelaw would have had to pay her $300,000 in cash if he wished to replace her. Our production no longer had that kind of cash in its coffers. It was lucky if it had enough cash to build sets for the new second act.

Despite the obstacles, we began to see minute improvements with each preview once Shelley had recovered from the flu and returned to work. What was more reassuring, the preview audiences seemed to enjoy the show. Joe Stein took all the credit for this. This infuriated my father, who, in one of the rare moments I'd ever heard him stick up for me, lashed out at Stein's boasting one night in Luchow's Restaurant. 'What the fuck are you talking about, Joe — you wrote the show? My son and his partner wrote it. You just added a few jokes. And not very good ones, in my opinion.'

It was gratifying to hear Groucho say that. For the first time in many months I felt like giving him a hug.

I felt less like giving him a hug after I learned that he had been going around Manhattan telling all his friends and newspaper columnists that *Minnie's Boys* 'looks like a real turkey'. He even told John Lahr, critic on *The Village Voice*. Not that he wasn't entitled to an opinion; he should just have kept it to himself. When word circulated through the theatrical community that even Groucho didn't like the show, the adverse publicity spread like a measles epidemic.

When we finally opened, on 26 March 1970, the word was already out that we had a 'bomb' on our hands. Notwithstanding, the show went ahead in front of a celebrity-packed audience. Zeppo and Gummo were there. And so was Groucho's ex-wife Eden Hartford, whom my father flew East to be at his side on opening night.

Everything clicked into place that night. Shelley Winters wasn't half bad. But what made the show was Lew Stadlin's brilliant portrayal of Groucho. After the final curtain call, which included several standing ovations for Stadlin, Groucho was brought on stage to say a few words.

Looking old, frail and ill, he said to Lew Stadlin, 'You're better than I was.' He rambled on after that, praising a few others in the cast, and then started talking about how uncomfortable it was to be walking around with a catheter in him.

Following that, there was the usual opening night party to

wait for the critics' verdict as to whether we had a hit or not. The audience reaction had been so enthusiastic that we were fooled into thinking that somehow we'd turned a turkey into a hit. But unfortunately Clive Barnes on *The Times* didn't like the show – particularly the music. Strangely enough, all the rest of the reviews were favourable. But a rap from *The New York Times* was all that was needed to kill us off. *Minnie's Boys* closed on 30 May, after twenty previews and sixty regular performances, with a loss of over $500,000.

Naturally I was as disappointed that I couldn't give my father a successful show, as he was by the fact that his son had written a flop. Not that he ever mentioned it. He was too wrapped up in his other troubles brought on by advancing age.

35

Lois and I flew back to California the morning after we read Clive Barnes's review, and opened up our house again. After six months in New York without an income, we were pretty broke. And having been out of television for nearly nine months Bob and I couldn't even rustle up a television assignment.

However, we had a new play called *The Chic Life* that we had tried out the previous summer in stock, and that seemed fairly promising. Consequently, we weren't too discouraged about our playwriting careers.

But Groucho didn't seem to have anything to look forward to.

Back in California, he had to adjust to rattling around in a huge house by himself, except for his cook-housekeeper, Martha Brooks. Having been with my father through his last two marriages, this white-haired black lady quickly became his closest confidante.

On the evenings when he was home by himself, he'd shuffle into the kitchen after dinner while Martha was cleaning up, seat himself at the table, and tell her the happenings of the day and ask her advice about things.

Although his career was just about over, he still received mountains of fan mail, which, in his precarious state of health, he didn't have the energy to answer. He just let the mail pile up in what formerly had been Eden's studio.

During the day, he would very often have lunch with Arthur Sheekman, Nunnally Johnson and Harry Ruby, and sometimes even with me. But in the evenings when all his friends went home to their wives, he was very often alone, with just Martha and his television set.

Lois and I would invite him to our house at least once a week, but he generally turned us down because he didn't like to drive in the hills of Bel Air at night. Even when he was young and in good health he couldn't find his way very easily. But now, without a wife to guide him and read the street signs, he would become totally confused. Rather than risk losing his way, he chose to stay home alone. He was too proud to call up his friends and admit he was too old to drive and ask to be picked up. He was also too proud to admit he was in need of company.

Compounding the problem, he flunked his driver's licence test, in spite of the fact that he bribed the examiner with an autographed picture of himself, an autographed book, and several dozen expensive cigars. 'Not the cheap ones I usually give away,' he complained. 'And he still wouldn't pass me.'

The fact that he was no longer permitted to drive heightened the realization that he was truly getting old, and he began to disintegrate completely.

His worsening bladder condition, of course, contributed to the feeling that life was really not worth living. I remember him telling me in a moment of despair: 'What's the use of living? I can't drink. I can't smoke. I can't fuck. I can't even go to the bathroom without this damn catheter in me. Just to have another dinner at Chasen's? Who cares?'

For a while in 1970 he became a recluse. Lois and I tried to talk him into seeing another doctor. Perhaps an operation could solve his problem. But he stubbornly maintained that his own doctor said he was too old to go through a major operation. He was liable to die on the operating table.

Lois and I sought advice from Joe Kaufman, a friend of ours who was the head of urology at UCLA. He seemed to think that if my father's heart was in good condition, which it was, that there was no reason why he couldn't survive an operation on his bladder. Joe had successfully operated on men of his age many times.

We relayed this information to my father, who resisted doing anything about it for several months. I gave up trying to persuade him. But Lois persisted. One night in September 1970, while we were having dinner at his house and he repeated what his own doctor had told him, Lois said, 'But you said you don't want to go on living like this. You're not having any fun.'

He thought about it a moment, then said, 'You're right. I'd just as soon die on the operating table as live this way. Maybe I'll go see your friend Kaufman.'

We phoned Kaufman that night, and made an appointment for Groucho to be examined by him the following afternoon.

Lois and I drove him to UCLA and waited while he was being examined. Two hours later it was all decided. Kaufman told him that he had a ninety percent chance of surviving, as his heart was good and so were his other vital organs.

'There's no reason why you shouldn't have ten more good years in front of you,' said Kaufman.

'Let's do it,' exclaimed Groucho. 'Just be sure to get me a pretty nurse.'

The operation was performed on 23 September, and was totally successful. Not only was he strong enough to survive a two-hour operation, but he was out of bed that same evening, walking up and down the corridor on the VIP floor of the UCLA medical centre, wisecracking with the other patients and making passes at all the pretty nurses.

Home again, he was in much more sanguine spirits. But he was still lonely, and still too proud to ask us what we were doing on the nights he was alone and craved company.

On the night before his eightieth birthday, he phoned Melinda and invited her to come to a celebration dinner next day. When he told her that in addition to Lois and me, Eden would be there, Melinda refused to attend.

Annoyed, Groucho said, 'Nobody's going to tell me who I can have to dinner in my own house,' and he hung up. It might seem mean of Melinda not to attend his birthday dinner, but I could understand her feelings about Eden. After all the terrible things Eden had accused our father of when she was divorcing him, why was she suddenly being pally again? It even infuriated Irwin Allen, who was at the dinner. He took Eden aside that night, and said to her, 'What are you doing – coming back for the other million?'

When I asked Groucho myself why he kept seeing Eden, he replied rather pathetically, 'Look, what kind of a girl will go out with an eighty-year-old man?'

Realizing the extent of his loneliness, Lois and I bought a six-week-old white poodle bitch at the Farmer's Market and gave her to Groucho for a birthday present. He'd never been much of a dog lover, because he'd never learnt how to house-train an animal.

Now, however, he seemed delighted with the dog, and he immediately named her Elsie. For several days, she was his constant companion. She ate with him, slept with him and followed him to the mailbox every morning when he strolled out to see what the postman had left. But just when we thought Elsie had solved the problem, Groucho phoned our house one afternoon, and in between sobs, blurted out that the mailman's truck had accidentally backed up over Elsie when the two of them were out at the kerb getting the mail, and killed her. He had picked up the poor animal and had Martha drive him and Elsie to the vet. But there was nothing the vet could do. Elsie was dead on arrival.

Groucho said that he was so upset he couldn't possibly eat dinner by himself that night. We'd have to go over and keep him company.

Lois suddenly remembered seeing a litter of white poodle pups at the Clip Joint, where we had our own poodles groomed. She called up the owner and asked him if he had any puppies left. 'Just one,' he said. 'A female.'

'Well, I want her,' said Lois. 'I'll be right down to buy her.'

The puppy looked like Elsie's twin. Lois bought her on the spot, and immediately drove to Groucho's house. He was taking a nap in his armchair when she arrived, so she tiptoed into his room and put the puppy on his lap. Awakening, he smiled at the furry white bundle, picked her up in both hands, and said, 'This is the best present I ever had.'

He immediately named her Elsie the Second, and his spirits rose again.

That night at dinner, he said to us, 'You know, when that dog was killed, I felt worse than when Harpo and Chico died.'

Later that night, the three of us went to a re-run of Chaplin's *Modern Times*.

'I'm a member of the Academy,' he said to the girl in the box office. 'Can we get in for nothing?'

'This isn't an Academy showing,' she said. 'Why should I let you in for nothing?'

'Because I'm Groucho Marx – a living legend.'

She nervously consulted the manager, who shook my father's hand and let the three of us in without paying.

Groucho might have been old, and on the verge of senility, but he still knew how to save a buck.

Being a living legend was no cure for loneliness. Neither was having a French poodle that not only couldn't talk to him, but which refused to be house-trained. Six weeks after we gave him Elsie the Second he telephoned us and said, 'How would you like another poodle? I can't handle Elsie any longer.' Groucho was back to Martha Brooks for steady company.

Because of our own commitments, Lois and I couldn't be with him every night. Melinda was married and living in Mendocino in Northern California with her second husband and first child, Miles. Partly because she couldn't afford it, and partly because her relationship with her father wasn't that good, she made the trip to Southern California infrequently. After a small stroke in 1971, which impaired his mind and slowed down his speech, even his good friends, much as they loved him, weren't as keen to be in his company as they had been when he was in full command of his faculties.

And much as Groucho loved Martha, she could never take the place of what he considered to be the ideal companion: 'A girl who looks like Marilyn Monroe and talks like George Kaufman.'

As a result, my eighty-one-year-old father was as vulnerable as a duck in a shooting gallery when he received a phone call from television producer Jerry Davis in August 1971, inviting him to dinner. It seemed that Davis's wife had a girl-friend visiting from New York who was a fan of Groucho's and who had expressed a desire to meet him. Would he like to meet *her*? Her name was Erin Fleming.

36

At the time she met Groucho, Erin Fleming was twenty-nine. She was born in Ontario, Canada, and her father was a physician. She'd always wanted to be an actress, so she migrated to Manhattan. She was married briefly to a lawyer for a New York labour union. She had a nervous breakdown after failing to get a part in a Broadway play, and consequently spent a few months in a sanatorium in either Connecticut or upstate New York. And before leaving for California she had acquired something of a reputation around Manhattan for erratic behaviour and exhibitionism.

Between 1969 and 1971, she had lived in an apartment building on Manhattan's East Side – the same building in which television writer Tony Webster and composer Burt Bacharach also had apartments.

Another writer who lived in the same building told me of an occasion when he was working on the Kraft Music Hall with Webster in the latter's apartment.

'Tony was kind of a square,' recalls the writer, 'but he was between girls and wanted to meet someone. So I told Erin about him and told her to come to the apartment one morning to meet Tony. When she knocked, Tony was at the typewriter, so I went to the door. I was shocked to see Erin standing there stark naked. Without saying a word, she walked right in and sat down in a chair, facing Webster. Webster was embarrassed, too, but he tried to play it cool and went right on typing.'

According to Webster's collaborator she pulled a similar stunt with Burt Bacharach: one morning he opened the door in response to the bell, and found Erin, stark naked with an empty cup in her hand. 'I'd like to borrow a cup of sugar,' she said in the baby voice she used when she wanted to be sweet and charming.

'That story livened up a lot of dinner-table conversations around New York,' recalls the writer today.

In brief, that was Erin Fleming's résumé up until she met Groucho at Jerry Davis's.

No matter how well that first evening at the Davises went – and it must have gone swimmingly, because in a matter of days Groucho had hired her to be his secretary, to supervise the answering of the hundreds of fan letters that were cluttering up his house – my father had no intention of ever marrying again. He didn't want to risk another divorce and have to part with more of his money.

What he was looking for was just companionship, without commitment. 'For that, you need a different kind of girl,' he had said in an interview he had given to the *Berkeley Barb*, an underground newspaper in the San Francisco Bay area, before meeting Erin Fleming in 1971. 'You need a girl who normally you wouldn't marry, or you wouldn't try to lay. But if a fellow gets both, he's a very fortunate man. If he gets a woman he enjoys sitting with and talking to and she understands what he's saying, he's a lucky fellow. You see, I don't believe there's such a thing as love. I believe two people can like each other, and I think that's more important than love. Love just means going to bed and fucking. You can get that anywhere, if you're young and partially attractive.'

Judging from what Groucho said in the rest of the interview, he needed more than a companion. He needed a manager and/or keeper to prevent him from saying things that got him into deep trouble. On the subject of politicians, he said, 'I think the only hope this country has is Nixon's assassination.'

In the United States, it is, of course, a Federal crime even to suggest such a thing, and Groucho wouldn't have said such a thing, even in jest, had he known the two long-haired reporters he was talking with were from the *Berkeley Barb*, a paper renowned for its left-wing anti-establishment views. In his confused mind he somehow believed his interviewers were from *Esquire Magazine*, which he figured would never publish such a remark, at least not without asking permission to quote it.

Within hours after the Nixon remark was published, it went out on all the wire services. It was also picked up by *The New York Times*, *Time*, and *Newsweek*. Before Groucho realized it, he was the centre of a storm and the subject of a Federal investigation for conspiracy.

In his inevitable comic style, Groucho defended himself by saying, 'I deny everything, because I never tell the truth. I lie about everything I do or say — about men, women or any other sex.'

Yet his disclaimer was not accepted by the Nixon administration, and in a file numbered CO 1297 009205 Groucho Marx was listed as a potential threat to the life of the President.

Later he complained that his telephone had been tapped. 'What can you expect from a President who has no sense of humour?' he said to me when we were discussing the incident, a few months before Erin Fleming came into his life.

Because she had no residence yet, Groucho willingly encouraged Erin to move into his Trousdale house during those first few months of their relationship when, as his 'secretary', she was getting his business affairs in order. Although she never officially lived there, she did sleep over occasionally in the guest room.

Groucho found it extremely pleasant to have a live-in companion to whom he didn't have to prove anything sexually.

Erin had found the key to an old actor's heart — flattery. She convinced him that he was not 'washed up', that there was still a demand for Groucho Marx, as proven by the sudden resurgence of popularity of Marx Brothers films, sparked, mainly, by the sixties generation of college kids, now thronging to see *Animal Crackers* and *Duck Soup*.

It never occurred to Groucho that Erin Fleming's interest in him might have been self-serving. Despite his protestations over the past that he didn't believe in 'love', it was apparent, not very many weeks into their relationship that Groucho, always a closet romantic, was very much in love with Erin Fleming, and that she was, as he said, 'stuck on me'.

But Erin's behaviour almost from the very beginning made it

pretty obvious, at least to me and my wife, that she had an ulterior motive in wanting to be Groucho Marx's 'companion'.

Lois and I met her for the first time one evening at Hillcrest Country Club, where Groucho had invited us to have dinner with him and the new girl he wanted us to meet, about whom he had only good things to say.

When he introduced us to her in the club's dining-room, I could see that Erin Fleming was young enough to interest him, with a fairly good figure and a face that bore a slight resemblance to the late English actress, Vivien Leigh's. She was dressed modestly, in a skirt and sweater, quite laid back, very respectful and very happy to meet us: 'Groucho's told me so much about you two.'

She certainly wasn't aggressive. If anything, she was prim and mousey, even to the point of refusing a drink. This made a good impression on Groucho, who, she must have known, would find teetotalism something of a rarity in a woman – at least among the ones he knew.

But after a few minutes of small talk, something that seemed to be troubling Groucho came to the surface.

Erin, he complained, had written a letter on his stationery to Bob Evans, President of Paramount Pictures, castigating the studio head for not giving her a part in a film her agent had suggested her for. 'What's worse,' said Groucho, 'she signed my name at the bottom and mailed it off to Evans without my permission.'

He was furious with Erin for doing this, claiming that she had now caused him to make an enemy of the most powerful studio head in the business.

He then pulled the letter out of his pocket and showed it to me, asking what I thought. I told him I had to agree with him. It wasn't a very smart thing for Erin to have done. But she just batted her eyes demurely and said she didn't believe it was so bad. Evans deserved it. Besides, Groucho Marx was world famous, he wasn't in any jeopardy, and just maybe the letter could do her some good.

Groucho doubted that. He said the letter put him in an embarrassing position, and how would he ever live it down?

The relationship between them seemed to be pretty uncomfortable during the rest of dinner. As they drove off later in his Mercedes, with Erin behind the wheel, I wouldn't have been surprised if he had booted her out of his life that night.

My wife's comment on the way home proved nearer the mark. 'You know something, Arthur,' she said to me, 'I don't trust that girl a bit. I think she's going to give us all a lot of trouble.'

37

During my life with Groucho, I'd seen him safely through a number of relationships with kooky girls who wanted to use him either as a stepping stone to stardom, or just as a means to get into the Hollywood fast lane. For instance there was the blonde, well-constructed tournament tennis player who was twenty when he was fifty-eight. There was the attractive, dark-haired, highly neurotic daughter of a Chicago department store owner, who had been one of the contestants on *You Bet Your Life*, and to whom Groucho had taken an immediate fancy and invited to dinner at his house all the time. This relationship ended when she embarrassed him by wearing décolleté dresses cut almost to her navel. There was the blonde lady who arrived unannounced on his doorstep one day bearing a bottle of cheap California wine and a honey cake she had baked expressly for him. 'I just thought you might be lonely,' she said, introducing herself. They went steady for several months, but when the lady mentioned the word 'marriage', Groucho told her to go peddle her honey cakes elsewhere. There was the brilliant but neurotic ex-wife of a world famous novelist who wound up incinerating herself by falling asleep in bed with a cigarette in her hand. There was the proprietress of a famous knit shop on Sunset Boulevard, who also made the mistake of mentioning the word 'marriage'. There was the well-known girl-about-Manhattan who was the love of Groucho's life until he discovered that she was the love of everyone else's life in the New York theatrical crowd, too. And there were a few others whom I've gladly forgotten.

But no woman ever succeeded in endangering my relationship with Groucho until Erin Fleming came along. In fact, I'd always been his confidant where his love life was concerned (even when I was an inexperienced fifteen-year-old). As a matter of fact, I'd been his confidant on most subjects, ranging from career problems to the travail he was having with my sisters, from his insomnia to how much money he had in the bank and to whom he was going to leave it when he died.

After his divorce from Eden, Groucho called me into his study one day and gave me the key to his front door, and the key to his desk, where he kept his will and a list of all his financial holdings, which amounted to approximately two million dollars, not counting his house. 'I'm not going to live forever,' he said, 'and I want you to know exactly where it's all going when I kick the bucket.'

There were no surprises in the will. Except for a ten thousand dollar bequest to Martha Brooks, his estate was divided equally between his three children. 'That should be about four hundred thousand each after taxes,' he said.

He even took me into his confidence and sought my advice during the first few months after Erin entered the scene. One afternoon I dropped into his house and found him and Erin in the midst of a heated argument.

Through his good friend Woody Allen, he had obtained Erin a two-minute part in the comedian's forthcoming comedy epic, *Everything You Wanted to Know About Sex But Were Afraid to Ask*.

Groucho was happy to have done that for her – until he read the script, which he had just finished before I arrived. He thought it sleazy and distasteful, particularly the 'Erection' sequence, the one involving Erin. She was to appear topless in the front seat of an automobile while she was having sex with her boyfriend.

'I can't believe that the movie business has come down to this,' he said.

Despite his strong objection, nothing was going to stop Erin from appearing in a Woody Allen film. And she did.

In an article about Groucho that was published in *Esquire* a few weeks later, he said, 'She does things in that film I've never been able to persuade her to do in the privacy of my own home.'

Early in 1972 Erin persuaded my father to hire Rogers and Cowan to do some advance publicity for his Carnegie Hall appearance in May. Their account had been turned over to Bill Feeder and Dale Olson, who also had Bud Yorkin and Norman Lear as their clients. After learning this, Erin was constantly after Olson to get her an introduction to Lear in hopes he might give her a part on one of his many TV series. 'I never did,' says Olson, 'but one day while Erin was in Bill Feeder's office next door to mine, with the door open, she heard my secretary call to me that Norman Lear was on the phone. While I was talking with Lear, Erin came running into my office and started taking off her clothes. I was naturally distracted and could hardly keep my mind on what Norman Lear was trying to tell me. Finally, when she was completely naked standing beside my desk, I was absolutely speechless. Lear said to me, "What's the matter, Dale?" And I said, "There's a girl here—Erin Fleming—taking off all her clothes. You know who she is?" And Norman said, "Yeah, that's the girl who's running around with Groucho." "That's right," I said. "What should I do?" And Lear said, "Hang up and screw her." I got rid of Lear as fast as I could and asked Erin what in hell she thought she was doing. And she said that she'd been trying to get me to tell Norman Lear about her for months, and I still hadn't. So she figured this would get my attention.'

My first major confrontation with Erin Fleming came as a result of Groucho's prospective Carnegie Hall engagement. Even before he had met Erin, the Carnegie Hall people had been after him to do a concert, but he had avoided a definite commitment because of his uncertain health, plus all the work involved preparing for a one-man show.

But once Erin took over his management, a deal was immediately firmed up. He was to get $10,000 for one performance. When a reporter asked him before the concert what he was going to do with the money, Groucho replied, 'I'll spend it on my secretary, which is a euphemism for this girl over here.'

Our argument came one night six weeks before the May

concert, when Lois and I were over at Groucho's house having dinner with him and Erin. The two of them were telling us with great excitement about the Carnegie Hall show and the record album deal they had also struck.

'What are you going to do on the show?' I asked him. When he said he hadn't decided yet, I suggested that he hire some writers. 'You can't just go out on the stage and ad lib,' I advised him.

'Why don't *you* write the show?' suggested Erin.

I thanked her, but said it would be better for my relationship with my father if he used writers other than his son. Besides, I was busy doing TV with Robert Fisher, my collaborator.

'I don't need writers,' he said. 'I'll just go out on the stage and start talking.'

'You can't do that,' I told him. 'Not in front of all those important critics.

'You'll make a fool of yourself.' At this point Erin lost her temper and accused me of trying to frighten him out of appearing, because I was 'jealous' of him.

I told her that I was in no way jealous of his performing, and that she should stop trying to make trouble between us.

She was rather cool to me for the rest of the evening. It was obvious she had a financial stake in bringing him out of retirement; also a professional one, for she hoped to play Margaret Dumont in the show.

If she thought she was helping the situation, she only exacerbated it when she invited us to dinner a couple of weeks later. She did not tell us that her psychiatrist, Milton Wexler, would be there. She wanted to spring him on us as a surprise.

It wasn't a surprise. We'd been tipped off about him by Martha, who'd phoned in the afternoon to warn us.

Lois and I were curious as to what Erin was trying to achieve by having her psychiatrist there, and so we turned up to have dinner with them, just as we had said we would, only we didn't let on immediately that we knew Wexler was a psychiatrist.

He turned out to be a tall, grey-haired, suave man in his sixties whom Erin introduced as 'my friend'. But when Groucho entered the den, where the four of us were gathered around the bar having drinks, he seemed uneasy about something. He didn't mention what it was, but something was bothering him.

I know one thing. He didn't have much respect for most psychiatrists.

After a few minutes of chit chat, the evening turned into a group therapy session. Wexler started off by telling me how much my father loved me and that I shouldn't try to prevent him from keeping the Carnegie Hall engagement. I said that wasn't my motive when I advised him he needed writers. I just didn't want him to humiliate himself in front of his New York friends such as Woody Allen, Neil Simon, Dick Cavett, and Mike Nichols. Furthermore, I said, I thought that Erin had a lot of nerve to push him into an appearance he really wasn't too keen to do in the first place, and then encourage him to go on unprepared.

'I don't need writers,' Groucho kept maintaining all through the evening. He said he was going on stage with some notes on index cards, and would tell anecdotes and ad lib.

Being a doctor, not a showman, Wexler didn't see anything wrong with that, but I insisted it was the route to disaster.

That prompted him to ask me why I resented Erin just because she was trying to be kind to my father and look after him at a time when he didn't have many friends left and his children had deserted him.

We, of course, replied that far from deserting him, we had persuaded him to see Joe Kaufman, the surgeon who had saved his life. As for resenting Erin, we felt we had a perfect right to. She was a complete stranger who not only didn't know the family, but knew nothing about show business. If he needed management and wanted to work, Groucho could have hired the William Morris Agency, which had represented him for fifty years.

At that point Wexler said that perhaps the reason we were concerned about Erin was because we were afraid she'd get some of my father's money. (He'd already bought her a new car and was talking about including her in his will with a $100,000 bequest off the top.)

I replied that I felt justified in being concerned. And so did my two sisters. What right did Erin have to come into our family circle and start taking money from my father on the pretence that *she* was re-making his career? He'd been a star before she was born.

As the argument heated up, Groucho became so upset that he excused himself from the table, disappeared into his bedroom and didn't return for the rest of the evening.

Wexler then accused us of being selfish. He said he was only there to help his friends. 'At how much an hour?' I retorted. As he stammeringly replied that he was doing this for nothing, Lois and I swiftly made our exit.

A week later I received the following letter from Groucho (typed by Erin) together with a cheque for a thousand dollars:

> 'Dear Art,
>   No matter what you think of Erin Fleming, I intend to keep her in my life. She's been very good to me, and I am very fond of her. The enclosed check you can use to buy yourself a new car.
>
>   Love,
>   Padre'

Evidently, the thousand dollars was intended as a peace offering, partially to even things up for the $1000 he spent on buying Erin the Ford Pinto she was currently driving.

When I phoned him to thank him for the cheque, I reiterated my view on the Carnegie Hall performance. I told him he definitely ought to get writers to punch up his act and give it some shape. He said it was too late to bother with that, and he assured me that somehow he'd manage.

'Don't forget, sonny, I've been in show business since vaudeville. I know how to handle myself.'

I didn't see much of Groucho or Erin during the weeks preceding the Carnegie show. Erin was keeping him extremely busy, capitalizing on the sudden and unexpected popularity of the Marx Brothers films – particularly *Duck Soup*. Because of its anti-establishment, anti-war sentiments, it was suddenly the rage among college students and peaceniks from coast to coast.

Consequently, Groucho was booked into Iowa State University for a warm-up appearance prior to Carnegie Hall. In keeping with the style of the times, Groucho arrived on the Iowa State campus wearing bell-bottom jeans, a blue blazer, a red sweater vest, a work shirt and a blue beret.

The Groucho name seemed to be magic, and brought out a swarm of students for a question and answer session before the night's performance.

Marvin Hamlisch, who wasn't the celebrity he is now, had been recruited to play the piano for Groucho, and Erin played the women in his life.

Despite his halting delivery, Groucho was unmistakably the star. Referring to index cards, he told anecdotes about his life, about Hollywood, about his family, and he sang some of his inimitable songs.

The show was a huge success at Iowa State, and Groucho and Erin were photographed by *Life* magazine strolling hand in hand through the campus. The image of the octogenarian romping through a college campus with a woman fifty years his junior captivated millions of readers, and inspired in more than a few men of his age the thought: 'What a way to go!'

The excitement of the tour pumped new life into Groucho's tired blood. At home alone, or with close friends, he was slow of both tongue and foot, but in front of an audience or newspaper reporters, he could still come up with some funny ad libs.

While Groucho was being interviewed in his Regency Hotel suite in Manhattan, prior to his Carnegie debut, a reporter asked him why he wasn't smoking a cigar. 'I'll smoke if it'll amuse you,' he said testily. 'I didn't know I was going to have to put on a show for you boys. You see, I just got out of the shower, and I generally don't smoke while I'm under water.'

Strangely enough, he wasn't nervous before he went on the stage at Carnegie Hall, Saturday night, 6 May. The hall had been sold out for weeks in advance, for it was fairly evident that this would be Groucho's swan song on a New York stage. The audience was jam-packed with such notables as New York's mayor John Lindsay and his wife, Senator and Mrs

Jacob Javits, Mike Nichols, Dick Cavett, Elliott Gould, Woody Allen, Diane Keaton, Art Garfunkel and Neil Simon.

I was unable to be there because I had television commitments on the West Coast, but I was pleased to see that the *New York Times* critic gave Groucho a very favourable review, even though the film projector hadn't worked when it was time to show the state-room scene from *A Night at the Opera*. Fortunately, Groucho had been able to ad lib his way through that screwup, and at the end of the show, the audience gave him a huge standing ovation.

Following this success, he and Erin flew to Cannes, where he received the French Commandeur des Artes et Lettres medallion. (Charlie Chaplin had been the first non-Frenchman to be so honoured.) As the President of the Festival tied the decoration around his neck, Groucho looked at the award and said indignantly, 'All the way from Beverly Hills for this! It's not even real gold.'

After a week of insulting all the dignitaries at Cannes, Groucho was approached by an emissary from the British Royal Family, inquiring if he would do his one-man concert as a command performance before the Queen.

Groucho was honoured and tempted – until he learnt that, according to tradition, all the proceeds from the performance would be given to charity. 'Tell the Queen that Groucho doesn't work for nothing,' he replied.

A diplomat my father wasn't!

Fatiguing as all this was for a man who'd be eighty-two on his next birthday, Erin had no intention of letting him rest; she had two more concerts booked for him that year – one in San Francisco soon after they returned to the States from Cannes, and one at the Taper Forum in Los Angeles in September.

He was able to fulfil the San Francisco engagement, and many considered it the best of his three performances. He was given four standing ovations.

But the Los Angeles engagement had to be postponed, because two weeks prior to it, he was hospitalized with a slight stroke.

My first knowledge of his illness came from Martha, who

phoned me Monday morning, 13 September, to say that when she came back from her Sunday off, she had found my father unconscious on his bedroom floor. She had phoned both Erin and his doctor, who had put him into Century City Hospital. There he had been given a series of tests, which showed some cardiac changes, plus a small stroke, which was what had caused him to pass out.

Martha said that Erin had told her not to tell anyone, including me, about the stroke because we would try to talk Groucho out of doing the show at the Taper Forum. 'And I'll lose money,' she told Martha.

As a result, Martha had to wait until Erin left the house for the hospital before she could phone me.

I then called the doctor, who said my father's prognosis was as good as could be expected for a man his age. He hadn't suffered any ill effects, such as paralysis of any limbs, from this 'minor stroke', but just to be on the safe side he was going to keep him in the hospital for observation for about a week.

I asked if he thought Groucho was up to doing the Taper show in two weeks, and he replied, 'Definitely not.'

That afternoon, Lois and I visited Groucho in his private room at the hospital. Erin was already there. He was sitting up in bed having dinner. He looked ashen and frail, and had to be spoon fed.

Later the three of us repaired to a visitors' waiting-room where Erin immediately raised the issue of the Taper concert. I told her that the doctor had advised against it. 'Well, Groucho has got to do it,' she insisted. 'I'll lose money if he doesn't go on.'

After a week had passed, and Groucho didn't seem to be any stronger, Erin agreed to a compromise. She would cancel the September date and get a later one. Fortunately, the earliest new booking she could get was 13 December 1972.

In her announcements to the press, Erin laundered the real reason for the cancellation from the reporters. She denied it was a stroke or heart attack, but simply a 'severe depression over the killings of the Israeli athletes at the Munich Olympic Games.'

While my father was in the hospital, Lois and I noticed that

Erin was beginning to boss everyone around. Not only us, but the nurses and Groucho's doctor whom she criticized for his opinion that Groucho wasn't fit enough to do the Taper engagement on its originally scheduled date.

Another problem arose while Groucho was in the hospital, and that had to do with his finances. Who would pay the bills and sign the cheques now that he was more or less out of action? For years the business management firm of Alexander Tucker & Company had made out the cheques, but Groucho, trusting no one with his money, had an arrangement whereby he was the only one permitted to sign them. But now there were bills that had to be paid, and he was in no shape to sign forty or fifty cheques.

Some of the bills could be let go, but more urgent were hospital and nursing charges, and some fairly large bills from a furniture upholsterer and a drapery shop that were overdue. Lois was responsible for the latter as she was redecorating his living-room at his request.

At the time of his hospitalization, there were about $15,000 worth of labour and material costs owing, and since we couldn't afford to lay out that kind of money ourselves, and the shops were dunning us, and my father couldn't sign cheques, we asked Groucho's lawyer, Marvin Meyer, if he couldn't get some kind of power of attorney from my father to deal with the present difficulties, and also if this situation arose in the future. Meyer seemed unwilling to do this, claiming that my father was perfectly competent and would be able to take care of the bills once he was released from hospital. 'But what am I supposed to do about these decorating bills?' Lois asked him. 'I don't want my credit to be ruined.'

Reluctantly, he and Alexander Tucker & Company worked out a compromise. They would get Groucho to sign one cheque for the amount he owed, made out to the Tucker office, who would deposit it in a separate account from which they would issue cheques, including those needed to defray the decorating expenses.

That was the best we could do inasmuch as Meyer absolutely refused to go to Groucho and suggest in any way that he might not be completely competent to handle his own affairs. The very idea seemed to frighten him. 'Groucho wouldn't like it,' he said with a slight shudder.

It was a frustrating situation, because at the pace Groucho's health was deteriorating, we knew there'd come a day, probably very soon, when he might not be strong enough to sign even one cheque. But there was nothing we could do about it. We accepted the compromise, and the financial crisis was temporarily averted.

On 12 October 1972, while still in the hospital, Groucho signed a written agreement employing Erin Fleming as his Executive Producer, Associate Producer, coordinator and secretary. The terms of her employment consisted of a salary of $100 per week, ten percent of his gross income from all his personal appearances, five thousand of the $17,500 he was getting for a Teacher's Scotch endorsement, and fifty percent of the net income he received from A & M Records for the album of the Carnegie Hall concert.

When Groucho told me of the arrangement I had a feeling he didn't know what he was signing. This was subsequently borne out in 1983 in the court case — Bank of America as executor of the estate of Groucho Marx vs Erin Fleming. Witnesses testified that Groucho had been unable to read or understand what he was signing at the time she got him to sign the contract.

Three weeks later, in November, following his release from hospital, Groucho signed another document hiring Erin as his personal manager, to be paid twenty-five percent of all his earnings after agents' commissions and other deductions. That was in addition to what she was to receive from the 12 October agreement.

By 13 December, my father had regained enough of his strength to be able to shuffle out on the stage of the Taper Forum in front of a packed house of Los Angeles celebrities and critics, and go through the motions of doing a concert.

It wasn't a bad performance. There were some amusing moments, in spite of Groucho's obvious lack of energy. He shuffled around the stage and on and off it as if he were afraid of falling if he moved any faster. He talked slowly, and forgetfully.

His eyes were so bad he could hardly read off his cue cards. And when he was telling a lengthy anecdote, he'd frequently lose the thread and wind up tacking on the end of another story instead. What's more he received little support from Erin, who played straight for him. All in all I was embarrassed to see my father, a legendary comedian, shuffling around the stage making a fool of himself.

In the *Los Angeles Times* next morning, critic Dan Sullivan wrote that Groucho was just a shadow of his former self, and suggested that if he wished to preserve in his fans' minds the memory of what a great performer he had been, that it was time for 'this Living Legend to retire.'

Fortunately Groucho took Sullivan's advice, and no more arduous concerts were scheduled. That didn't meant that Erin was putting him out to pasture, however. He was still available for assorted guest spots, TV specials, and talk shows.

If the spots were short enough, Groucho could generally handle them without a problem. He might even come up with a witty line or two that hadn't been written for him. On one of his last appearances on the *Dick Cavett Show*, he appeared wearing a knitted tam with three large, ball-shaped tassels hanging from it. Sharing a spot with Groucho that night was the late Truman Capote, who had at one point monopolized the conversation with a lengthy diatribe against the United States Government for taxing him too heavily.

Groucho kept trying to interject his opinions, but neither Cavett nor Capote would acknowledge his presence, until finally he said, out of sheer annoyance, 'If you were married, Truman, your taxes would be smaller. Why don't you get married?'

'No one has asked me,' lisped the quick-thinking Capote, who, of course, was gay.

'I'm available,' said Groucho with a pert toss of his head that caused the three balls on his tam to bounce around merrily. 'Why don't you marry me?'

Piqued, Capote retorted, 'Because, Groucho, you have three balls.'

In January following his unhappy experience at the Taper,

Groucho signed to do a short interview spot on the *Bill Cosby Special*. The show was taped, and he was one of the last to go on. He sat patiently waiting in the wings for what must have been two hours, thoroughly bored with what was taking place in front of the cameras. Finally he was called by the director to do his spot.

'Tell me, Groucho, do you have any unfulfilled ambitions?' asked Cosby.

'Yes,' replied Groucho, 'to end this interview.'

As his manager, chauffeur and girl-Friday, Erin was naturally present at all Groucho's stage appearances. As she started to feel her power, she began bossing around the people with whom he was working, as if she were the producer and not just the guest star's agent-manager. Digby Wolf, who was head writer on the Cosby Show at the time, told me afterward: 'She kept giving Groucho pep pills to keep him from falling asleep while he was waiting to go on with Cosby. At another point, she unbuttoned her blouse, took out her left tit and ran around backstage saying, "It's time to feed Groucho, it's time to feed Groucho." She evidently thought that was funny. I thought it was shameful. Your father acted like her prisoner.'

Whether or not he was her prisoner, Groucho was certainly under her spell. He'd never do anything without first getting her approval, and anything she wanted was hers for the asking.

Right after the Cosby show, Erin told my father she wanted to buy a house on Vista Grande. It was a few blocks down the hill from his Trousdale home, and to the left or east of Doheny Drive. She said it was a good buy at $56,000 and close enough to Groucho's house for her to be there at his calling in a matter of minutes.

On 10 January he gave her a thousand dollars for the deposit to hold the house until a bank loan could be arranged, and an escrow deposit of $4,650. She then got a $25,000 mortgage from the bank, and on 28 February my father loaned her $31,000, interest free, to make up the difference.

The house was recorded in Erin Fleming's name in March 1973.

In 1974, Groucho wrote 'Paid in Full' across the note and

signed it, 'Julius H. Marx'. Notwithstanding, she was never able to prove that she actually did pay back the loan from him.

It was in the first four or five months of 1973 that I started to notice a change in my father's behaviour.

Ever since I had moved out of his house to marry my first wife, in 1943, he had always phoned me around six in the evening to see how things were. And on my birthdays and at Christmas he would always send me a pretty generous cheque, or give me a few shares of stock in some company that his adviser had recommended he buy for his own portfolio.

After Erin's arrival, however, he stopped phoning completely. And Christmas 1972 was the first time he hadn't marked that holiday, even with a card. But the gifts or lack of them weren't nearly so important as what was happening to him. At times he seemed sharp, almost like his old self, but very often, if I was taking him out to lunch, for example, he seemed withdrawn and far away, as if he'd been sedated.

Whatever was causing his strange behaviour – strokes, Erin's influence on him or just old age – his feelings towards me suddenly became very ambivalent. One minute he loved me, another minute he had a bone to pick with me and was threatening to cut me out of his will. I never paid much attention to his threats. Eventually we always made up. But the longer Erin was on the scene, the more difficult it became to achieve these reconciliations.

By the spring of 1973, family tensions were stretched pretty taut. Any little spark would set off an explosion.

Although Erin lived in her own house on Vista Grande Drive, she was at Groucho's house most of the day, ate most of her meals with him, and in general gave people the impression that she was his girlfriend. And even though theirs wasn't a sexual relationship, Groucho did nothing to dispel the notion that they were lovers. At every opportunity he proclaimed loudly how much he loved her.

As assiduously as she was promoting the Groucho trademark, she was simultaneously pursuing her own acting career.

For a couple of weeks that spring she appeared in an avant garde play at the Taper Forum. The role required her to play one scene naked from the waist up.

Lois and I had driven Groucho to the performance, and he was shocked to see his 'secretary' performing topless in public. Evidently she hadn't told him what the part required of her. 'I don't know, what's happening to show business?' he complained to us in the car on the way home. 'What became of good clean family comedy?'

While talking to Groucho on the phone one morning several weeks later, I discovered that he was going to be alone for dinner that night. When I asked him where Erin was, he said she would be attending an acting class. 'I figure if she learns to be a better actress, someone will give her a part sometime where she can keep her clothes on.'

Not wanting him to be alone, I invited him to dine with Lois and me at Matteo's, a popular Italian restaurant in Westwood. 'Thanks, but I'm not up to going out. I'll just stay here and eat by myself.'

That night in the restaurant, we saw Erin walk in with a good-looking young man whom I'd never seen before. She didn't notice us as she and her friend sat down in a booth in a quiet corner, and it was obvious from the coy, flirtatious way she was behaving, that her companion wasn't her acting teacher.

Lois was so annoyed that Erin had lied to Groucho that on our way out of the restaurant, she made a detour past Erin's booth and poured a glass of ice water over her head. Erin was so taken aback that she just sat there, wiping the water off her face as it trickled down, and saying nothing.

I knew I'd soon hear about that, and I did. The next morning, early, Groucho phoned and said, 'Come over here. I want to see you.'

When I arrived, he was sitting in his armchair, in his combination bedroom-study, glaring balefully at me. As I waited for the explosion, he said quietly, 'Why did Lois do that?'

'Because she was very upset about seeing Erin with another man when she had told you she was in acting class.'

'That was Erin's agent,' he said, not wishing to face the truth. 'And if Lois doesn't apologize to Erin, I'm cutting you out of my will.'

We didn't apologize. Neither did we see them for several months.

Groucho's mind around this time had been on a forthcoming book, to be titled *The Marx Brothers Scrapbook*, that he was working on in collaboration with Richard Anobile. It was mostly a collection of photographs covering the lives of the Marx Brothers, but there was a running text that my father had spoken into a tape recorder during the several months he was working with Anobile.

It was an interesting collection of family photos, but my father's observations about the show business scene and the people he had known and worked with, together with their sexual proclivities, were brutally frank. Some of the anecdotes bordered on the libellous, and many of them were liberally sprinkled with four letter words. It wasn't how my father would speak had he been in complete control of his mental faculties, and he was so distraught when he finally saw a copy of the finished book that he tried to sue Darien House, the publisher, claiming that he had never given his approval to the final text. Despite this disclaimer, I knew that he had, because I had happened to be in his study late one afternoon when Anobile was going over the finished manuscript with him. I even watched as he affixed his signature to the document giving his approval.

Before he could bring suit, he was hospitalized on 21 August 1973 with another stroke, possibly brought on by the business over *The Marx Brothers Scrapbook*. Once again it was Martha Brooks who told me he was in hospital. His condition was officially diagnosed as 'probable pneumonitus, acute anteroseptal myocardial infarction, arteriosclerotic cerebrovascular disease and chronic urinary tract infection secondary to bladder retention.'

In short, old age was catching up with him.

He was out of hospital in a week, but back in again in September with the same problems.

Following his release from his second stay in hospital, he filed a one million dollar lawsuit against Darien House Inc. and W. W. Norton & Company, the book's distributors. He also attempted to get an injunction against *Penthouse* magazine, which had bought the first serial rights to the book and was planning on publishing excerpts from it in December.

A New York judge lifted the injunction against *Penthouse* three days after Groucho's suit was filed, and a week after that the injunction was lifted against the book publishers, stating that Groucho had signed a contract that allowed the distribution of the book in whatever form the publisher chose.

In his *New York Times* review, Wilfred Sheed dismissed the *Scrapbook* as being 'filled with sleazy breaches of trust'.

By mid-October Groucho was out of hospital for the third time, still frail but trying to be his old feisty self. One Friday I got into an argument with him over who should make the television pilot for a comedy series based on *Minnie's Boys*, the musical I had written with Robert Fisher.

Two people were after the rights, which were owned by Bob and me. Irwin Allen, producer of *The Poseidon Adventure* and *The Towering Inferno*, wanted to produce it and hire me and Bob to write the script, feeling we were the logical ones to adapt our property for television.

Simultaneously an offer came to my father through Arthur Whitelaw, the original producer of the musical on Broadway, who had become friendly with Erin and knew exactly how to get Groucho to swing the pilot deal his way: he offered Erin the position of Associate Producer.

If Whitelaw produced the pilot, he was going to hire Larry Gelbart to write the script, and Bob and I would be cut out.

When Groucho got wind of the fact that we were going to write the pilot for Irwin Allen, he phoned me and said he wanted Erin to get the job, and that we should bow out.

I pointed out that Bob and I had written the original play, and we'd hardly made a nickel on it. This was a chance for us to recoup some of our losses.

'But Whitelaw's going to give Erin a job on the show,' insisted Groucho.

'And we'll wind up with nothing,' I said. 'No way am I going to let Gelbart write it.'

'If you don't,' he threatened, 'I won't approve the deal.'

'I own the rights,' I said.

'Yes, but it's my life. No network'll touch it unless they get a written release from me.'

I knew he was right.

'You know something?' I said. 'I used to think you were different. But you're just as selfish and self-centred as every other movie star I know.' And I hung up on him.

I was so upset my hand was trembling as I put the receiver down. I'd never spoken that disrespectfully to him in my entire life.

Two days later the phone rang. I was afraid it might be Groucho calling, and I was right.

'Arthur,' he said meekly, 'I want you to come over to my house right away. I want to give you a cheque.'

'What for?'

'Because I can't stand to have my own son think of me as just another selfish actor.'

'Forget I ever said it. And keep your cheque. I don't want it.'

'Look,' he said, 'if you don't come over here right now and pick up this cheque, I'll never speak to you again.'

When Lois and I arrived at his house, he was alone except for Martha, who opened the door for us and led us into the den.

As soon as he saw us, he struggled to his feet, gave us each a hug and a kiss. Then he reached into the pocket of his smoking jacket and handed me a cheque for $100,000 scribbled in his own shaky handwriting. I'd never seen a cheque that large before, and I couldn't believe it was the real thing or that it wouldn't bounce if I tried to deposit it. I'd never known him to keep so much cash in his personal account before.

'Look,' I told him, 'I can't take this kind of money from you. It's too much. I don't even know if you have that much in your account. Do you?'

'If I don't, the bank will cover it. Now I want you to take it or we're through.'

'Is this a bribe?' I asked him. 'So that I'll let Erin get the job?'

'No,' he assured me. 'You can have the pilot deal too.'

'But why do you feel you have to give all this to me?' I asked.

'Because I don't want you to think your father's a son of a bitch! Now put the cheque in your wallet before you lose it.'

38

In 1974 Groucho's physical condition steadily worsened so Erin hired two trained nurses to be with him in the house round-the-clock to look after him and see that he took his medicine and ate properly. Erin didn't think that Martha was capable of preparing the low cholesterol diet that his doctor had insisted on.

Erin didn't like Martha much, anyway, and vice versa. Martha resented being bossed around by this comparative newcomer who had usurped her position in the household and Erin felt (and rightly so) that Martha was suspicious of her motives in taking over Groucho's life.

With due respect to Martha's hurt feelings, it must nevertheless have been a relief to her to have trained nurses care for Groucho. She didn't have to worry about leaving him alone on her days off, or taking him for walks, which was part of his daily routine when the weather was nice.

Every morning the day nurse would drive Groucho down to the 'flats' of Beverly Hills and walk with him, at a snail's pace, either through the park in front of the Beverly Hills Hotel or up and down Rodeo Drive in front of novelist Sidney Sheldon's house. Sheldon and Groucho were good friends, so my father would often drop in on him during his walk and chat with him and his wife, Jorja. Occasionally, Erin would take Groucho on his morning constitutional instead of the nurse.

Sheldon took advantage of the opportunity to pump my father about his present life, and Groucho was only too willing to talk, never dreaming that Sheldon might be contemplating a novel about an old comedian and a young woman. Although Sheldon disclaims it, there's little doubt in my mind that Groucho's circumstances inspired the idea for his *roman à clef, A Stranger in the Mirror.*

When this was published in 1976, Sheldon vehemently denied that the character of Jill Castle, who hitched her wagon to a star comic named Toby Temple, was based on Groucho and

Erin. He even dedicated the book to Groucho, and thanked him in a foreword for his help in giving him information on comedians. It was an old and proven writer's ploy to fool the characters on which a *roman à clef* novel was based into thinking it wasn't about them. But he didn't fool me. Sheldon had worked at MGM when he was in his twenties, had won an Oscar for writing *The Bachelor* and *The Bobby Soxer*, and had been around comedians all his life. He didn't need Groucho Marx to tell him what made a comedian tick.

In any case, the novel wasn't a very flattering portrayal of either the comedian or the young woman. Fortunately Groucho never read the book, and Sidney Sheldon continued to be his friend.

As far as his career was concerned, 1974 was a better year for Groucho than 1973. For several years he and John Guedel, the producer of the *You Bet Your Life* series, had been trying to persuade NBC to re-syndicate the show. Both felt the series had more mileage in it, but the executives of the network maintained that the programme was too slow and old fashioned to justify syndication. However, Guedel, at Erin's urging, was able to work out a royalty deal with NBC that was favourable to the network, and a local Los Angeles TV channel, KTLA, agreed to take a 13-week chance on the *Best of Groucho*.

Fourteen years of films of *You Bet Your Life*, which had been kept in a warehouse in New Jersey, were shipped to Groucho's house. There, my son, Andy, a recent graduate of UCLA, was hired by Groucho at a modest salary to sift through all those cans of film and put the shows in some semblance of chronological order.

With due credit to Erin *You Bet Your Life* was extremely successful in its local airing, and went on to become again one of the most popular re-runs in syndication all over the country. It was even a hit in Canada.

Some time in 1973 I had written to the President of the Academy of Motion Picture Arts and Sciences, suggesting the possibility of Groucho Marx getting an 'honorary' Oscar at the 1974 Academy Awards. Unbeknown to me, my father's good friend, screenwriter Nunnally Johnson, had written a similar letter.

To my surprise, the Board agreed to our suggestions, and in February of 1974, the Academy announced that Groucho Marx would be given a 'special' Oscar for 'the brilliant activity and unequalled achievement of the Marx Brothers in the art of motion picture comedy'.

Simultaneously, Universal Studios, who owned the film version of *Animal Crackers* but had been reluctant to put it on general release again because they didn't believe there was a large enough market to warrant striking fresh prints, bowed to the wishes of thousands of fans and decided to re-release it. Instrumental in their decision was a petition bearing several thousand signatures of UCLA students demanding that the picture be re-released. This action was spearheaded by a young Marx Brothers buff named Steve Stoliar.

As a result, *Animal Crackers* was released in limited engagements at the United Artists Theater in Westwood and the Sutton Theater in New York City. It broke attendance records in both houses.

The flood of fan mail following the revival of *Animal Crackers* was such that Erin, who had more important things to do, had to hire someone to deal with it. She hired the young student, Steve Stoliar, and put him on my father's expanding payroll.

The Academy Award show was held on the night of 2 April 1974, at the Music Center in downtown Los Angeles.

The morning of the Academy show, I received a frantic telephone call from my father's nurse. She told me that Erin had gone 'berserk', and had slapped the night nurse for not giving Groucho his Valium. Consequently he had had a restless night. Erin was saying she was going to fire everybody on the staff. If that happened, Martha was going to quit, too. The nurse asked me if there was anything I could do. I told her I didn't think there was.

Groucho, however, was very upset by the turbulence in his household, and even though he had the Awards on his mind, he phoned me ten minutes after the nurse had hung up and said he wasn't going to fire anybody, and that 'Erin needs a psychiatrist'.

After the traumatic goings-on in his home that morning, I was surprised that Groucho made it to the Music Center at all to pick up his award. But in the true show-must-go-on tradition he was on hand when Jack Lemmon presented him with his Oscar.

He looked old and frail as he shuffled out on to the stage in his tux and blue beret. He was greeted by a prolonged standing ovation, following which he said, 'I only wish Harpo and Chico could have been here — and Margaret Dumont, who never understood any of our jokes. She used to say, "Julie, what are they laughing at?" But she was a great straight woman, and I loved her. And then I'd like to thank my mother, without whom we would have been a failure. And last I'd like to thank Erin Fleming who made my life worth living and who understands all my jokes.'

A few evenings later, Lois and I found ourselves sitting in a restaurant next to my Uncle Gummo and his wife Helen. They greeted us warmly and Gummo said that he was thoroughly disgusted with Groucho for mentioning Erin in his acceptance speech — 'You'd think she had something to do with the success of the Marx Brothers,' he complained.

He also told us of a recent incident when Erin had deliberately tried to come between Groucho and himself. 'She told Groucho I had called her some four letter names, which is absolutely untrue. But Groucho believed her and said I had to apologize to her or he'd never speak to me again.'

Gummo was a mild-mannered man who to my knowledge had never used a profanity in his life. He and his wife were furious with Erin, whom they believed was plotting a deliberate campaign to alienate my father from his family and close friends.

A week later Andy phoned me to say that Erin had overruled my father's wishes and had fired both Linda and the night nurse.

Martha was so upset by all this that she came to see us the next morning and announced she was thinking of quitting, in spite of her love for Groucho, and in spite of the fact that she knew she was in his will for $10,000 if she remained in his employ until he died.

'It's not worth it if I have to be around *that* woman,' she confessed.

She was sure Erin was deliberately trying to estrange my father from his friends and relatives. She didn't want them to be around to see how she was manipulating him and getting her own way. She told us that Erin had screamed at Groucho and threatened to hit him if he wouldn't loan her the money to buy a house. Martha also said that Erin was deliberately trying to poison my father's mind against me by telling him that I thought he was senile and that he should be put in a home for the aged – Groucho's biggest fear since childhood. I had no such intention, of course. As long as he had the money to maintain himself in his present style, there was no necessity to take such a drastic step. My only concern was that I didn't want him to run out of money while he was still alive – and at the rate Erin was spending it, that might very well happen.

Martha also told us that she was aware of the $100,000 my father had given me: Groucho had told her himself that he had only given it to me so that he wouldn't feel guilty about giving $100,000 worth of his savings bonds to Erin.

We tried to persuade Martha not to quit, as she was our main link with what was going on in Groucho's house. Finally Martha agreed to stay on, but said she wasn't sure how much longer she could take Erin's tantrums and maltreatment of Groucho.

Though it was becoming more and more difficult for me to be in the same room as Erin Fleming without losing my temper, I managed to keep my relationship with Groucho on a fairly even keel through the rest of 1974, mainly by visiting him only in the mornings, when I knew Erin wouldn't be around. We were rarely invited to dinner any more, because Erin was starting to cultivate a whole new group of friends for Groucho. The one exception was his birthday dinner. When we arrived at the house I gave him a copy of my latest book, *Everybody Loves Somebody Sometime – Especially Himself*, the story of Dean

Martin and Jerry Lewis, and signed it to him. As I placed it in his hand, he looked at it critically and said, 'Why do you want to write about Jerry Lewis? I'm funnier than he is.'

When I was visiting him a few mornings later, he seemed uneasy, as though he had something unpleasant to tell me. Finally he blurted out, 'I'm going to leave the house to Erin.'

I hated discussing wills with a man who was so close to the grave, but since he had brought up the subject, I felt I owed it to myself and my two sisters to remind him that the house was worth at least three quarters of a million dollars — which was more than any of us children would get.

Until I told him that, he didn't seem to be aware that his house was that valuable. 'So you think that's too much to leave her?' he said.

'I can't tell you what to do,' I said, 'but why does she need this house? She already has two of her own which you bought.'

'I just gave her the money for the down payments. She's paying them off.'

'Well, I still don't think it's fair to the three of us.'

He considered it for a moment, then said, 'Okay, I'll leave the house to you three, and just put her in for $125,000 cash off the top.'

I couldn't believe he had acquiesced so easily, or that Erin wouldn't get his ear at a later date and persuade him to leave her the Trousdale house. But when he showed me his new will later in the summer, I saw he had remained true to his promise.

Unfortunately, there were more disturbing developments soon to come. In mid-October, I received a call from Bob Morgan, who handled Groucho's account in Alexander Tucker's office.

He told me that he was extremely worried about Groucho's financial situation. Groucho was spending more money than he was earning, which was unlike him, and Erin was signing Groucho's name to his personal cheques, causing substantial overdrafts in his personal account. This had necessitated Morgan to liquidate some of Groucho's investments in order to pay $40,000 in overdrafts. Not only that, but Erin was talking about cashing in all of his securities and bonds, and putting the proceeds into a company he had formed with her in July called Groucho Marx Productions. He and Tucker had advised Groucho, and so had his stockbroker in the East, Salwyn Shufro, that this was not the prudent thing to do. Erin had flown off the handle, screamed obscenities at Tucker and threatened to fire him and also to get rid of Salwyn Shufro, who'd been Groucho's good friend and financial adviser since the 1929 market crash.

When I asked Morgan what he advised, he said I ought to see my father's lawyer and do something about becoming his conservator. 'If you don't, there's liable to be nothing left. I really don't think he knows what he's doing any more.'

I phoned Marvin Meyer and expressed Morgan's concern, as well as my own, again. But again he said he didn't believe my father was in the kind of shape yet that required a conservator. 'Besides,' he added, 'it's Groucho's money. And he's allowed to spend it any way he wishes.'

'But you're his lawyer. You should look out for his interests. I don't want him to wind up penniless, and he might if he lives long enough.'

When I couldn't get anywhere with Meyer, I consulted Joe Ball, a top trial lawyer in Los Angeles, and his associate John McDonough.

They were very discouraging about the prospect of persuading a judge and jury that Groucho needed a conservator. They said the legal fees and court costs would be astronomical, and that I'd almost certainly lose the case.

'One wisecrack from your father in court,' said McDonough, 'and he'd have the judge and jury in stitches and convinced he was perfectly capable of handling his own affairs.'

'Then you suggest we do nothing?'

'Not exactly. There's a simpler way. Get your father to voluntarily sign a paper making you his conservator.'

'Are you kidding?' I told him. 'First of all, nobody who's senile will admit it. Because if he knew it he wouldn't be senile or in need of help. Secondly, he wouldn't do anything for me, he's so under Erin's influence. And she's certainly not going to permit my taking over. And she has his ear twenty-four hours a day.'

'Then I think you have to wait until he's a little worse before you can do anything,' he advised. 'Sorry to sound so discouraging, but that's the way the law is set up – to protect the elderly from being manipulated by their children.'

'But it's not set up to protect the elderly from being manipulated by outsiders, is it?' asked Lois.

'That's about the size of it,' said McDonough with a wry grin as he showed us to the door.

After being advised not to do anything, I made up my mind to forget trying to rescue my father from his own incompetence, and get on with my own life. I had a new play going into rehearsal later that autumn at the Royal Alexander Theater in Toronto, and making a success of that was going to take all of my energy and mental resources.

Just before leaving for Toronto, however, in response to the concern expressed by one of Groucho's nurses and several of my father's friends, I took a shot at seeing another lawyer, J. Brin Schulman. He was more encouraging than the other two had been, but he had the same reservations about going to court to obtain a conservatorship. The trouble was, he told us, we didn't have any 'hard' evidence to back up our charges. It was all circumstantial, and if we didn't have hard evidence, it would turn into a circus, with Groucho making jokes, and we'd end up looking foolish.

He recommended, however, that we keep notes on incidents involving Groucho and Erin, together with the times and dates. When we had some hard evidence, that would be the time to reconsider. Meanwhile, he said, we should keep our eyes and ears open. He felt that eventually Erin Fleming would make a slip.

Since we'd now been advised by three of the best attorneys in town not to risk a court battle, Lois and I abandoned the idea of seeking a conservatorship and left for six weeks in Toronto. Satisfied we'd done all we could to prevent an unhealthy situation from getting worse, we put the matter out of our minds.

My play, *Sugar and Spice*, opened on 11 November 1974 at

the Royal Alexander Theater in Toronto. Because my plot was based on a well-known murder case of the Sixties, it contained violence, drug-taking and some nudity. This shocked some of the opening-night audience, causing a few elderly ladies to leave the theatre before the final curtain. We also heard some booing from the balcony.

Despite this, the play received one rave review, a mixed review and a very bad one. However, it played out its three week limited run engagement to full houses and later sold to the movies.

On my return to Southern California, in mid-December, I received a phone call from Groucho one morning, demanding that I drop what I was doing and 'come over here and see me right now. I want to talk to you'.

I couldn't imagine what the urgency was, but since I hadn't seen him for about six weeks, I figured this was as good a time as ever.

When I arrived, he was in his bathrobe, pyjamas and slippers, sitting in his usual place – an armchair in front of the TV set in his bedroom. He seemed to be furious about something. When I asked him what was troubling him, he accused me of having written an uncomplimentary article about Erin in one of the Toronto newspapers. He threatened to cut me out of his will if I didn't apologize to her immediately.

When I told him the truth – that I'd never written anything about Erin in my life – he accused me of lying. I asked him to show me the article. He said he couldn't, because he didn't have it. Then how did he know about it? I asked. From Erin, of course. Canadian by birth, she had friends in Toronto. And I knew where they were, I suddenly realized – in the balcony of the Royal Alexander Theater on opening night.

I told him that I had had more important things to do in Toronto than waste my time writing about Erin. He could not resist the taunt that I had written a play that was so bad the audience had booed (the story had made the wire services). I reminded him that the only play he had ever written was so bad it closed in New York after a three-day run. He denied this, claiming *Time for Elizabeth* had been a big hit, and again

310

demanded that I apologize to Erin or suffer the consequences.

I told him I'd be glad to apologize as soon as he could produce the article. 'You're no good,' he said.

Completely frustrated, but feeling sad that our relationship had finally come down to this, I walked out of his house, determined never to return.

I didn't see him again until September 1976. Much as I loved him and felt sympathy for his creeping senility, and tried to be understanding of his devotion of Erin, I just couldn't take his abuse any longer.

In the interim year and a half, it was easy to keep track of his activities, either through my son Andy, who was still working for him, or from what I read in the papers or heard from his friends and former business associates.

During that period he became further alienated from Melinda and Miriam, both of whom refused to see or speak to him while Erin was there. His old friends were no longer on the scene either.

Groucho's two long-time buddies – Arthur Sheekman and Hary Ruby – had died, and his other good friend, Nunnally Johnson, was hopelessly ill and bed-ridden with emphysema.

Nat and Helen Perrin, and Gloria Sheekman also, had as little to do with Groucho and Erin as possible. They weren't openly hostile to Erin, but they made their disapproval felt by turning down invitations to have dinner at Groucho's house.

Since these people were old-guard Hollywood, who couldn't do much for her, Erin wasn't too upset over this. When my father was up to having company, and even when he wasn't, she filled the house in the evenings with a more 'current' crowd. People like Sally Kellerman, Bud Cort, Bill Cosby, Charlotte Chandler, Bernadette Peters, Shields & Yarnell, Carroll O'Connor, Jack Lemmon and the long-haired singer, Tiny Tim.

Although he preferred being with writers, Groucho did enjoy the company of some of his new friends. For instance, he loved Bill Cosby's sense of humour, and when he was up to it got a big kick out of singing harmony with Carroll O'Connor, who gave him a bongo drum in appreciation of their friendship. And he liked Jack Lemmon's piano playing and old-time soft-shoe

311

dance routines, which the actor performed at Erin's after-dinner musicales, in which she too appeared.

There were other important changes besides my father's social life. In January 1975 Erin 'retired' Martha Brooks and replaced her with John Ballow, a male cook. Also to go were Salwyn Shufro, the Alexander Tucker Business Management office, and Groucho's attorney, Marvin Meyer. These three, plus Rogers & Cowan, were replaced by a long string of other attorneys, business management firms and personal managers of Erin's choosing, all of whom either quit or were fired for one reason or another.

Shortly before Martha Brooks was fired, she told me that Erin was trying to persuade my father to adopt her against his will. Martha said she knew it was Erin's idea and that my father wasn't for it, because he had come to her one day and told her, rather plaintively, 'Martha, I already have two daughters. What do I want with another one?'

She also told me that Erin had been coaching my father on how to act in front of the psychologists who would have to examine him prior to any adoption procedure.

Since this seemed a possible case of coercion, I decided to seek the advice of yet another attorney, Martin Gang. I knew Gang well. He had been Bob Hope's attorney for many years, as well as my ex-mother-in-law's, and I knew him to be an honourable man who would probably look out for my interests, if Erin became too demanding.

'It seems a bit unusual,' Gang admitted after I had told him about Erin's plans to have herself adopted.

'I think it's a case of undue influence,' I said. 'Maybe a conservatorship is in order.'

When Gang, too, said he thought it would be unwise to try to seek a conservatorship, I said, 'Then why don't you become his attorney, and try to dissuade him from adopting her? I know he's looking for a new lawyer, because he asked me to suggest someone when I was still talking to him. I even gave him your telephone number.'

Subsequently, Groucho and Erin did engage the services of the Gang office.

Despite his good intentions, I don't think Martin Gang was too successful in dissuading Erin from her adoption scheme, because adoption papers were filed with the court sometime in early 1975. Fortunately, and despite Erin's coaching, when the two doctors appointed by the court relative to the adoption procedure did examine Groucho in the autumn of 1975, their findings were that (1) Groucho was 'terrified that Erin would leave and abandon him', and (2) 'his IQ was at such a diminished level that his ability to respond to all but the most routine kinds of things was essentially gone.'

That put an end to Erin's plans to become Groucho's daughter.

39

Groucho spent a great deal of time in bed during the last two years of his life. He got up usually only to eat his meals or to go out for an occasional lunch or to watch television after dinner in his den. Once a while, if business called for it, Erin would take him to New York.

He didn't have much of an appetite, and Erin had to treat him like a small child, cajoling and often berating him, in order to get him to eat his vegetables. Occasionally he would lash back at her, saying, 'Who do you think you are? I work hard. I'm supporting you. Do you think *you* paid for all this? I'm Groucho Marx, and what I did for you I can do for anyone.'

These rare moments of resentment may have been sparked by the fact that Groucho missed his children. Sensing that it all might backfire and that he might turn against her – because he could still assert himself on occasion – Erin told Groucho, when the two of them were in New York on a short trip in August 1976, that she was not going to return to California until he made peace with his children.

In September I received a telegram from Groucho which read:

PLEASE CALL ME. WANT TO SEE YOU.
LOVE FATHER

I knew that someone else had actually composed the telegram, because he would have signed it 'Padre', the nickname Miriam and I had called him by ever since we'd taken Spanish in school. But I didn't care. I knew that he had to be behind the peace overture, so I phoned his number as soon as I got the message. I didn't reach him personally. I got a young man who introduced himself as Henry Golas who said, he, too, was working for my father now. He said Groucho was sleeping, but was anxious to have Lois and me over to dinner soon. I said, 'How about tomorrow?' And he said fine.

When we arrived we were let in by Henry Golas, who was blond, nineteen, and a part-time college student and full-time Marx fan. I learned during the evening that Erin had hired him to catalogue Groucho's film collection and to run the projector whenever he wanted to screen Marx Brothers films for their guests.

Golas seemed friendly enough, if a bit nervous, but Lois and I couldn't help feeling as we walked into the den where Groucho was waiting to greet us, that we were inside the 'enemy camp'.

My father hadn't changed much, a little older and thinner. He kissed me on the cheek, hugged Lois, and pointing to the bar, invited me to 'name your poison, but you'll have to fix it yourself. I don't drink any more. In fact, I don't do anything that's fun.'

He said that Erin was in New York, which was fine with me. At least there'd be no arguments. But I still didn't like the feeling I had about the household as the evening wore on.

Apart from Steve Stoliar, his entire household staff was new. In addition to Henry, there was a new secretary, a new nurse, a new cook, and a new live-in housekeeper who had replaced Martha.

Perhaps I was being paranoid, but I didn't feel able to talk freely to Groucho in front of them. Anything I said to him was sure to be reported back to Erin. She might not have been there, but her presence was palpable, and it was eerie.

Sometime during dinner Groucho started extolling Erin's virtues and telling us how much she was doing to further his career. 'She set up this company for me – Groucho Productions,' he said. 'We both own fifty percent of the stock.'

When I asked him the purpose of the company, he said it was to capitalize on the Groucho trademark: there would soon be Groucho dolls, watches, T-shirts, greeting cards. Also, the money being made from the re-syndication of *You Bet Your Life* would go into Groucho Productions.

'That looks like a pretty good deal for Erin,' I said. 'Better than for you. She's going to get fifty percent of *You Bet Your Life*, which she had nothing to do with, plus a management fee from all your income, including from *You Bet Your Life*.'

Groucho didn't see anything wrong with that, but my statement seemed to have made the rest of the people at the table nervous, especially Henry Golas, who offered Lois and me a look at my father's 'books'. I didn't see how a callow youth – practically a complete stranger to my father's ménage – could possibly take responsibility for making that offer on his own. He was obviously under instructions from some higher authority.

So what was the point of looking at the books? What would there be to see that Erin didn't want us to see?

The other members of Groucho's household sat at the dinner table with us, and at no time during the evening were we allowed out of their sight.

All in all I felt uncomfortable, and was glad when Groucho announced at nine o'clock that he was tired and wanted to go to bed. Before we left, he gave me an autographed copy of *The Grouchophile*, another collection of photos and Marx memorabilia, compiled by Hector Arce.

He must have considered the evening a success, however, because a couple of weeks later he invited us to his eighty-sixth birthday party.

I debated whether or not to attend, because I was sure the guest list would be mostly Erin's friends, hangers-on and assorted sycophants. I knew none of Groucho's old friends would be there, because the ones who were still alive were refusing to have anything to do with Erin.

But in the end, knowing it could very well be his last birthday party and that it would please him to see me there, I decided to go. Lois, however, just couldn't face the scene, and told me to make up some sort of an excuse if Groucho missed her.

There were so many people milling around in his living-room, including Jack Lemmon, George Burns, Sally Kellerman and Elliott Gould, that I doubted if Groucho would even notice me, let alone miss Lois. But he surprised me, and when I told him Lois couldn't make it, he immediately shuffled over to the telephone and dialled our number.

'Aren't you coming to my birthday party?' he asked.

'I can't,' said Lois. 'I have a bad cold. I'm sorry, Grouch.'

He looked crestfallen. 'I'm sorry you're not coming, Lois. I'm eighty-six today.'

Bill Marx (Harpo's adopted son) was also at the party. He'd been invited to play dinner music on the piano and to accompany the singers during the musicale that inevitably followed.

Groucho and Erin led off the entertainment with a comedy song from his vaudeville days which had a number of verses similar to this:

'My mother called Sister downstairs the other day.
"I'm taking a bath," my sister did say.
"Well, slip on something quick: here comes Mr Brown."
She slipped on the top step and then came down.'

Somehow Groucho remembered the words, but his voice was barely audible.

'Okay,' called out Erin when they finished to perfunctory applause, 'let's do "Oh, How That Woman Could Cook" for an encore.'

As if by rote he went into another old number from his vaudeville days.

I squirmed. Watching Erin call the shots somehow reminded me of a trained monkey being told what to do by his organ-grinder boss.

The entertainment ended with a soft-shoe dance number done by Jack Lemmon, George Burns, Elliott Gould and Groucho. The only thing I remember about it is that my father crumpled to the floor half way through it. True to the show-must-go-on tradition, the others kept right on dancing. I guess everyone was too preoccupied to notice the nurse come in and help me pick up Groucho and carry him to his bedroom.

I kissed him goodnight, watched the nurse put him to bed and left without saying good-bye to anyone.

My relationship with Groucho continued on a fairly even keel for the rest of that year. Since eating dinner with him meant I'd have to be with Erin, I generally tried to see him at lunchtime, at his house, or else I'd take him to the Polo Lounge.

I preferred the latter, because I still didn't feel free to talk to him in his house. Either Henry Golas or Steve Stoliar would be at the table, or perhaps both, along with the nurse. If there was anything I needed to say to him alone, then I definitely had to take him out.

I remember one such incident. Edy Addams, the comedienne, had told my agent, Rita Chandler, that she'd had dinner with Groucho the night before, and when my father refused to eat his vegetables, Erin had lost her temper and slapped him on the cheek with all her might. 'Edy thinks you ought to do something about it,' Rita Chandler told me. 'She says your father is scared to death of that woman.'

I immediately called him up and invited him to the Polo Lounge. On our way there in the car, I asked him directly, 'Are you afraid of Erin? Edy Addams said Erin hit you last night.'

Groucho thought about it for a moment, and said, with a sheepish smile, 'That's all right. I hit her once in a while, too.'

It was fairly obvious to me that he was intimidated by Erin, and that he was afraid to admit it. Obviously that's why she had such power over him. It became apparent to me at that moment that I could never get him out of her clutches unless I kidnapped him. He'd never leave her or kick her out voluntarily.

Another time, Groucho mentioned to me that Erin had just bought a new Mercedes sports coupé.

'Who paid for that?' I asked.

'She did. She's doing very well now.'

'Doing what?'

'Acting,' he replied. 'She's getting a part in a new Woody

Allen movie. That's why she isn't here. She's in Switzerland trying out for the part.'

I informed him that there was no Woody Allen movie being made in Switzerland. She must have had another reason for going there.

'No,' he insisted, 'she's going to be in Woody's new movie.'

Notwithstanding, she never appeared in any other Woody Allen movies, made in Switzerland or anywhere else.

Between January and March 1977, I had lunch with Groucho three more times.

He wanted to give me his membership of Hillcrest Country Club. I thanked him but said I didn't particularly want it as I was a tennis player and a member of Beverly Hills Tennis Club, and in any case he still enjoyed using the club. Groucho said he never went there any more – everyone at the Round Table was dead.

'I don't know if you can just give it to me,' I said. 'You'll have to look into their rules. And what about Erin? Does she know about this?'

'She's out of town. She doesn't have to know everything I do.'

By the following week he had learned that he could give me the membership, provided I was approved by the board, but that there would be a $6500 transfer fee. 'Which I'll pay,' he offered.

'Just keep the membership,' I said. 'I don't want you to pay it.'

'No, I insist. I can afford it.'

The third time we had lunch, about a week later, Erin was back in town, but not with us. 'I changed my mind about paying the transfer charge,' he said. 'You'll have to pay it.'

'Look,' I said, 'it's no gift if I have to pay $6500. If I wanted it, that would be something else.'

He sulked all the way back to his house in my car. When I dropped him off at his house and walked him up the steps to his front door, where his nurse let him in, he was quite cool to me.

Sad to say, that was the last time I ever saw him on his feet.

Groucho went downhill rapidly after that, both physically and mentally. Notwithstanding, Erin did her best to keep him involved in the Hollywood social swirl.

When they were invited to the Hugh Hefner Playboy mansion

to a huge soirée celebrating George Burns's eighty-first birthday, Erin accepted for the two of them. She saw another opportunity to entertain in front of important producers and writers.

The morning after the party I received a call from Norman Krasna, who had flown in from Switzerland. He'd been at the party, and told me that Groucho had collapsed on the dance floor when he was dancing with Erin before dinner. Luckily, a prominent Beverly Hills heart specialist happened to be there. After examining my father he told Erin that he believed Groucho might have suffered a 'small heart attack'. He advised her to take Groucho home immediately, put him to bed, and call his regular doctor.

According to Krasna – and Irwin Allen, who also was there – Erin was reluctant to take Groucho home. She said that she and Groucho were expected to entertain after dinner and she didn't want to disappoint Hugh Hefner.

The specialist told her that in no way was Groucho in any shape to perform a number. He was liable to drop dead in the middle of it. Moreover, he would hold Erin personally responsible if she didn't take him home immediately.

Reluctantly, she followed his advice.

When I phoned my father's doctor, he said he had found no evidence of a heart attack. There was just a general deterioration of his body caused by old age. He simply needed rest, he said.

However, Groucho was in the throes of preparing for a syndicated TV special in which he was to star as the host at a series of parties with his famous guests in his home. A pilot film was to be shot in March. Every afternoon Groucho rehearsed his songs with an accompanist. After rehearsing one day, he went to bed exhausted. The next morning he suffered another small stroke which left him completely disoriented.

He was put back to bed, and according to his biographer Hector Arce, who was there, the house suddenly took on a morbid air. 'Everyone seemed to sense that this was the end.' He wasn't hospitalized, but his doctor came to the house and gave him medication, and recommended plenty of bedrest. The proposed TV show had to be cancelled.

He remained weak and disoriented for several days. Despite this, Erin took Groucho out of bed one morning, seated him at a desk and according to Arce, placed several legal-looking papers in front of him. Then she handed him a pen and ordered him to sign them without telling him what they were.

Hector Arce, who witnessed the scene, was very disturbed. He knew it wasn't like my father to sign papers without his attorney present to tell him what he was signing.

Once the signing was over, Groucho was helped back to bed.

My father's condition improved slowly over the next two days. He even got out of bed and dressed one morning in order to receive a visit from the actress Olivia De Havilland. But as he started to walk down the hall, he fell again. When the nurse helped him to his feet, he complained that his hip hurt. She put him to bed, where he received Olivia De Havilland in his pyjamas.

After her visit, Groucho complained to Erin of a pain in his right leg. He was then driven to Cedars Sinai, where it was discovered that he had a floating fracture of the right hip.

If he were to walk again, he would have to undergo a hip replacement operation immediately.

Groucho himself made the decision to have the operation, and it was performed the very next morning.

40

Since I hadn't been in touch with Groucho for about three days, I didn't know anything about his fall and the resultant hip operation until two days after the surgery, when I received a call from my father's attorney, Martin Gang. He said my father had come through the operation nicely, that he was in the intensive care ward at Cedars Sinai, and that he had asked to see me.

When I arrived in the small cubicle in the intensive care ward, I found Groucho curled up in his bed, in a white hospital gown, sleeping fitfully under the sedation he'd been given to ease the pain.

Evidently sensing someone's presence, he stirred slightly, opened his eyes and stared at me.

'How do you feel?' I asked.

'Fine,' he said weakly, an answer he would have given had he been in mortal pain. I never heard him complain about his health, except as a joke. And he was in no joking mood today.

'Is there anything I can do for you?' I asked.

'Yes. Get me a newspaper.'

When I returned with a copy of the *Los Angeles Times*, he had fallen into a sound sleep. I waited to see if he would wake up again, and when he didn't I folded the paper, put it on the night table within reach of his hand and tiptoed from the room.

On my way out of the hospital I met my son, Andy, with Hector Arce. They asked to see Groucho, so I led the way back to the intensive care ward.

When we arrived, I found Erin standing over my father's sleeping form, cooing at him. I left without saying a word to her.

Later, Arce told me that Erin had said Groucho's blood pressure had 'risen dangerously' as a result of my visit. That evidently was to validate her reasons for not telling me about the operation before it took place. When I checked with my father's doctors and told them what Erin had said, both agreed it was 'utter nonsense. It'll do him good to see you.'

After I left the hospital, I drove over to Groucho's house, to see if everything was all right there. But when I tried to let myself in the front door with the key my father had given me expressly for emergencies like this, I discovered that the locks had been changed. So I rang the bell and was let in by Mrs O'Donnell, the housekeeper.

According to her, the rest of the staff was not there, under Erin's orders. Evidently she didn't want anyone snooping around, even her most trusted employees, while she was out.

'But I know it's all right with Mr Marx to let you in,' she said.

As I walked up the hall to Groucho's room, I saw that there were dozens of cardboard cartons stacked up in both Erin's and Steve Stoliar's office. These contained legal papers, I discovered, that had been returned by the many attorneys Erin had hired and fired during the years of her tenure.

In Groucho's room, I attempted to open his desk drawer, but I should have known better – the desk key my father had given me wouldn't work. A new lock had been installed. Fortunately, he'd already given me copies of his will and holdings to take home.

That afternoon Groucho had recovered sufficiently to be moved out of intensive care and into a large, comfortable private suite on the seventh floor.

Lois and I dropped in on him the next afternoon. We entered without knocking and found Erin sitting on the couch with Warren Berlinger, an actor who had an insurance business, whom she had put on the payroll of Groucho Marx Productions at a five hundred dollars a week salary. For this he was expected to give Groucho business advice, handle his insurance, and administer a costly health insurance plan Erin had set up to benefit herself and the company's other employees.

Groucho was sitting up in bed, and seemed genuinely happy to see Lois and me. Each of us gave him a kiss on the forehead, and he said to me, 'I love you.' This raised Erin's eyebrows, and she glared at us while we remained at my father's bedside.

Feeling the tension, Berlinger got up and walked out into the corridor.

When I asked Groucho how he was getting along, he kept saying, 'My money! It's down the hill and to the left.'

I could only guess what that meant, but Erin didn't like him saying it one bit, and immediately came over to the bed and started cooing at him, hoping to get his mind off the subject of what had happened to his money.

I wanted to explore the subject further, but Erin continued hovering over him and soon suggested that we leave and 'let Groucho get some rest'.

During the next week I made several attempts to see my father without her or any of her spies in the room. But she saw to it that I was never left alone with him. If she couldn't be there, then it would be Berlinger or one of the nurses from home that she had brought in and felt she could trust.

In spite of this, Groucho twice more said to me that his money was down the hill and to the left. While it is possible that these words were just the ramblings of a confused old man, I am sure it was more than a coincidence that both Erin's houses, which he had paid for, were down Hillcrest Road from his home and to the left of Doheny Drive.

During the rest of his two-and-a-half week stay in the hospital, Erin made it more and more uncomfortable for me to visit Groucho. She absolutely refused to allow me to see him alone and finally left instructions with the private nurses that we weren't to be allowed to see him at all, because it upset him and caused his blood pressure to rise.

Towards the end of Groucho's hospital stay, when I was more or less banished from his room, his good friend Norman Krasna came into town from Palm Springs, where he and his wife had been vacationing. When I told them what had been going on with Erin, the two of them were shocked.

Krasna, who'd been after me for months to take the bull by the horns and become my father's conservator before it was too late, promised to look in on Groucho at the hospital the next day.

He did, and that evening I got a call from him. He said, 'Arthur, you have to do something. I met Hector Arce after I saw Groucho. He was interviewing me for the book he's doing, and he told me some terrible things about Erin. He said he saw her trying to force Groucho to sign a paper giving her title to the house so she can sell it. He also said that she's had real estate people coming through to appraise it.'

'I've been trying to do something,' I said, 'but I can't get any lawyer to take it on.'

'Well, I want you to talk to Arce,' said Krasna. 'He's got the goods on her. I'll bring him over tonight.'

I was elated that Norman had been able to talk Arce into siding with me. Having lived with my father for the last four months while he researched his book on Groucho, there were few goings-on that he hadn't been witness to.

Unfortunately, Arce had had second thoughts about helping me by the time Krasna brought him to my house. He admitted that Erin was power-mad and was trying to gain complete control of Groucho as well as title to his house. But he said he felt a certain amount of loyalty to my father for giving him a chance to write his book, and to Erin for giving him such complete access to his subject and his subject's friends.

'If Groucho were in his right mind, he'd never let this happen,' Krasna told Arce. 'You have to help Arthur.'

'Groucho's so dependent on Erin,' said Arce, 'that I'm afraid he'd die if Arthur took Erin away from him.'

Realizing we'd get no co-operation from Arce, Krasna and I decided to monitor the situation for a few days to see what developed. The next afternoon we dropped in on Groucho. Erin, who was sitting in the hospital room with Berlinger, had left orders not to allow me in. Krasna burst in anyway, saying 'Arthur's his son, and he has every right to visit his father.'

'It upsets Groucho to see him,' said Erin.

'Bullshit,' said Krasna. 'He loves Arthur.' And with that he pulled me into the room.

Erin got up and left with Berlinger.

Though it was difficult for Groucho to speak – he was having some respiratory problems – and what he said didn't make a great deal of sense, we remained at his bedside until he dozed off.

The next morning, Lois and I decided to go to the hospital early, before Erin or her cohorts arrived. We hoped that without the pressure of Erin's presence, perhaps my father would have a few lucid moments and tell us what exactly was troubling him. But when we pushed open the door to his hospital suite, we found the room mysteriously empty. There was not even any evidence that anyone had occupied it lately.

We learned from the floor nurse that Erin had come at seven in the morning, with a nurse and a tall black man, whom she said was her 'driver', and who had carried Groucho out and down to their car. She hadn't bothered to check him out of the hospital officially or obtain his doctor's permission.

Lois and I drove straight to Groucho's house. The

housekeeper told us that Groucho was in bed. Erin was out. When we walked into his bedroom, where one of his nurses was on duty, my father was sleeping.

As we stood by the bed, the phone rang. Lois picked up the receiver. It was Groucho's doctor, and he was so angry I could hear him too. 'What are you doing, taking Groucho out of the hospital?'

'We had nothing to do with it,' Lois replied. 'Erin did.'

The doctor was shocked, and said Groucho was in no condition to leave hospital. His life could be in jeopardy, as well as the hip operation.

However, the doctor made no move to counter Erin's wishes: 'Now that he's there, he might as well stay.'

At home, I immediately phoned J. Brin Schulman, and said I believed I finally had enough ammunition to go to court and be appointed my father's conservator. He asked us to come over right away.

In Schulman's office we quickly apprised him and his associate of the events of the past few days, together with our suspicions that Groucho was in no condition, either mentally or physically, to be making decisions affecting his financial and real estate holdings. To us it seemed a sure case of 'undue influence'.

Although the latter allegation was purely circumstantial, all things pointed to that in the 1983 court case: The Bank of America vs Erin Fleming. At the trial, it was successfully shown that while Groucho was in the hospital following his hip operation Erin Fleming had him sign a document transferring title to the Mercedes Benz she was driving, and which was registered in the name of Groucho Marx Productions, to her own name. Similarly it was shown that in early 1977 she had made Groucho endorse a $93,000 cheque out of his personal account to the corporation – of which she owned fifty percent – presumably so that there would be sufficient funds in the corporation to pay Erin her $1,000 a week salary.

Although, at the time, most of our complaints against Erin were just allegations, Schulman agreed that they raised serious concerns. He suggested that we go down to the Santa Monica

Superior Courthouse as soon as his secretary could prepare the papers, and file a petition naming me my father's conservator, and the Bank of America conservator of his estate. (The bank was chosen because in the will I had shown Schulman Groucho had named the bank as co-executor.)

I was surprised that that was all we had to do – file a petition naming me. Supposing my father or Erin objected, which they surely would? And wouldn't there have to be some kind of hearing to determine my father's capability?

While the three of us were driving to the Superior Court later that afternoon, Schulman explained that the petition was just to have me named 'temporary' conservator in order that there be someone to look after my father until a formal hearing could take place, which would be in three or four weeks. In the meantime, he said that either a process server or I would have to place the petition in my father's hand.

I said that presented a problem. Even if I could get into Groucho's house, I felt it was inappropriate for me to serve my own bedridden father with a legal paper.

'Sending a process server would be worse,' said Schulman. 'At least maybe you could say something that would ease his fears.'

By five o'clock that afternoon, we had filed my petition with the Superior Court and notified Heide Galke, the head of the Bank of America's trust department, of what was about to happen.

At ten the next morning, Schulman, his associate Vin Fichter, Lois, Heide Galke and I marched in a phalanx up to Groucho's front door. I hoped Erin wouldn't be around that early, and that the housekeeper would co-operate if she was told we were 'under court order'. My heart was pounding.

I hadn't slept all night for worry. But the scene at my father's turned out to be even worse than I had anticipated.

After a deep breath, I rang the bell. Immediately the door was opened, just a crack, by a black man who seemed about seven feet tall and very muscular. I told him who I was and that I was there to see my father. 'Who are you?' I asked.

He said he was Groucho's physiotherapist and that my father

wasn't seeing anyone. In fact, he said, he couldn't let anyone in without checking with Erin Fleming, who was not there. Then he slammed the door in our faces.

I rang the bell again, and when the same man opened the door, Schulman spoke up and said he was my lawyer and that he was there with a court order, and demanded to be let in.

This time the man said he'd phone Erin, and again shut the door firmly.

The five of us waited on my father's doorstep for about a half an hour. Around eleven we were let in and ushered into the den. The black man stood guard at the door to make sure I didn't make any attempt to see my father until Erin arrived with her attorneys.

When Erin arrived, her faction, including Warren Berlinger, Hector Arce, Hermione Brown of the Gang office, and Bob Payson, the attorney for Groucho Marx Productions, took over the living-room.

Soon our lawyers were huddling with Erin's lawyers in a neutral zone – the dining-room. After a while Schulman and Fichter came back to our camp with the disturbing news that my father had apparently signed a document in 1974 naming Erin Fleming as his personal conservator and the Bank of America as conservator of his estate in the event of his ever reaching the stage where he couldn't handle his own affairs. According to Schulman, if Erin could produce such a document, my petition would probably be an exercise in futility.

Erin's attorneys contacted the Superior Court and requested an immediate hearing so that they could present this paper they claimed my father had signed.

While we were waiting to hear back from the court, Erin was running around saying Groucho was as sharp mentally as he had ever been. To validate this, she had his nurse bring him into the living-room in his wheel chair, stopping at the piano. He seemed unaware of the gathering storm, and not at all interested in what all these strangers were doing in his house.

At Erin's bidding, he tried to play the piano and sing. But all he could manage was a tuneless croak as he listlessly kept playing the same note over and over on the piano with his forefinger.

I felt sad as I walked over to him – not to serve him with a paper, but just to give him a kiss on the forehead and ask him how he was feeling. 'Fine,' he said, looking at me suspiciously.

It was like being with a complete stranger. I felt as if he had been totally brainwashed as he turned back to the keyboard and resumed hitting the same note.

About one that afternoon, word came from the court that a judge had agreed to entertain Erin's motion that afternoon.

The hearing was short and sweet. Schulman presented our petition, along with a quick review of the pertinent facts. Then Hermione Brown produced a document that my father had signed in 1974 (while I was in Canada), naming Erin as his conservator should he ever need one. Groucho's signature had been witnessed by Milton Wexler, Erin's psychiatrist, who verified on the document that he had examined Groucho and that he was alert and in full control of his mental faculties at the time of the signing.

In view of the fact that Groucho was not yet well enough to come to court and speak on his own behalf (which the judge had recommended) Schulman said there was nothing we could do but honour the document. 'That's the bad news,' he said. 'The good news is that the Bank will be in charge of his money, so she can't mess with that any more.'

Helpless to do more, I conceded defeat and agreed to Erin officially being named my father's conservator on the day the court set for the final hearing – Friday 15 April three weeks away.

On the Thursday evening before the hearing, Schulman telephoned. He had received a call from a detective on the Beverly Hills Police Force named Judy Trunk.

According to her, drugs and syringes containing traces of barbiturates had been found hidden in the storm drain in front of Groucho's house; I wasn't surprised. One of my father's nurses, who had been fired, had told me that Erin had smoked marijuana and that she had once tried to persuade my father to try it.

When I asked Schulman why all this was surfacing now, he explained that a few days before, Erin had hired two private detectives, Norman Perle and Fred Wolfson, to determine if there were any listening devices hidden in Groucho's house or on his grounds. For some reason, she apparently suspected me of bugging the place so I could get evidence on her.

But what the detectives had discovered, instead of the listening devices, were the drugs and syringes. They took their findings to Judy Trunk, along with the testimony that when they were searching Groucho's bedroom for bugging devices, they had witnessed Erin trying to browbeat him into signing some papers against his will.

Judy Trunk had read about the Groucho Marx hearing coming up the next day. Consequently she had phoned Schulman and told him that he ought to know about what Perle and Wolfson had found and seen.

'What does all this mean?' I asked.

'It means I'm not going to allow you to turn over the conservatorship to Erin. With evidence like this, we can take the conservatorship away from her, no matter what your father signed in 1974. It would be a disservice to him for us to do otherwise.'

When court convened at nine o'clock, under the aegis of Judge Edward Rafeedie, Erin's attorneys, Brown and Payson, expected the approval of Erin's petition to be just a routine matter, since I'd already withdrawn my petition. They were therefore shocked when Schulman told the judge that I had reconsidered the matter in the light of some evidence against Erin that had surfaced the night before, and which he would like to present to the court.

The judge overruled the complaints of the opposition, and asked Schulman to present his evidence. Schulman said he would rather put detective Norman Perle on the stand, and let the court hear it directly from the person who had discovered it.

The judge agreed, and Perle was sworn in.

Under Schulman's adroit questioning, Perle testified that he had found drugs and syringes in the storm drain, and that when he had told Erin about them, she disclaimed any knowledge of them. She said that they had probably been planted there to frame her. Moreover, she had suggested to Perle's partner, Fred Wolfson, that the matter should not be taken to the police. She recommended that the drugs and syringes be 'buried in Groucho's yard'.

After Perle left the stand, Schulman told the judge that he had other witnesses he wanted him to hear, all of whom would show that Erin Fleming was not fit to be this 'great man's conservator'. Rafeedie said he would be very interested in hearing the evidence of Wolfson and Judy Trunk, but unfortunately he had a whole slate of cases to hear that day, and had not allowed room for a lengthy debate.

'Consequently I'm going to hold your hearing over until Monday morning at nine o'clock,' he said, pounding his gavel. 'Next case.'

41

Although I'd been warned by all three attorneys I'd gone to see to expect a 'circus' if I ever petitioned for Groucho's conservatorship, I wasn't quite prepared for the explosive happenings of the next few days or for some of the disclosures in court regarding Erin Fleming's behaviour that shocked even me.

When Lois, Schulman, Vin Fichter and I arrived at the courthouse there were already some reporters and photographers standing outside waiting for the litigants to arrive.

When they spotted our party, they immediately cornered us and started asking stupid questions such as 'Where's Groucho?' 'What's he think of all this?' ... 'Is it true, Arthur, you had his place bugged?'

Schulman advised us to say that we couldn't comment on the subject right now, and invited the reporters into the courtroom to hear the case for themselves.

Since Lois and I weren't expected to testify — at least not in the morning session — we took seats at the back of the courtroom, trying to be as inconspicuous as possible. By the time the bailiff called the courtroom to order, the place was spilling over with more spectators, courtwatchers and media people than there was room for. Word was evidently circulating that there were about to be some fireworks.

After being sworn in, the second of the two private detectives took the stand and confirmed what Perle had told the court previously – that Erin had suggested that the drugs and syringes be 'buried in Groucho's yard'. He also said that he and his partner, after leaving Groucho's house, had discussed the matter with an attorney, who advised them to go to the Beverly Hills Police.

Judy Trunk took the stand next and testified that traces of short-acting barbiturates were found in the syringes, according to the finding of the toxicologist. She said that a criminal investigation was under way.

While Schulman was drawing the details out of the two witnesses, Vin Fichter was on the phone in the corridor outside the courtroom, contacting all the household help and nurses and lawyers and accountants who'd been hired and fired by Erin, and asking them to testify. Several were eager to help, including the cook, John Ballow, who'd retired to Palm Springs, and of course Martha Brooks, who was the only one who lived near enough to be able to get to court in time for the afternoon session.

After the detectives, Martha led off the parade of witnesses.

She gave a pretty complete account of life in Groucho's household under the Erin Fleming regime, telling how Erin had insisted that he work when he wasn't up to it; how she had tried to keep his first stroke secret so that his doctors wouldn't prevent him from making the Taper concert, from which she would reap financial gain; how Groucho's old friends did not come to see him as frequently as they used to, and then only when invited. When she had mentioned this to Groucho he had told her that Erin kept the guest lists and invited her friends. Martha also told the court how Erin kept telling Groucho that his family didn't care for him, would put him in an old people's home, and were only after his money. And finally she told of Erin encouraging Groucho to tear up photos of Melinda and his grandchildren, Miles and Jade, because she had made him believe his daughter no longer loved him.

In the cross examination, Erin's lawyer tried to make out that Martha's testimony against Erin Fleming was biased because Fleming had fired her and she was no longer entitled to the $10,000 bequest that under the terms of Groucho's will would have come to her if she'd still been working for him. But Martha made it pretty clear to the court that she was testifying because she loved Groucho and his family and didn't give a hoot about his will.

Two days later, the two private detectives were unexpectedly back on the stand, in the light of some new evidence that had just surfaced against Erin. It seems there had been a confrontation with her the previous night in the courtyard of a Los Angeles condominium, where one of Groucho's former nurses lived. Erin had gone there to seek out the nurse, because she had accompanied the detectives on their surveillance mission of Groucho's grounds, and Erin was afraid she too would ally herself with my side. The detectives charged that upon seeing them at the condominium, Erin had threatened to kill them.

While all this testimony was important, it was the accusations of my father's former private nurses that were the most devastating to Erin's case. One alleged that Erin had given Groucho tranquillizers against his physician's orders. All said they had seen Erin physically abuse Groucho, and try to turn him against his family by saying we were only interested in his money and intended putting him in a home.

With the allegations against Erin becoming more damning and sensational each day, the case was beginning to attract nationwide, if not worldwide, media attention.

One of Groucho's former nurses, Terry McCord, who had not yet been contacted, phoned Schulman to say that she'd been reading the newspaper coverage, and she had some testimony that she thought would help our case.

That turned out to be an understatement.

After Schulman had got the quiet-spoken and ladylike McCord to confirm the allegations of other witnesses, she related an incident that took place in 1975. A nurse, who was supposed to relieve McCord, had come into the house smoking and high on marijuana. McCord complained to Erin about this, but Erin only began shouting obscenities at her. In response, McCord said she was quitting, whereupon Erin had threatened her and yelled further obscenities. McCord said that Fleming then unzipped her jump suit, and took off her clothes, leaving just panties on, and started fondling her pubic hair. She said to McCord, 'Isn't that good looking? What's the matter? Haven't you been fucked lately? Why don't you fuck me?'

According to McCord, John Ballow and a new maid had witnessed the scene.

McCord quit the job on the spot, and so did Ballow a few days later, after having worked for Groucho for two years.

When Ballow testified in the Bank of America versus Erin Fleming court case following Groucho's death, he confirmed Terry McCord's story, and then said that Groucho had taken his leaving very hard. He said that Groucho had told him that he couldn't get rid of Erin because he feared her. 'Quite frankly, I think she would kill me,' he had said.

Groucho had also told Ballow that Erin would give him no peace and was always screaming at him that they had to do another TV show or another concert or some charity work. 'He told me,' said Ballow, 'that all he wanted to do in his last days was to watch TV and that he wanted to retire and enjoy his success.' All of this belied Erin's contention that work was good for him.

The case Schulman was presenting went on for about a week and a half in front of Judge Rafeedie, with what seemed like an endless stream of witnesses with something negative to say about Groucho's 'secretary'.

During this period, on 21 April, Groucho's brother, Gummo, died of heart failure. Knowing how he felt about Erin, I'm sure he'd been following our case closely.

Groucho, who was bedridden most of the time now, still suffering from a respiratory ailment in addition to a hip that was not healing as well as it should, was not told of Gummo's death, for fear that the news would contribute to a further decline in his health. Not that there was much room for further decline. His mental condition was abysmal. He was showing no interest in reading – one of his favourite pastimes – or watching his own re-runs on television.

Consequently, he wasn't even aware that across town a court-room drama was unfolding in which he was the principal actor, even though he wasn't there.

By the time Schulman rested our case, after nearly two weeks of testimony, and cross testimony, without ever putting me or Erin on the stand, it was apparent to everyone concerned that Judge Rafeedie could not possibly rule in favour of Erin Fleming.

Nevertheless, I was on tenterhooks while we waited for the judge to come out of his chambers, where he'd been deliberating all afternoon.

When he finally, did take his place on the bench again, he looked in my direction and said, 'After reviewing the facts, I have decided to name Arthur Marx his father's conservator.'

As a cheer went up from everyone, except Erin and her faction, tears came to my eyes.

But my victory was short-lived. Even before the commotion in the courtroom had died down, Stanley Gold, one of Erin's attorneys, had leaped to his feet and was saying, 'But, your honour, the defence hasn't had a chance to present its case yet. And therefore it's highly unusual for you to have found in favour of the plaintiff without hearing both sides.'

Looking surprised that anyone had thought of that, Rafeedie said that the reason he hadn't listened to both sides was because the hearing had already gone on for ten days and to have it continue for another week or more would be a disservice to Groucho, who was badly in need of a conservator *right now*.

'In that case,' suggested God, 'why doesn't the court allow Groucho to decide if he wants Arthur to be his conservator?'

'But I thought he was too ill to leave the house,' said the judge.

'Then let's all go there,' said Gold. 'Miss Fleming says she visited him this morning, and that he is perfectly lucid.'

Schulman objected on the grounds that that would be unfair to me inasmuch as the court had already been shown how afraid Groucho was of Erin Fleming. Notwithstanding, Judge Rafeedie overruled Schulman's objection, saying he would be better able to make a determination after he'd met Groucho.

As a result, court was adjourned in the Santa Monica courthouse, to be resumed in Groucho's bedroom as soon as we could drive there.

Erin arrived there ahead of everyone in order to prepare Groucho for his interview with Judge Rafeedie.

Whether he was in any shape to be coached by Erin and retain anything, I do not know. But I do know that after Rafeedie talked to him behind closed doors, with only the opposing attorneys present, my father's decision was not favourable to me. According to what Schulman later told me, Groucho was not 'with it' mentally, but he did seem to understand what the judge was saying when he asked, 'Would you like your son, Arthur, to take care of you?'

'No,' Groucho croaked out tearfully.

When the judge and lawyers and respective litigants gathered in Groucho's living-room, Rafeedie announced that there would have to be a compromise. Refusing to name either Erin or me, he suggested that we come up with a candidate – a relative or close friend of the family – who would be acceptable to both camps, who would serve as a temporary conservator until the legal matters could be resolved.

This was Friday. We were given until Monday to submit a list of names.

Lois and I and Schulman spent the weekend mulling over possible candidates. Since most of my father's friends were either dead or ill, our options were few – either Bert Granet, a movie producer who was fairly close to Groucho, or Nat Perrin, who had been an attorney before turning Marx Brothers scriptwriter.

We approached Granet first, but he turned us down after being told the job might last longer than three weeks. Perrin told us he'd take it on if it didn't last too much longer than three weeks.

The only person on Erin's list turned out to be Zeppo Marx, the youngest and last remaining Marx Brother except for Groucho. But Zeppo was living in Palm Springs.

Nice as it would have been to have one of Groucho's brothers looking after him, Zeppo wasn't acceptable to me for three reasons: (1) He lived too far away, and was too old to commute, (2) He was an incorrigible gambler, (3) He was beholden to Erin because she had prevailed on Groucho to give Zeppo $1,000 a month to live on now that he had no income of his own and had no savings.

However, both candidates had to show up at the Superior Courthouse to be interviewed by Rafeedie before either one of them could be chosen.

When Zeppo arrived, in a Rolls-Royce and jazzy-looking sports jacket and slacks, he hammed it up for the benefit of the media on the courthouse steps. Questioned as to what he thought of Erin Fleming, he replied, 'I think she's a wonderful girl. She's been great for Groucho, and I'm all for her.'

Rafeedie immediately eliminated him.

Nat Perrin, a kindly, easy-going man and a brilliant intellect, easily won the job of temporary conservator. He'd have the responsibility of taking care of his friend until another hearing, in which Erin would present her case, could be held. Rafeedie set 13 May for that hearing, and said that at the end of it he would name either myself or Erin Fleming to be Groucho's permanent conservator.

42

During his brief regime, Nat Perrin brought some semblance of order and serenity to Groucho's household, and with this a little bit of happiness to the dying comedian. Gone were the tumultuous days when Erin had free access to the house; gone were the daily displays of her fiery temper and bullying ways, and gone were her kooky friends and unemployed hangers-on.

One of the first things Nat Perrin did was to arrange separate visiting hours for Erin and me, so that there would be no confrontations and upsetting scenes in front of Groucho. I was allowed to see him for an hour or so in the morning; Erin came late in the afternoon and usually stayed through dinner.

In between, Perrin allowed one visit a day from Groucho's

old friends: George Fenneman, who'd been his announcer and straight man on *You Bet Your Life*; Norman Panama, of the great comedy writing team of Panama and Frank; Julie Epstein, author of the film classic *Casablanca*; Steve Allen, and occasionally Carroll O'Connor.

On good days, Groucho would be allowed out of bed to be wheeled into the living-room, where he would sit by the window in the sun, and fondle his cat Suki. Sometimes he might plunk a few notes on the piano, with Steve Allen playing along with him. Possibly, if he got the right feed line, he might be able to remember a punch line, such as the day when Julie Epstein told him that he was going to play poker at his house that night for 'small stakes'.

'And French fried potatoes,' cracked Groucho weakly, reaching back into the past for that line from *Animal Crackers*.

Perrin also arranged a rapprochement between Groucho and Melinda, by sending her the air fare to fly to Southern California from Mendocino. Thoroughly forgotten at this first meeting in two years were the bad feelings between them generated by Erin. On this day Groucho couldn't get enough of Melinda. Kissing her over and over again, he kept saying to his nurses, 'Isn't my daughter beautiful?'

When her visiting time was up, he begged her to stay a little longer. Which she did.

As the weeks went on, Erin began acting like herself again, staying longer and asserting herself more and more. She resented her lack of power, and she was still trying to turn everyone, including Perrin, against me and my wife.

One day, after both she and my father got stomach upsets from something the cook had prepared, she phoned Nat Perrin and accused Lois and me of trying to poison them. Although Perrin, who had known me since I was a child, knew better than to believe her, it worried him that she had such a notion on her mind. Consequently he ordered that nobody but the cook was to touch Groucho's food or to go into the kitchen, and nobody but the nurses were to feed him.

According to Perrin, Fleming was constantly badgering him about being the conservator. After four weeks, he could no longer take the strain of arguing with Erin or keeping the various factions from squabbling, and so he submitted to the court his application to be removed as temporary conservator. That, however, took several more weeks to process.

Meanwhile, Norman Krasna wrote to me from Switzerland, enclosing a letter to Groucho and asking me to read it aloud to him. He was afraid that if he sent it to Groucho directly, he would never get it.

Standing at my father's bedside, I read Krasna's letter aloud to him during my visit the following morning.

It was full of genuine sentiment, and its harking back to Hollywood's halcyon days, in the late thirties and early forties, when his relationship with Groucho was the closest, had both my father and me in tears by the time I finished reading the letter.

As Groucho wiped away his tears, he instructed me to get a paper and pencil. 'I want to dictate a letter right back,' he said.

As he was short of breath, his dictation was laboured, his voice quiet and halting.

'DEAR NORMAN,

'I MISS NOT SEEING YOU. WE HAD A LOT OF GREAT TIMES TOGETHER, UNTIL YOU MOVED TO SWITZERLAND.

'COME BACK. WE NEED YOU.

LOVE,
HACKENBUSH'

Probably sensing that he didn't have too much longer to live, Groucho felt it safe to display a rare moment of sentiment.

He even started showing his old warmth towards Lois, which had been missing during much of Erin's regime. One day when the two of us were visiting him, Lois bent over to kiss him. He put his arms around her and kissed her about fifteen times. 'He never would have stopped if Lois hadn't got tired of bending over,' remembers Nat Perrin today.

Groucho also said, in front of Perrin, 'I love you very much, Lois.'

Perhaps he was compensating for his past treatment of her.

338

Early in May, the hearing to determine Groucho's permanent conservator was postponed until 18 July by Judge Rafeedie. This was to allow Erin's new attorneys time to prepare her case in which she'd try to defend the allegations made against her at the first hearing.

As a result, Nat Perrin agreed to stay on as temporary conservator until the July court date.

In early June, Groucho was back in Cedars Sinai once again. The new hip joint had become dislocated and had to be replaced with another one. The hospital public relations department kept telling the media every morning that Groucho Marx was 'doing nicely and is his old wise-cracking, nurse-pinching self again'.

From my visits to him, I knew that he wasn't. His breathing was laborious, and even though the physiotherapist forced him to get out of bed and try to walk a couple of days after the surgery, I could see that he was no longer capable of it.

Notwithstanding, he was released to go home after a week. Twenty-four hours later, however, he was back in Cedars Sinai. His lungs were filling up with water. He was diagnosed as having pneumonitis, normally a benign form of pneumonia, but dangerous to an eighty-six year old with low resistance. Having to be constantly on his back in a hospital bed caused his lungs to fill up with fluid, and he had to be on an aspirator most of the time.

Meanwhile, Schulman had not been idle. He had taken a lengthy deposition from John Ballow in preparation for the final conservatorship hearing that had been reset for 18 July. The *Los Angeles Times* printed excerpts from the deposition which had been filed with the court. In it, 'Ballow alleged that Erin had bullied and drugged Groucho, and he likened the atmosphere in the house to a 'battlefield'. Coming on the heels of the nurses' testimony in court, Ballow's deposition further strengthened our case.

During this time Nat Perrin was still Groucho's conservator and becoming awfully tired of the responsibility, especially of having to act as referee between Erin and me. He told the court he would serve only until the end of July.

Since it was obvious from the latest developments that Erin

would never be approved as permanent conservator, and just as obvious that she would never approve me without a long drawn-out court battle, I suggested that my son Andy, who was twenty-seven years old, be named permanent conservator. He was bright, he loved his grandfather, and I was reasonably sure that he would be acceptable to Erin inasmuch as she had liked him enough to hire him to help with the cataloguing of Groucho's *You Bet Your Life* films.

My hunch turned out to be partially correct. Erin approved Andy as temporary conservator, stating that she wanted a few extra weeks to 'evaluate his performance', before agreeing to his being installed in the job permanently.

As a result the final hearing was reset for 31 August 1977.

Another court session had to be held in order to make Andy's temporary conservatorship official. This time the hearing was held in Groucho's hospital room at Cedars Sinai. By then, 27 July, it must have been clear to Erin's attorneys that her case was hopeless, and in a complete switch, they agreed to the appointment of Andy Marx as permanent conservator.

It was a victory of sorts for our side – if there was such a thing as victory amidst such unhappy circumstances.

43

Why it was necessary to hold the hearing in Groucho's hospital room I do not know. My father could barely talk, but he did seem aware enough of what was going on to nod – barely perceptibly – when Rafeedie asked him if it was all right with him if his grandson Andy took care of him.

During the final days of his life, I visited Groucho every afternoon. There couldn't be any conversation with the aspirator – a long tube attached to his nose and mouth – pumping away twenty-four hours a day. His vision was bad, and I don't think he recognized anyone. It was just a question of being there so he wouldn't feel deserted should he become aware of his surroundings. I brought a book or a newspaper along, and read while he dozed.

On Friday 19 August, around eleven in the morning Andy

called me. He said, 'You'd better come to the hospital, Dad. The doctor's just phoned me and said Groucho's blood pressure is down to forty.'

Lois and I rushed to the hospital and remained in the room until 5.30 in the afternoon. His breathing was becoming more and more laboured and his blood pressure was still sinking. His eyes were permanently glazed and seeing nothing.

We left the hospital at five-thirty to go home and feed our dogs before meeting Andy for a quick bite of dinner across the street from Cedars Sinai. Afterwards we would go back to stand watch at Groucho's bed.

But just as we were leaving the house we received a call from the doctor urging us to rush right over.

When we arrived in Groucho's hospital room, we found Erin standing by his bed, holding his hand. His heartbeat, according to the doctor, who was standing by with a stethoscope, was becoming fainter and fainter. I walked over to the other side of the bed and took hold of Groucho's other hand. Erin looked at me contemptuously and left. Lois and I and Andy waited, as he became weaker and weaker. At 7.25, it was all over.

I had been apprehensive about watching him, or anyone else die, but I had nothing to fear. It was as if peace had finally descended upon my troubled father. He looked completely at rest.

I kissed him good-bye on his forehead, which was still warm, the doctor closed his eyelids and then pulled the sheet over his face. And then we all had a good, long cry.

I knew he didn't want to have a funeral. He considered them barbaric. He had told me that many times. He just wanted to be cremated and he didn't care what became of his ashes. He didn't believe in an after-life, but had once jokingly told me that if there were one, he'd like to be in the same place as Abraham Lincoln, William Shakespeare and George S. Kaufman.

Consequently, there was no funeral or any kind of religious service. Just a memorial gathering of friends and relatives, including Harpo's widow and my sister, Miriam, at my house Saturday afternoon.

The media waited at the bottom of my driveway, hoping to

catch some celebrities. But there were none. I had forgotten to invite George Jessel and George Burns, and Zeppo had refused to come because I had objected to his being named conservator.

Erin conducted her own memorial service somewhere else in town at which, I imagine, were gathered all of Groucho's 'new' friends, including Elliott Gould and Sally Kellerman and Carroll O'Connor.

A few days after Groucho was cremated, and his ashes interred in a vault at Malinov & Silverman's cemetery in the San Fernando Valley, a letter addressed to me was found among his effects. In it he requested that he not be cremated. He preferred to be buried at the Westwood Cemetery alongside the body of Marilyn Monroe.

The same old Groucho. Even after he had shuffled off this mortal coil, he wanted to lie throughout eternity alongside the most glamorous sex symbol of the age.

Epilogue

In the autumn of 1977, the Bank of America, as Executor of Groucho Marx's estate, filed a suit in the Superior Court against Erin Fleming, seeking recovery of certain moneys and properties obtained by Fleming over a six-year period. The suit sought damages based on fraud, undue influence, breach of fiduciary duty, conversion, duress and menace, and declaratory and other equitable relief, including a rescission of four contracts and imposition of a constructive trust over certain properties, including two houses, one half the shares of Groucho Marx Productions Incorporated, and a Mercedes Benz alleged to have been obtained in violation of Groucho's rights, and to have the assets transferred to Groucho's estate. The action also sought punitive damages.

The case didn't reach court until 1983. After a ten-week trial the jury returned a verdict for the plaintiff against Erin Fleming awarding $233,118.09 compensatory damages. Punitive damages of $250,000 were also awarded for a total jury verdict and judgement entered on 1 April 1983 of $473,118.09.

It must have been an April Fool's verdict, for the judge later took away the punitive damages.

Almost immediately, Erin Fleming and her attorneys, Melvin Belli and Associates, took the case to the California Court of Appeals, which didn't hear it until 1986. The Court of Appeals upheld the original verdict of 6 February 1987, whereupon Belli petitioned the California Supreme Court for a reversal of the jury's findings.

In July 1987 California Supreme Court refused to hear the case.

Another victory?

I doubt it. There are no winners in cases like this, only losers. Attorneys' fees and court costs had eaten up most of Groucho's estate by the time it was distributed to the family, in 1988, *eleven years* after his death.

Bart Mills
Marilyn on Location £9.99

Marilyn on Location is a celebration of the work of the young model called Norma Jean who, with a combination of talent, sheer determination, and sex appeal became Hollywood's most glittering star.

Bart Mills explores her career, film by film, from walk on parts in B Movies like *Scudda Hoo! Scudda Hay!*, to classics like *The Seven Year Itch* and *Some Like It Hot*.

Lavishly illustrated with stunning stills from all of her movies, *Marilyn on Location* shows just why Marilyn remains Hollywood's most enduring legend.

Eartha Kitt
I'm Still Here £5.99

To Orson Wells she was 'the most exciting woman in the world'.

To herself she was 'Rejected, Ejected, Dejected, Used, Accused, Abused.'

One of the enduring legends of show business tells the incredible story of her transformation from poor little 'yella gal' Eartha Mae, to the legendary songstress Eartha Kitt.

Throughout a career spanning theatre, film and television, Eartha Kitt triumphed with classic gold records like 'Old Fashioned Girl', I'm Still Here' and 'Santa Baby'. And survived the racial abuse that led to the CIA branding her a 'sadistic nymphomaniac'.

Passionate, forthright and revealing — Eartha Kitt looks back on her life with an ironic edge as sharp as her gun-metal lamé.

Miss Peggy Lee
An autobiography £4.99

'Louis Armstrong said I always knew how to swing . . .'

Born Norma Egstrom in North Dakota, Peggy Lee turned her back on an unhappy childhood when Benny Goodman gave her a job singing with his band.

One of the most respected jazz singers in the business, she has survived stormy marriages and frequent battles with illness but continues to captivate audiences with her smokey, haunting voice.

Here, Peggy Lee tells her remarkable life story with the same intimacy and winning directness that characterises such hits as 'Fever', 'Is That All There Is?', 'Mañana' and many many more . . .

'Reading her book is a bit like going through a 'Who's Who' of the stars of music and film throughout the '40s, '50s and '60s'. TIME OUT

'Age cannot wither her, nor custom stale her infinite variety. The voice, the rhythm, the phrasing, the emotion are all still there'.

RICHARD BOSTON, THE GUARDIAN

All Pan books are available at your local bookshop or newsagent, or can be ordered direct from the publisher. Indicate the number of copies required and fill in the form below.

Send to: **CS Department, Pan Books Ltd., P.O. Box 40, Basingstoke, Hants. RG21 2YT.**

or phone: 0256 469551 (Ansaphone), quoting title, author and Credit Card number.

Please enclose a remittance* to the value of the cover price plus: 60p for the first book plus 30p per copy for each additional book ordered to a maximum charge of £2.40 to cover postage and packing.

*Payment may be made in sterling by UK personal cheque, postal order, sterling draft or international money order, made payable to Pan Books Ltd.

Alternatively by Barclaycard/Access:

Card No.

Signature:

Applicable only in the UK and Republic of Ireland.

While every effort is made to keep prices low, it is sometimes necessary to increase prices at short notice. Pan Books reserve the right to show on covers and charge new retail prices which may differ from those advertised in the text or elsewhere.

NAME AND ADDRESS IN BLOCK LETTERS PLEASE:

....

Name ————————————————————————————

Address ————————————————————————————

——————————————————————————————————

——————————————————————————————————

——————————————————————————————————

3/87